T0142033

The Science and Art of Simulation I

Michael M. Resch • Andreas Kaminski •
Petra Gehring

Editors

The Science and Art
of Simulation I

Exploring - Understanding - Knowing

 Springer

Editors
Michael M. Resch
High Performance Computing
  Center (HLRS)
University of Stuttgart
Stuttgart, Germany

Andreas Kaminski
High Performance Computing
  Center (HLRS)
University of Stuttgart
Stuttgart, Germany

Petra Gehring
Institute for Philosophy
Technical University of Darmstadt
Darmstadt, Germany

ISBN 978-3-319-85739-8   ISBN 978-3-319-55762-5   (eBook)
DOI 10.1007/978-3-319-55762-5

Cover illustration: FEM model by NCAC, Simulation and Visualization by Thomas Obst. HLRS, Stuttgart Germany

Printed on acid-free paper

This Springer imprint is published by Springer Nature
The registered company is Springer International Publishing AG
The registered company address is: Gewerbestrasse 11, 6330 Cham, Switzerland

Contents

Introduction

Michael M. Resch, Andreas Kaminski, and Petra Gehring

It is quite rare to witness a radical change in science—not just the advent of a new topic or a new idea, and not just a change in a single field or scientific discipline, but a transformation of the way in which science works in general.[1] In this kind of situation, it is difficult to understand what is going on. Our perceptions are not yet accustomed the novelty; no scholarly language has been refined and developed to reflect on what's going on.[2]

When faced with such challenges, societies and science often respond in one of two ways: (1) The first strategy is to increase the contrast. This makes a virtue of necessity. Familiar concepts and language games are used to survey the difference between "old" and "new," and a comparison between the traditional and the novel is expected to provide information about the ongoing change (see Husserl 1939; Luhmann 1988). The advantage of this strategy is that it does not require any presuppositions about what is essentially new. We validate our hypotheses on a familiar baseline and we are from the outset prepared to determine differences step by step. This, however, comes with certain disadvantages. Our results will be a

---

[1] It is easy to say, following Kuhn, that we are observing a paradigm shift (Kuhn 1970). In fact, it is too easy, because the scientific shift necessarily includes a corresponding shift in the philosophy of science. Kuhn's approach establishes a different "paradigm" of observing and understanding science. Thus, both the philosophy of science and its subject are in motion. See also Winsberg's remarks on their correlation (Winsberg 2010).

[2] Fleck (1981) describes this challenge for scientists in detail, but it applies to philosophers and historians of science as well.

M.M. Resch (✉) • A. Kaminski
High Performance Computing Center Stuttgart (HLRS), University of Stuttgart, Nobelstr. 19, 70569 Stuttgart, Germany
e-mail: resch@hlrs.de; kaminski@hlrs.de

P. Gehring
Institute of Philosophy, TU Darmstadt, Dolivostr. 15, 64293 Darmstadt, Germany
e-mail: gehring@phil.tu-darmstadt.de

© Springer International Publishing AG 2017
M.M. Resch et al. (eds.), *The Science and Art of Simulation I*,
DOI 10.1007/978-3-319-55762-5_1

measure of distance or difference, commonly expressed as similarity or dissimilarity, but they will not give us a profound understanding of the new kind of practice itself. Comparisons of "old" and "new" practices can only serve as a starting point to understand the new. (2) The second strategy is a risky one. It can be called "experimental" in the broad sense of the term and it tends to turn science into engineering and/or into art. Due to the lack of reliable knowledge about the ongoing transformation, we try to develop models. Science as art creates a merely possible basis for a new understanding. Novels, movies, and music map out strategies to cope with radical transformation.

From our (and not only our) point of view, computer simulation is radically changing science in general.[3] The transformation affects not only hard sciences such as physics, chemistry, and engineering, but also sociology, psychology, political science, and even mathematics. Computer simulation changes (and will increasingly change) the way political decisions are made, uncertainty is handled, and the future is understood. Tool metaphors, therefore, are misleading. Computer simulation is not at all just a new device, an instrument, but rather a medium[4]—and a *dispositif*, in which thinking, decision-making, and understanding itself are shaped.

The two responses mentioned above can be witnessed in current debates on simulation sciences. A lot of scientific literature (ours partially included) revolves around the question of whether computer simulations are more similar to experiments than they are to theory and argumentation, or vice versa.[5] In other words, familiar concepts are used to measure the distance between classical methodologies and new ones. This results in a certain lack of concepts specific to computer simulation. Commonly, the adjective "simulation" must serve to identify the objective: Instead of "models" or "experiments", one speaks of "simulation models" or "simulation experiments". While this strategy ensures discursive continuity, it also delineates the frame of possible thoughts. When it comes to computer simulations, the result is tangible: A narrowed epistemological approach dominates. The second strategy, understanding computer simulation through the medium of art, is not without its weaknesses either. Narratives of machines that become intelligent and humanlike, or of Laplace's demon, which can calculate everything, are prevalent.[6] By inappropriately mythologizing computers, these narratives complicate our understanding.

How might such shortcomings be resolved? Bearing in mind that the strategic options for responding to ongoing transformations are limited, it may be useful to

---

[3]For just a few examples, see Winsberg (2010), Humphreys (2004, 2009), Lenhard (2015a, b), and Küppers and Lenhard (2006).

[4]For a media studies perspective, see Pias (2011). For an approach based on the philosophy of technology, see Hubig (2006, 2007, 2015).

[5]For two well-developed studies, see Gramelsberger (2008) and Beisbart (2012).

[6]Cf. the movies *Transcendence* (2014) or *Lucy* (2014). For a more experimental approach cf. *Black Mirror* (2011–2016).

reconsider some of the preliminary decisions and to reorganize the collaborative research on computer simulation step by step. This is the guiding idea of the *Science and Art of Simulation* series (SAS). Its intention is to enable theoretical work on the basis of possible (and possibly appropriate) conceptual frameworks. Furthermore, its aim is to open up perspectives for improved 'hands-on' research on computer simulation. To that end, SAS connects science and art in a threefold manner:

1. The arts—understood as the humanities, social sciences, and philosophy—enter into a more comprehensive exchange with practitioners of computer simulations. In addition to epistemological perspectives, the SAS series addresses normative, political, historical, and aesthetic questions.
2. Art—understood as a craft put into action by practitioners—is related to the methods and procedures described in theory. For this reason, the tension between the science and engineering of computer simulations, between epistemology and technology, as well as between theory and practice, takes center stage. In addition to such an "accompanied research", the SAS series offers practitioners a collegial and occasionally critical voice.
3. Art—understood as skill or artistry to reflect and make decisions based on the outcome of computer simulations—is considered in social and political contexts. In addition to the science and practice of computer simulation, the SAS series explores the possibilities of relating to computer simulations from a social or political point of view.

The High-Performance Computing Center in Stuttgart (HLRS) is the ideal home for the SAS enterprise. With around a hundred engineers, scientists, mathematicians, and computer scientists, it is one of the global pioneers in computer simulation. The newly founded Department for Philosophy of Computer Simulations at HLRS, consisting of four Ph.D. students and two postdoctoral researchers, enables interaction between disciplines which are normally separated and offers insight into the practical side of simulations studies and high-performance computing. Together with the Department of Philosophy at TU Darmstadt, which contributes its expertise in the philosophy of science, technology, and engineering, we have founded the complementary SAS workshop series, which attracts an interdisciplinary group of scholars. Every fall, computer scientists, engineers, historians, and social scientists meet philosophers researching the science and art of simulation. In the spring, a second SAS workshop series, run in collaboration with Nicole C. Saam (University Erlangen-Nuremberg), focuses on sociological issues in computer simulation.[7]

The first volume of the series addresses three topics at the interplay of the science and art of simulation:

---

[7]We owe a great debt of gratitude to Madeleine LaRue for her diligent and brilliant proofreading and Charline Medernach for her superb support in implementing the style guide.

1 How to Explore Computer Simulations?

Philosophy began devoting attention to computer simulations at a relatively early stage. Since then, the unquestioned point of view has been that computer simulation is a new scientific method; the philosophy of simulation is therefore part of the philosophy of science. The first section of this volume discusses this implicit unchallenged assumption by addressing, from different perspectives, the question of how to explore (and how not to explore) research on computer simulations. Scientists discuss what is still lacking or considered problematic, while philosophers draft new directions for research. They explore the art of exploring computer simulations.

2 How to Understand the Results of Computer Simulations?

The results of computer simulations are integrated into both political and social decisions. It is implicitly assumed that the more detailed, and consequently more realistic, a computer simulation is, the more useful it will be in decision-making. This idea is by no means justified. Different types of computer simulations must be differentiated, which in turn requires the specific skill of understanding computer simulation results. The articles in this section examine the capabilities and limits of simulation results in political and social contexts, exploring the art of understanding computer simulation results.

3 How to Gain Knowledge Through Computer Simulations?

The advent of computer simulation in scientific practices today challenges the order of science. What kind of knowledge is gained through computer simulations is the key question of this section. Computer simulations are usually compared to experiments or to arguments. The transformation of our traditional scientific notions might be more challenging than expected. Ideas are put forward in the third section to conceptualize the art of knowing through computer simulations.

References

Beisbart, Claus. 2012. How can computer simulations produce new knowledge? *European Journal for Philosophy of Science* 2 (3): 395–434.

Besson, Luc. 2014. *Lucy*. DVD. Universal City, CA: Universal Studios Home Entertainment.

Brooker, Charlie, Barney Reisz, Annabel Jones, Otto Bathurst, Konnie Huq, Euros Lyn, Jesse Armstrong, et al. 2011–2016. *Black mirror*. TV Series.

Fleck, Ludwik. 1981. *Genesis and development of a scientific fact*. Chicago, London: University of Chicago Press.

Gramelsberger, Gabriele. 2008. *Computerexperimente: Zum Wandel der Wissenschaft im Zeitalter des Computers*. Bielefeld: Transcript.

Hubig, Christoph. 2006. *Technikphilosophie als Reflexion der Medialität*. Vol. 1 of *Die Kunst des Möglichen*. Bielefeld: Transcript.

Hubig, Christoph. 2007. *Grundlinien einer dialektischen Philosophie der Technik*. Vol. 2 of *Die Kunst des Möglichen*. Bielefeld: Transcript.

Hubig, Christoph. 2015. *Macht der Technik*. Vol 3 of *Die Kunst des Möglichen*. Bielefeld: Transcript.

Humphreys, Paul. 2004. *Extending ourselves: Computational science, empiricism, and scientific method*. New York: Oxford University Press.

Humphreys, Paul. 2009. The philosophical novelty of computer simulation methods. *Synthese* 169 (3): 615–626.

Husserl, Edmund. 1939. *Erfahrung und Urteil: Untersuchungen zur Genealogie der Logik*. Ed. Ludwig Landgrebe. Prag: Academia.

Kuhn, Thomas S. 1970. *The structure of scientific revolutions*. 2nd ed. International encyclopedia of unified science: Foundations of the unity of science. Chicago, IL: University of Chicago Press.

Küppers, Günter, and Johannes Lenhard. 2006. From Hierarchical to Network-Like Integration: A Revolution of Modeling Style in Computer-Simulation. In *Simulation. Pragmatic Construction of Reality* (Sociology of the Sciences Yearbook, 25), ed. Johannes Lenhard, Günter Küppers and Terry Shinn, 89–106. Dordrecht: Springer.

Lenhard, Johannes. 2015a. Kann Technik die Naturgesetze verändern? In *Ding und System. Jahrbuch Technikphilosophie 2015*, ed. Gerhard Gamm, Petra Gehring, Christoph Hubig, Andreas Kaminski and Alfred Nordmann, 171–186. Zürich, Berlin: Diaphanes.

Lenhard, Johannes. 2015b. *Mit allem rechnen - zur Philosophie der Computersimulation*. Berlin, Boston: de Gruyter.

Luhmann, Niklas. 1988. Familiarity, Confidence, Trust: Problems and Perspectives. In *Trust. Making and breaking cooperative relations*, ed. Diego Gambetta, 94–107. New York, NY, Oxford: Blackwell.

Pfister, Wally. 2014. *Transcendence*. DVD. Burbank, CA: Warner Home Video.

Pias, Claus. 2011. On the Epistemology of Computer Simulation. *Zeitschrift für Medien- und Kulturforschung* 2011 (1): 29–54.

Winsberg, Eric B. 2010. *Science in the age of computer simulation*. Chicago, London: University of Chicago Press.

Part I
The Art of Exploring Computer Simulations

Doing Research on Simulation Sciences? Questioning Methodologies and Disciplinarities

Petra Gehring

Abstract The application of computer-based simulation procedures has led to the formation of a compact body of methodological knowledge. But what about the methods and the practices of research in the social and human sciences addressing simulation-based research? Is there one authentic type of evaluative research on simulation research? Should it exist? And if so: what epistemic forms, what overarching methodological postulates are fruitful? The Paper looks into these questions.

The application of computer-based simulation procedures—including data-driven heuristics and/or visualization[1]—has led to the formation of a compact body of methodological knowledge that crosslinks and transforms the disciplines involved. But what about the methods and the practices of research in the social and human sciences addressing simulation-based research? Is there one authentic type of evaluative research on simulation research? Should it exist? And if so: what epistemic forms, what overarching methodological postulates are fruitful? The following discussion looks into these questions.

My deliberations are located on the level of the envisaged targets of methodology and research organization, or, to put it more loosely, they treat academic territorial politics. Even if recognizable trends point in a different direction, I argue programmatically. The concluding propositions are meant as a contribution to communication on regulation options. Although I formulate these reflections as a philosopher, I hesitate to ascribe them to my discipline, philosophy. Essentially, I am speaking simply to advocate that research *about* and *on* simulation research

---

[1] I speak of computer simulation in a consciously broad sense—to include everything that must be of interest to second-order research that also targets epistemic and social circumstances. By simulation I mean the model-based digital processing of complete experimental cycles. These can also be attempts at depiction or design, or exploratory cycles that synthesize their object. Hence, it is for my purposes not necessary to separate simulation and production, or to distinguish paradigmatically between simulation and data-driven exploration procedures (cf. Hey et al. 2009).

P. Gehring (✉)
Institute of Philosophy, TU Darmstadt, Dolivostr. 15, 64293 Darmstadt, Germany
e-mail: gehring@phil.tu-darmstadt.de

© Springer International Publishing AG 2017
M.M. Resch et al. (eds.), *The Science and Art of Simulation I*,
DOI 10.1007/978-3-319-55762-5_2

should be as comprehensive as possible, that is, I advocate meta-research and evaluative research in the social and human sciences.

The focus is on the academic environment in Germany with its specific division of research methods and domains in social and human sciences. Thus, I address a proximate environment in which it is possible to speak appellative sentences as it were to 'my own kin'. If the transition to simulation procedures does indeed amount to a radical innovation for science, then it seems to me that it should be worthwhile to reflect on how the social and human sciences see their future observer role and their function in research on simulation research.[2]

1 Unity Does Not Follow from Novelty: On Simulation as an Object of Research

The realm of simulation procedures is relatively new,[3] but it is large, indeed very large, and it is also strikingly heterogeneous. The term "simulation science" or "simulation sciences" is sometimes encountered, but it is something of a makeshift. There is no *single* science of computer simulation, at best those involved wish for a convergence of procedures, objects and interests. Today, problems in physics, biology and biochemistry, geology, materials science, architecture and structural engineering, generally complex engineering problems are explored by means of simulation, as are many research questions in economics and social sciences—from financing scenarios to traffic analysis and epidemiology.

Even with respect to the required mathematical and digital expertise, there is presumably no 'central' discipline of simulation-based research. All are dependent on all, and all join forces: expertise in mathematics, modelling, scientific calculation, computer science in its various forms including the individual computer and the software interacting within it. In general, simulation is not merely "complex", rather it is a highly composite procedure. Various disciplines share the work in what is called the simulation pipeline, and for this reason among others common overall concepts remain vague. Expressions such as "virtualization" function as synonyms

---

[2]Thus, the *use* of digital simulation procedures in the social and human sciences is not my topic; from the perspective chosen here, this would simply be simulation research like simulation research in the natural and technological sciences.

[3]The history of science is not readily able to identify a beginning. Needless to say, work with models (for example in civil engineering) has a long history, as has mathematical forecasting (consider ballistics); other forms of running things through could be interpreted after the fact as quasi 'analogue' simulation. By contrast, IT-based, that is, computer simulation emerged in the life sciences in the 1970s (cf. Varenne 2007); but it was only with the triumph of powerful multiple processors together with parallel computational procedures tailored to them in the past two decades that it has become the standard method in the applied sciences.

Fig. 1 Simulation based
sciences/simulation
sciences:
"computational..."
(Source: own elaboration)

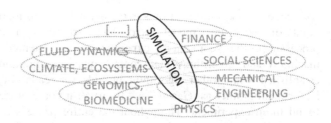

for simulation,[4] and paraphrases such as "modelling", "calculation", "projection" and "representation" (all used non-terminologically) as well as the prevalent characterization of the process and its results in terms of the tool used—"computational" or in German "computer-based"—express this difficulty (Fig. 1).[5]

Thus, it may well be the case that discourses on simulation are made coherent more by the striking status of their range of objects than by solid terminology that has undergone thorough theoretical discussion. It is astonishing—not only for the broad public, but also for the disciplines that actively apply simulation and for the disciplines that accompany it by way of description, conceptualization or evaluation: simulation research operates in the medium 'as if'. In so doing, it works with constructs that are no longer models because in digital processing, aspects of similarity recede far into the background, though they still play a certain part: certain isomorphisms or references concentrating on the treatment of input and output values. Rather, simulation resembles a chain of heterogeneous transformations, each for itself complex, which lead—ideally on a controlled path—to a result that has significance because the steps by which it was obtained are known and because these steps ensure that the result of the simulation shall retain its descriptive value. It is also disconcerting that simulation avowedly relies on threshold values; and under certain circumstances, this excludes "verification" from the goals to an extent that was previously only known in hermeneutic disciplines. In the various research fields in which simulation is used this abdication of verification is implemented differently,[6] but the analogy to experimental science or to a "real"

---

[4]"Virtuality" accentuates the lack of phenomenal presence (as a characteristic for the symbolic chains of operations typical of simulation: the "object" appears in absence), whereas—in purely conceptual terms—"simulation" addresses precisely what is operatively (see above) minimalized, namely the successful establishment of similarity with what is simulated (and thus the epistemically sufficient equivalence of the results obtained by way of simulation with results obtained by conventional means, say "empirically"). On reality within the framework of such "new media" (to which computer simulation can be reckoned), cf. Krämer (1998); on the distinction between virtual reality and virtual actuality [Wirklichkeit] (interpreting computer simulation as "transclassical technology") cf. Hubig (2006, pp. 187–188).

[5]The German Council of Sciences and Humanities (Wissenschaftsrat) distinguishes in a position paper (Wissenschaftsrat 2014, p. 11) between simulation sciences and simulation-based sciences, which would amount to computational ...

[6]When, for example, in engineering simulation results are commonly compared with 'fresh' experimental data, verification claims are undoubtedly implicated more than in climate or biosphere simulation or in macroeconomic and financing scenarios based on rational-choice models.

construction procedure is always explicitly referred to merely as an analogy. The point of departure (model-based data structures prepared for algorithmic processing), the "computed" experiment (task-oriented algorithms encounter machines and algorithms that control machine operations) and the digitally established result (other algorithms provide for readability or visualization, that is, for intelligibility as 'Gestalt' and form) all involve process features that are not found in an experiment. Throughout the entire process leading to the result the "empirical" contact points, however they may be established, are lacking[7]; moreover, maxims of technological problem solving absorb methodological questions (cf. Kaminski et al. 2016). It is obvious that through this disengagement from classical, material objectivity as well as from the classical laboratory, something serious has changed in research—up to the point that experimental and simulation procedures are linked crosswise with each other in a novel manner.

Modified object worlds and lost relatedness to objects[8] are indeed not the sort of thing that will establish a new epistemic unity: Novelty as such will not alone constitute a new discipline; rather, it remains so to speak scattered over the tools and over the knowledge of methods that has to be adapted in various ways according to the discipline concerned. Thus, as an umbrella term "simulation" already covers a very broad field in the sciences using simulation-based procedures: questions of modelling and the mathematical and algorithmic procedures used permeate this field, as do problems of computing and of computers up to the presentation procedures selected in the end to make the results obtained plausible, to demonstrate results in a perceptual form and thus to make them literally "evident". In order to do justice to all this, expertise in simulation science remains in itself collaborative, and knowledge of the simulation procedure itself has the character of an ancillary science. This for its part means that in contact with and between experts questions concerning basic concepts are sometimes dropped because in case of doubt work is started on a trial basis inasmuch as the heuristic aspect is predominant and the utility of results counts. Thus, simulation seems to be a name that to a certain extent operates in the manner of a placeholder.

---

[7]For a case of this kind, Niklas Luhmann speaks of "cybernetic methodology": Data, axioms and combinations of the two are not related back step by step, rather warrants (and retrovalidations) are postponed in favour of the assumption that "certainty can only reside in the process itself"; scientific compatibility no longer presupposes testing procedures aiming at validation, but rather "more or less daring . . . assumptions with control reservations" are sufficient (cf. Luhmann 1993, pp. 418–419). A similar thought recurs in the discussion of simulation when simulation procedures are criticized for mixing up mere validation and genuine verification (cf. Winsberg 2010, pp. 9–10).

[8]Above all, those who believe in "nature", that is, in a guarantee of reality 'behind' the sciences and beyond the objectivity typical of the various disciplines, will presumably see in simulation a break with what constitutes 'hard' science.

2 Who Researches How Simulation Research Does Research? Interrelating and Extending the Observer Perspective

Though the name simulation binds heterogeneous things, with a certain justification it acts as a signal that in the future a "homogenous discipline"[9] may well be formed. However, the internal complexity of the wide range of producers, users and operators of simulation-based data and research results is not at all my real topic. The double-barrelled question that I mainly want to pose is as follows: How does observing and second-order science research position itself with respect to simulation? And how does it constitute itself so as to grasp and do justice to its—obviously multidimensional—object?

At any rate, research done by the social and human sciences also does not have an unequivocal answer to the question as to what can be called the object of research using simulation.[10] Does simulation examine modelling? Does it procure data-based, generic perceptualities of its own? Is ultimately only the arrangement of computing procedures that are used determinable as its object? Should the methodology be understood as a "medium", as a "technique" or even as a form of art?[11] The fact that the residual relationship of simulation procedures to reality cannot be readily determined also has to be included in this catalogue of questions.[12]

Without a doubt it was philosophy of science oriented on theory of science that addressed the status of simulation at a very early stage—and internationally—and it now dominates the discussion in the literature. There were and there are on-going, intensive discussions as to whether a paradigm shift to a new type of science is impending, whether simulation initiates a completely transformed relationship of model and world, whether it involves alternative realities (Galison 1996) or at least a "unique epistemology" (Winsberg 1999, 2010) and thus in philosophical terms a new ontology, or whether it is sufficient to characterize it simply as a "ubiquitous technology" (Wissenschaftsrat 2014).[13] The second major field is interdisciplinary theory of science oriented on social science: science studies, science and technology studies, technology assessment. Here, German-speaking research discusses,

---

[9]According to the German Council of Sciences and Humanities (Wissenschaftsrat), which explicitly draws a parallel to the emergence of computer science from mathematics and electrical and electronic engineering (Wissenschaftsrat 2014, p. 11).

[10]A world of objects that is typified for the sake of presentation? A family of presentation procedures? The realm of possibilities that it delineates and in a certain manner uses? The future?

[11]Indeed, the turn of phrase speaking of the "art and science" of simulating (cf. Shannon 1998) is freely used in the simulation community.

[12]Since I am sceptical about any scientistic realism, questions of the relation to reality seem to me to be less dramatic than problems of the unclear character of the object of the simulation (thus also questions of its reference). Realists may well assess this differently.

[13]Cf. the criticism of Frigg and Reiss (2009); as a reply to Frigg and Reiss cf. Humphreys (2009); for a comprehensive inventory Lenhard (2015).

among others, the case studies "climate" (Gramelsberger and Feichtner 2011) and "energy systems" (Möst et al. 2009). Beyond this, so to speak between these discipline areas, researchers from the fields of media history (Pias 2011), visual studies (Schneider and Nocke 2014) and the philosophy of technology (Hubig 2006) have addressed simulation as an object of research.

Let me turn to the promised programmatic view: it nonetheless seems to me to be conspicuous that the forms of observation that have so far been developed—we could call them "second order" forms of observation—are relatively closely tied to only certain perspectives of the social and human sciences (Sect. 2.1). These perspectives pay little attention to each other and do not solicit the expertise of neighbouring disciplines (Sect. 2.2); this results in large but unnoticed gaps in the spectrum of the disciplines involved. Consequently, research *on* simulation does little to approach simulation research (which for its part is heterogeneous) in the manner of a discussion partner (Sect. 2.3). For this reason, the worlds of simulation research and those of their satellites in the social and human sciences remain communicatively apart from each other—controversies or reciprocal "learning" exchanges do not take place. In this case I think that the observers are making things too easy for themselves. Finally, the conditions for theory formation are therefore not very good (Sect. 2.4). Overall, the present state of research in the social and human sciences does not represent what accompanying evaluative and reflective research on simulation research with a comprehensive interest in this field of objects could ideally be (or at least what could be desired). On all four points let me present a brief diagnosis and propositions.

2.1

Philosophy of science, if you will permit me to make some sweeping judgements for the sake of argument, is a dynamic scholarly community in Germany, too, but it is primarily oriented on science theory. This community is only loosely connected even with directly neighbouring subjects such as history of science, sociology of science or science and technology studies. There is little connection in the form of citation or basic concepts to fields such as philosophy of technology, theory of technology, technology assessment (TA) or policy analysis with respect to fields of application (Fig. 2). If we plot the focal points of evaluative research interests against the series of processes in the simulation pipeline, philosophy of science focusses primarily on questions of model formation and the mathematical view of the simulation event (Gramelsberger 2008 is an exception)—and then on questions of presentation concerning results that are "images".[14] The fact that simulation

---

[14]For critical discussions centred on questions of visualization, brain research has proved to be a paradigmatic research field (in addition to the controversial case of climate scenarios); according to its own claims, however, in brain research digital visualization procedures are not used to

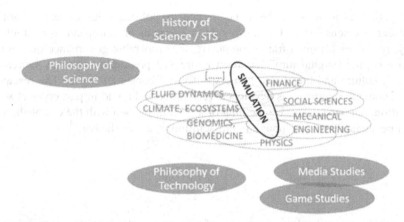

Fig. 2 Research on simulation sciences—to few, only loosely connected? (Source: own elaboration)

presents a different appearance with each "computation", with the limited conditions of a large-capacity computer (perhaps of a certain type), with the art of dealing with problems of scaling or with the significance thresholds of the "patterns" obtained—including the visual and verbal communication of what "is the case" according to the simulation—all this is thus more or less left out of the picture, probably quite unintentionally. Thus, the division of labour among simulationists almost seems to be reflected on the level of second-order research.

2.2

Normative problems—which genuinely belong to the scope of the social sciences and humanities—are somewhat neglected in the analysis of simulation, and it is not the pertinent disciplines that pose the questions and pursue them. Thus, at least the sparse German-speaking research does not get beyond a wide-ranging historical–diagnostic approach to the "political" aspect of simulation—research efforts on climate politics (cf. pars pro toto Edwards and Miller 2001; Edwards 2010) are an exception in this connection. Although philosophy of science also poses critical questions on simulation and subtly seems to link concern about research policy with its claim that a "new paradigm" has emerged, political science, law and ethics are not represented in research on the status, practice and rhetoric of simulation.

---

simulate, but rather to measure or display; correspondingly, the epistemological models of neuroscience distinctly distinguish between a "third-person perspective" (with a claim to objectivity) from a subjective "first-person perspective". There is ample critical literature on this, as an example cf. Janich (2009).

16

Equally, there is no debate in the social sciences or political science—at least not in the research discussion in Germany—about German or European infrastructure policy, resources for main-frame computers or comparable governance questions. Up to now, the "digital turn" has been addressed predominantly as a switch in everyday culture and thus from the perspective of consumer goods. The research field of computer games was developed very early and could in part connect with simulation, but has followed something of a path of its own with the establishment of "game studies", which, though interdisciplinary, are exclusive.[15]

2.3

The ability to understand the changeover from empirical–experimental research to the computer-aided simulation experiment as a method presupposes close acquaintance with the object level as well as something like "field contact".[16] Furthermore, the question arises as to whether beyond this something like an interdisciplinary capability for communication is required between simulating disciplines and the social sciences and humanities involved in simulation research. Simply with a view to refining their own judgement, but also to promote more reflection in the overall science system, the "second-order" disciplines should not only enhance the exchange of views among themselves, but also with the disciplines that are the objects of their research, the simulation sciences. Science research always involves reciprocal elucidation of partial epistemic views. Even Niklas Luhmann, who was quite pessimistic about the chances that epistemic observers could ultimately find a shared perspective, channelled his research on other disciplines and their objects (which was severely abstractive and provocative to those concerned) into the discourses of the disciplines concerned.[17] In other words: second-order research on simulation research should be able to speak with simulation research—not simply as a matter of politeness or due to research ethics, but rather to promote reciprocal accountability and along with it reflection. The methods followed by social science and humanities research in the field of simulation research must not be a "black box" for the simulation experts themselves. Simulation research should be able to take a stand and argue with evaluative researchers.

---

[15]For a critical characterization of game studies as a community at a loss for basic concepts and thus relatively helpless in the face of its object, cf. Feige (2015, pp. 10–11); and let me add: this helplessness may well be due to a lack of links to the discourse of academic disciplines.

[16]It seems clear to me that this can also be acquired by reading (of, say, specialist literature in simulation science), that is, that it need not be "empirical", for example, when concept and discourse analysis are concerned.

[17]Consider in particular his discussions of education science, which were projected as dispassionate descriptions from an external perspective, but nonetheless published together with representatives of the discipline with the aim of mutual understanding; cf. Luhmann and Schorr (1982).

2.4

New topics that are only weakly integrated in the discipline generally do not provide good presuppositions for well-founded theorizing; rather, the registration of objects by means of distinctions, some new, derived from the external world is preponderant, whereas theory is oriented on concepts, and theorizing is susceptible to (re-)integration when transformations take place.[18] Nonetheless, the difficulty in developing sufficiently reliable concepts in social sciences and humanities becomes greater with increasing communication gaps between the (sub-)communities involved. Basic concepts such as "technology", "media", "real" and "actual",[19] "virtual", canonic contexts and methodological terminology can hardly be adapted to each other—or they become uncontrollably detached from sound theoretical traditions when instead of building interdisciplinary bridges they form completely new, multidisciplinary communities, in the worst case promoting jargonizing detrimental to reputation and to the topic as a whole. Thus, the need for the development of good theory in the social sciences and humanities addressing simulation, that is, the need for a sufficiently consistent theory with responsive potential within and among the disciplines involved is an argument against insularized evaluative research and in favour of contact that is as intensive as possible.

3 Interdisciplinary Evaluative Research: Taking Simulation Sciences Seriously

It is quite possible that my preceding outline of 'second-order' research is not completely apposite, and that this caution applies not only to matters of detail. It is only intended to raise awareness for questions of the academic organization of research on simulation research. What paths should be taken, what paths *could* be considered *if* it were possible to employ a suitable development of social science and humanities research on simulation research?

Permit me to state a few propositions in addition to the answer that I have already given to the preliminary question "whether at all": yes, indeed, it is good to

---

[18]Cf. Luhmann (1993, p. 407): "It is not the object that guarantees the unity of theory, but rather the theory guarantees the unity of the object according to the slogan that everything that is a unity for an autopoietic system is a unity by virtue of the autopoietic system."

[19]The distinction in the German philosophical tradition between "real" and "wirklich" (actual) has been utilized especially by Christoph Hubig towards a better understanding of modelling and computer simulation; cf. Hubig (2015, pp. 144–157).

hold a serious discussion on as broad a basis as possible on an agenda for evaluative research on simulation research.

3.1

Differentiated communities that have already been formed in (sub-)disciplines and have specialized on selected aspects of simulation and simulation research and/or on certain methods should become open to each other in reading, discussion and at conferences to promote work on a common field of objects. Ideally, research on simulation does not constitute a fragmented domain (islands), but rather a kind of ring (Fig. 3) in which exchange is practised, while various perspectives and tools are used in search of equidistance to the object.

3.2

Gaps in the ring of evaluative research must not be accepted inasmuch as social significance is indeed attributed to the new phenomenon of computer simulation and science based on simulation results. Expertise that is lacking should therefore be sought and solicited—for example expertise pertaining to the governance and organization of simulation research or expertise that treats questions in terms of political science or economics more intensively than up to now. The current overabundance of descriptive analyses in the philosophy of science and science and technology studies is especially conspicuous. Hence, contributions from normative disciplines are much needed to complement the discussion of simulation; for example, light should be shed from a legal perspective on the diffuse area which is publicly viewed more in terms of ethics.

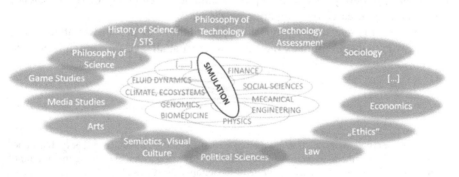

Fig. 3 Research on simulation sciences: a possible future? (Source: own elaboration)

3.3

The image of a ring in which there are neighbourhoods[20] intentionally suggests that a variety of disciplines and methods is important. Evaluative research that is intended to do justice to the complex implications of the changeover of science (together with economic action, social forecasting, political decision-making, everyday discourses and so on) to simulation procedures should not prematurely coalesce to an ad hoc discipline ("simulation studies" or the like) that is only purportedly unified and detached from the disciplines concerned. A specialization symbolically sailing under its own flag is more visible, it promises mutual intelligibility (oriented on paradigms, for example) and reduces competition. In the middle term, however, there is a danger of disengagement, lack of theory and marginalization. Many small islands are replaced by one somewhat larger island.

3.4

Social science and humanities research should organize dialogue forums, each for itself and jointly, in which simulation research itself is given the floor. On the level of reflective deliberation, mutual observation will not blur the difference between research and evaluative research ("second-order" research). Enhancing the precision of research approaches and discourses can only be beneficial to dialogue (and academic disputation).[21]

3.5

One phenomenon could emerge in an especially interesting manner in the constellation described: the plurality, in a manner of speaking a secondary plurality, resulting from the fact that simulation research is itself plural. Social sciences and humanities will not likely be subjected to criticism because they tend to equate

---

[20]In the following discussion I leave the question open as to whether the appearance of this neighbourhood should be similar to the contiguity of the actors in simulation research so as not to speak too much about simulation research; my topic is second-order research. In any case, the disciplines that do research into simulation research are integrated by a common object (how does simulation research operate?). This may well mislead us to close the discourse more than does the application of simulation methods to very different objects, which is constitutive of simulation sciences "as such".

[21]I thank Andreas Kaminski for helpful comments and discussions. This essay was written during a stay with the research group *Medienkulturen der Computersimulation* (MECS, media cultures in computer simulation) under the auspices of the German Research Association (Deutsche Forschungsgemeinschaft); accordingly, I would like to thank the MECS.

simulation with simulation—specifically, for example, transferring conclusions drawn from climate simulation without further ado to other fields of application of computer simulation. How inappropriate this is can be best learned in interdisciplinary discussions. This would also be the fitting place to hold comparative discussions in which light can be shed not only on the various methodological approaches of evaluative research, but also on the diversity of simulation research itself together with its results, which correspondingly require different treatments. When sociologists study the simulation of a construction component, both the sociological toolbox and design engineering as the field of application (say as the section of the simulation pipeline under examination) will specify what is ultimately addressed as "simulation".

4 In Lieu of a Conclusion

At the beginning, I characterized my remarks as programmatic and as a draft of an ideal state of academic policy. It is obvious why the world does not match such an ideal state. Social sciences and humanities are only sporadically interested in studies *about* simulation research, but above all it is problems of research organization that deter them from models of serious cooperation; such models require first of all abstention from the pattern of the quickly united "community", and in the second place these models require that the second-order researchers seek dialogue with the simulation researchers under study even though these researchers, as explained, occupy a heterogeneous field. Nonetheless, I adhere to my plea for a reflective interdisciplinary approach—on both sides and also on the great bridge between research and evaluative research where contact is quite *possible* and indeed immensely productive—isn't that what it's all about?

Translated from the German by Donald Goodwin.

References

Edwards, Paul N. 2010. *A Vast Machine. Computer Models, Climate Data, and the Politics of Global Warming*. Cambridge, MA: MIT Press.
Edwards, Paul N., and Clark A. Miller, eds. 2001. *Changing the Atmosphere: Expert Knowledge and Environmental Governance*. Cambridge, MA: MIT Press.
Feige, Daniel M. 2015. *Computerspiele. Eine Ästhetik*. Berlin: Suhrkamp.
Frigg, Roman, and Julian Reiss. 2009. The philosophy of Simulation: Hot new issues or same old stew? *Synthese* 169 (3): 593–613.
Galison, Peter. 1996. Computer Simulation and the trading zone. In *Disunity of science: Boundaries, Contexts, and Power*, ed. Peter Galison and David J. Stump, 118–157. California: Stanford University Press.
Gramelsberger, Gabriele. 2008. *Computerexperimente. Zum Wandel der Wissenschaft im Zeitalter des Computers*. Bielefeld: Transcript.

Gramelsberger, Gabriele, and Johann Feichtner, eds. 2011. *Climate Change and Policy. The Calculability of Climate Change and the Challenge of Uncertainty*. Berlin and Heidelberg: Springer.

Hey, Tony, Stewart Tansley, and Kristin Tolle, eds. 2009. *The Fourth Paradigm: Data-Intensive Scientific Discovery*. Redmond, WA: Microsoft Research.

Hubig, Christoph. 2006. *Die Kunst des Möglichen*, vol. 1, *Technikphilosophie als Reflexion der Medialität*. Bielefeld: Transcript.

Hubig, Christoph. 2015. *Die Kunst des Möglichen*, vol. 3, *Macht der Technik*. Bielefeld: Transcript.

Humphreys, Paul. 2009. The philosophical novelty of computer simulation methods. *Synthese* 169 (3): 615–626.

Janich, Peter. 2009. *Kein neues Menschenbild. Zur Sprache der Hirnforschung*. Frankfurt a. M.: Suhrkamp.

Krämer, Sybille. 1998. *Medien, Computer, Realität. Wirklichkeitsvorstellungen und Neue Medien*. Frankfurt a. M.: Suhrkamp.

Kaminski, Andreas, Uwe Küster, Michael Resch, and Björn Schembera. 2016. Simulation als List. In *List und Tod. Jahrbuch Technikphilosophie 2016*, ed. Gerhard Gamm, Petra Gehring, Christoph Hubig, Andreas Kaminski and Alfred Nordmann, 93–121. Zürich und Berlin: Diaphanes.

Lenhard, Johannes. 2015. *Mit allem rechnen. Zur Philosophie der Computersimulation*. Berlin and Boston: de Gruyter.

Luhmann, Niklas. [1990] 1993. *Die Wissenschaft der Gesellschaft*. 3rd ed. Frankfurt a. M.: Suhrkamp.

Luhmann, Niklas, and Karl E. Schorr, eds. 1982. *Zwischen Technologie und Selbstreferenz. Fragen an die Pädagogik*. Frankfurt a. M.: Suhrkamp.

Möst, Dominik, Wolf Fichtner, and Armin Grunwald, eds. 2009. *Energiesystemanalyse*. Karlsruhe: Universitätsverlag Karlsruhe.

Pias, Claus. 2011. On the Epistempology of Computer Simulation. *Zeitschrift für Medien- und Kulturforschung* 1:29–54.

Schneider, Birgit, and Thomas Nocke, eds. 2014. *Image Politics of Climate Change. Visualizations, Imaginations, Documentations*. Bielefeld: Transcript.

Shannon, Robert E. 1998. Introduction to the Art and Science of Simulation. In *Proceedings of the 1998 Winter Simulation Conference*, ed. D. J. Medeiros, Edward F. Watson, John S. Carson and Mani S. Manivannan, 7–14. Los Alamitos, CA: IEEE Computer Societey Press. http://cecs.wright.edu/~fciarall/ISE195/Readings/ShannonSimulationART.pdf. Accessed 16 May 2016.

Varenne, Franck. 2007. *Du modèle à la simulation informatique*. Paris: Vrin.

Winsberg, Eric. 2010. *Science in the Age of Computer Simulation*. Chigago: University of Chicago Press.

Winsberg, Eric. 1999. Sanctioning Models: The epistemology of Simulation. *Science in Context* 12 (2): 275–292.

Wissenschaftsrat. 2014. *Bedeutung und Weiterentwicklung von Simulation in der Wissenschaft. Positionspapier*. Dresden. http://www.wissenschaftsrat.de/download/archiv/4032-14.pdf. Accessed 16 May 2016.

On the Missing Coherent Theory of Simulation

Michael M. Resch

Abstract Simulation as a methodology is a widely used tool in scientific research, as well as in industrial product development. As simulation has become an established practice in many fields of scientific research, discussions arise about what simulation is. While engineering and natural sciences take a technical position in this discussion, philosophy tries to classify and identify simulation by means of scientific theory and the epistemology of science. This article will attempt to look at these approaches by formulating, from a technical background, questions relevant to philosophy and social sciences in order to understand simulation. In the end, we will find that a coherent theory of simulation is missing, although key building blocks for such a theory do already exist.

1 Introduction

As a tool in scientific research and industrial product development, simulation has become a solid component of our world. This is why simulation itself has become an object of scientific research. Within the framework of information technology, this is frequently referred to as the third paradigm or third pillar of science (Hey et al. 2009). According to this paradigm, simulation is a third way of attaining knowledge, next to logic and experimentation. However, this perspective will not be merely accepted, but instead consciously questioned.

In this paper, the subject of simulation is introduced with a short outline of what simulation is in a technical sense. Subsequently, simulation is observed from various angles. Different issues surrounding the subject of simulation are then discussed. Due to the pillarization and specialization of sciences, these issues and questions are currently found in a no man's land between disciplines. Because these questions have not been clarified, confusions in scientific discussions and a collective silence within disciplines about the essence of simulation have often resulted.

M.M. Resch (✉)
High Performance Computing Center Stuttgart (HLRS), University of Stuttgart, Nobelstr. 19, 70569 Stuttgart, Germany
e-mail: resch@hlrs.de

© Springer International Publishing AG 2017

M.M. Resch et al. (eds.), *The Science and Art of Simulation I*,
DOI 10.1007/978-3-319-55762-5_3

A quote by Karl Popper should be stated at the beginning of these considerations, as it can prove fruitful to further contributions on this subject:

> A scientist engaged in a piece of research, say in physics, can attack his problem straight away. He can go at once to the heart of the matter: to the heart, that is, of an organized structure. For a structure of scientific doctrines is already in existence; and with it, a generally accepted problem-situation. (Popper 1992, p. xv)

With these words, Karl Popper introduced "Logik der Forschung. Zur Erkenntnistheorie der modernen Naturwissenschaften" (The Logic of Research: On the Epistemology of Modern Natural Science) in 1934. Regarding the subject of "simulation" against this background, one question that emerges is whether a "structure of scientific doctrines" for simulation exists. Of course, the first question that arises is whether simulation is an individual science. This also raises the issue of whether it is possible and useful to establish a systematic structure of scientific doctrines for simulation, as it has been done in the case of physics.

However, not even a "generally accepted problem" can be stated: From the point of view of engineering and natural sciences, simulation is considered to be an established, well justified, and easily available method. Since it is used, it exists, and therefore there is no need to question it. Similarly, in social sciences, simulation is typically perceived as a mere fact so that only its effect or impact is examined. In contrast, the meaning and the nature of simulation are often relegated to a secondary position, due to the general marvel of modern supercomputers' gigantic processing capacities.

In summary, the scientific view of simulation is in large part uncritical, and therefore unscientific. Consequently, it is not possible to speak of the existence of an academic facility. Questions that could lead to such a well-structured scientific doctrine ("organized structure") still need to be established.

2 The Technical-Scientific Conception of Simulation

What simulation is, from a practical point of view, may seem initially unclear—even when simulation experts refer to the existence and importance of simulation. Frequently, simulation is described as a process whereby a series of instructions are passed through and are terminated in a computer-generated result. Reference should be made here to the examples of Winsberg (2010) and Resch (2013, p. 240). Both refer to a series of steps that can be thought of as a "Simulation Pipeline", which can also be found in detail in further literature on simulation (Bungartz et al. 2013). The meaning of all the individual steps of such a pipeline will not be further considered here, nor will the problem of accuracy and correctness. See Kaminski et al. (2016) for a detailed discussion of a series of adjustments and restrictions for the approach outlined here (Fig. 1).

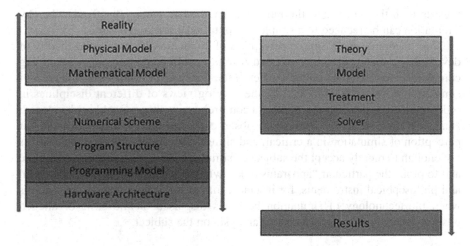

Fig. 1 Schematic description of processes within a simulation by Resch (*left*) and Winsberg (*right*). (Cf. Resch 2013, p. 240)

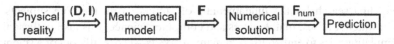

Fig. 2 Simulation pipeline by Szabó (2015)

A conception comparable with my previous work (2013) and Bungartz et al. (2013) can be found in a recently published mathematics article by Szabó (2015). However, there, the simulation-pipeline is reduced to only a few steps (Fig. 2).

It is notable that all of these concepts seem to be incomplete. Winsberg focuses predominantly on the "treatment" and sees the core of simulation precisely therein (in the choice of correct framework conditions and parameters). As the director of the High Performance Computing Center Stuttgart, I unsurprisingly emphasize the programming and hardware aspects. Szabó concentrates primarily on the mathematical and numerical issues, as he is a mathematically trained fluid mechanics engineer.

Each of these three models, when compared with the other two, exhibits considerable gaps. These gaps may perhaps be perceived as professionally induced blind spots on behalf of the authors. However, upon closer examination of these blind spots, it can be observed that a homogenous concept of simulation does not exist.

Essentially, Winsberg sees a mathematical problem in simulation, mainly defined by the correct boundary conditions and choice of parameters, which, in turn, are derived directly from a model or from the experience of the simulator. In contrast, Szabó concentrates primarily on a mathematical scheme which aims to solve a given equation that is an accepted model for reality. While Winsberg sees mathematics as a given fact mainly varying in its numerical implementation, Szabó regards both the model and the numerical method as essentially fixed, whereby simulation can be reduced to a simple computational solution process.

This "incompleteness" in the perception of simulation leads to the difficulty of developing a theory of simulation and results in different disciplines developing completely varying views on the subject. If the goal is to develop a sensible view of simulation, then we have to analyze the varying views of different disciplines in order to identify gaps and see whether a comprehensive theory could be developed. Here, we must have the courage to observe the impact of disciplines on our perception of simulation in a critical, and simultaneously pragmatic, manner. It is not enough to merely accept the subject of simulation in each respective discipline and to probe the particular "apparatus of knowledge." The application of historical and philosophical instruments, for instance, may result in less fruitful conclusions when the technology of simulation becomes disguised on the basis of alleged positive results that prohibit a critical analysis on the subject.

3   Core Sciences of Simulation

We will first search for the fundamentals of simulation in the core subjects and fields in which it arises: mathematics and computer science. It is also in these fields that simulation tries to embed itself in many respects—especially out of a scientific-organizational motivation. A focus on these two sciences does not indicate that one or even both of these sciences should be regarded as the only fundamental parts of simulation. When we speak of a "core," we refer to visible aspects around simulation that form the basis for the scientific and public perception of the concept of simulation.

3.1   Mathematics

Assuming that mathematics is a language for describing the world, simulation could be viewed as an enhancement of this language. Consequently, simulation would only be a mathematical way of describing the world. And using this description, simulation would only be transforming these descriptions through formal processes (e.g., programming, program sequence, visualization) in a mathematically defined way to achieve an image of reality. The computer would supply the output of these mathematically defined processes without making any contribution of its own, just as a slide rule automatically supplies the correct output for any given input.

In the process, however, mathematicians fail to account for two problems in simulation. First, they fail to address the question of correctness of their models, i.e., the bias inherent in any modelling process that transforms perception (*Wahrnehmung*) into a formal description. They rely on the assumption that this problem is of a purely philosophical nature, which can only be resolved epistemologically. Furthermore, they do not factor in the inaccuracies of the calculations, or the correctness of the processed output. Instead, they consider this to be a problem of a technical nature that can be "treated" by error assessment.

The model correctness problem (mathematical models resulting from experiments and perceptions) may appear to be negligible. Mathematicians may adopt the view that mathematics cannot be better than epistemology itself. This interpretation may be responsible for a number of misunderstandings regarding simulation in several fields. For example, in order to fully understand our climate, simulation requires the direct awareness that there is no completely accurate model describing the world climate based on experiments, or on fundamental physical laws. It would, however, be as fatal to conclude from that that no climate simulation is possible at all, as it would be to simply trivialize or discard its relative incorrectness.

Beyond this, mathematicians do not acknowledge that the computer is not a mathematically exact machine. Therefore, simulation leaves the mathematical sphere and cannot be approached only by mathematical means. Typically, mathematicians view this as a mere problem of precision, but not as a fundamental issue. Kaminski et al. (2016) point out in great detail, however, how and why these flaws of the machine can have a profound effect on the outcome of a simulation. Eric Winsberg (2010) offers a similar critique, emphasizing the material aspect of simulation in the use of computers.

Conclusively, the increased use of mathematics and the attempt to describe the world in mathematical terms takes away from our capacity to develop scientific descriptions for models beyond the reach of mathematics, which may, however, be critical and helpful for our understanding of the world.

3.2 Computer Science

From a computer science point of view, like so many mathematical problems that can be analyzed by computer processing, simulation is merely another application of computer science and therefore a specialty of the field. According to this definition, simulation is principally subject to the rules of information-processing science. Historically, simulation has been seen to have low significance to computer science—even been considered entirely void of such relevance—which is why computer scientists frequently dismiss the problem of the right input for their simulation, reducing it to terms such as "input error" and "vague assumptions." Following the first law of computer science, "garbage in—garbage out," all of the responsibility that the maker of the model has toward the scientific content, is delegated elsewhere.

In general, computer science has largely turned away from the concept of simulation in favor of more lucrative topics such as the "Internet of Things" and "Big Data."

One is tempted to say that this is indicative of a direct effect of federal aid measures on academic sciences. In reality, however, we are observing the retreat of the scientific character out of the wide open view—as described, for example, by José Ortega y Gasset (1988)—into the warming flow of Weber's niche, well protected by "blinders" (Weber 1992, p. 312). The scientist wearing blinders is reanimated, a golem amidst living science.

At the same time, the focus on vaguely defined terms such as "Big Data" presents a retreat of computer science from science at large. Consistently, computer scientists are already proclaiming the "end of theory" (Anderson 2008), suggesting that, after analyzing huge amounts of data, it is possible to reach a result without a theory and that Big Data renders theoretical attempts obliterate. The concept of what is "feasible," based on the accelerated performance of computers and increased memory capacity of modern database systems, is gradually replacing the concept of the "logical." Consequently, we cannot hope for computer science to contribute meaningfully to a logical or rational concept of simulation. On the contrary, computer science as a natural continuation of the concept of interpreting huge masses of data rather promotes the idea of huge parameter studies. Their framework is the hope for gaining deeper insight into simulation systems via numerous parallel processing simulations and sensible calculation of mean values.

4 Applied Sciences of Simulation

In the area of applied science, simulation takes on the function of an instrument. Depending on the degree of the user's prior knowledge, simulation is used as a black box (no knowledge of its functioning) or as a grey box (sparse knowledge of its functioning). The result is astonishing: Through the use of only very small and occasionally simple interventions and by altering the parameters, it is possible to generate any desired result, supported either by commercial or open-source software.

These approaches and their corresponding views of simulation are not surprising when scientific theory is redirecting the focus from the actual topic of simulation toward the epistemological meaning of these parameter variations and adjustable mathematical-information technological instruments. However, from the perspective of a simulation expert, these variations do not represent the essence of simulation, but, instead, the derivation from the essence of simulation. Consequently, the adjustment of the method to the desired result (in the simplest case, curve-fitting) weakens the scientific credibility of simulation.

In today's applied sciences, there is no awareness of the use of simulation or a computer's likeness to a measuring device. Although, on the one hand, the alteration of data derived from experiments—aside from any scientific justification—is considered dishonorable, on the other hand, the willful alteration of parameters for the purpose of achieving better results can be applied freely without any repercussions. Due to current standards, such manipulations often go unnoticed, especially in cases when very fast and expensive computers are used and when a repetition of the course of simulations is not feasible for the external examining scientist.

In conclusion, although the applied sciences make an important contribution to the scientific development of simulation, they are taken up and formalized by mathematicians and computer scientists. That being the case, they also contribute to damaging simulation as a scientific tool.

5 Science Theory of Simulation

Currently, no scientific theory of simulation has reached a broad level of academic engagement. Within the visible contributions to date, there are two tendencies that can be briefly mentioned here.

First, there is a quasi-positivistic approach in the scientific theory of simulation. According to this view, simulation is seen as a truth whose effect is to be examined, but whose essential nature is not relevant. Such an approach is typical of those who consider simulation only as a further "triumphal entry" of computers. This being the case, it coincides surprisingly well with certain unreflective approaches of the applied sciences.

Second, those who take a more critical view of simulation understand the problem presented by diversified representations and models, but they tend to get lost in the haze of basic and applied sciences. Their analyses of simulation do not concentrate on the more common aspects of simulation, but instead on visual and unfinished aspects.

Consequently, social scientists, humanities scholars, and philosophers prefer to focus on simulations of climate or astrophysics, where simulation exhibits both its greatest strengths and its most profound shortcomings. Although understanding such shortfalls may offer productive results, it does not address the true "essence" of simulation. Accordingly, simulation experts lack an understanding of the scientific theories behind simulation. The latent approach of technical scientists toward their colleagues in the social sciences—saying that they lack the required "expertise" to fully understand technology—is enhanced by the focus on areas such as climate change.

Given this situation, we find a key for the process of working out a theory of simulation. For such a theory, clear communication between technical scientists and social scientists and humanities scholars would be required. But, ironically, technical scientists fail to notice that it is precisely their vague descriptions of technology that mislead social scientists. To take a step towards a theory of simulation, we will have to get rid of the vagueness of technical descriptions of simulation.

6   Socio-Scientific Theory of Simulation

A socio-scientific theory of simulation does not exist. Because simulation is so far removed from the focus of specialized socio-scientific research, it can at best be seen as a field within the theories produced for "information societies" or "knowledge-based societies." Even when examining the historical development of computer sciences, simulation only played a prominent role at the beginning of nuclear weapons-related research.

Simulation usually disappears in the flow of the glorious historical victory of the computer. In rather grotesque ways, the personal reminiscences of directors of data centers get in the way of scientific exploration. Two essential criteria, however, should radically transform the attitude of the social sciences.

6.1   Meaning of Simulation for Political Action Processes

In the political decision-making process, simulations represent the possibility of supplying a reliable, scientific basis. The fields in which this can be done are many. The most prominent one is climate simulation, where simulation is a key tool for gaining insight into the behavior of our climate. But there are other fields that politics looks to for support: Financial simulations, for example, are seen as a way to support economic decision-making. Social simulations are seen as a tool to better understand society and to better design rules and regulations.

To allow for the use of simulations in the political decision-making process, a sound theory of simulation is required. This would allow scientists to put their work in perspective and convey relevant information to the political decision-makers. Moreover, it would allow politicians to rely on standardized information gained from standardized and reliable simulations.

6.2   Meaning of the Perception of Simulation in Society

At the same time, simulation is forcing its way into public life. Simulation then becomes the basis of critical decisions and the essence of the critical narrative. Again, climate research serves as the most prominent example. A series of societal developments cannot be understood if simulation's role in influencing them is not taken into account. Some powerful forms of social expression such as the media, especially films,[1] are currently contributing to a distorted understanding of the meaning of simulation for society. Films project a wrong picture of simulation as

---

[1]See, for example, Besson (2015) or Pfister (2014).

they have to simplify the view on computers. By contrast, social sciences are only beginning to reach an insight into simulation.

This is all the more surprising as social scientists have a number of methodologies at their disposal to analyze this phenomenon. Both Niklas Luhmann's Theory of Society (Luhmann 2005) and Power (Luhmann 2012) and Michel Foucault's way of analyzing social phenomena (Foucault 1995) and knowledge (Foucault 2012) offer methods for critical analysis. These and other approaches are, however, not currently being applied. Instead, social scientists concentrate on simulation as an instrument for social research. There is, on the one hand, a critical view of the problems relative to exact simulation in social sciences (Braun and Saam 2014), and on the other hand, optimism about its potential and usability (Pentland 2015).

While Byung-Chul Han (2015) offers an interesting insight from a philosophical perspective, he does not go beyond a critique of computers, which obscures the underlying social and philosophical concepts instead of illuminating them. Specifically, his interpretation of information as a "smooth surface" of all things is a problem for information theorists, who take the opposite view: information is what surprises (Weaver and Shannon 1963). Beyond that, philosophy has begun to examine simulation in greater depth within the context of the theory of knowledge, if, however, only within a purely scientific debate and framework (Winsberg 2010; Humphreys 2009).

7 Questions

Based on the previous considerations, a number of questions arise on the practical users of simulation. Answers to these questions may eventually lead to a theory of simulation:

1. How does the concept of simulation fit with our understanding of woman and her ability to acquire knowledge?
2. What potential knowledge does simulation offer in fields that cannot be described primarily through mathematical formulae?
3. How can social sciences and humanities contribute to the understanding of the phenomenon of simulation?
4. What can simulation contribute to solve social and political problems?

The enterprise of understanding simulation, may not lead to answers, but it is still vital to examine these questions in a dialogue between applied scientists and their counterparts in the social sciences and humanities.

References

Anderson, Chris. 2008. The End of Theory: The Data Deluge Makes the Scientific Method Obsolete. *Wired Magazine*, June 23. http://www.wired.com/2008/06/pb-theory/. Accessed 25 October 2016.

Besson, Luc. 2015. *Lucy*. DVD. Universal City, CA: Universal Studios Home Entertainment.

Braun, Norman, and Nicole J. Saam. 2014. *Handbuch Modellbildung und Simulation in den Sozialwissenschaften*. Berlin and Heidelberg: Springer, Springer VS.

Bungartz, Hans-Joachim, Stefan Zimmer, Martin Buchholz, and Dirk Pflüger. 2013. *Modellbildung und Simulation: Eine anwendungsorientierte Einführung*. Berlin and Heidelberg: Springer, Springer Spektrum.

Foucault, Michel. 1995. *Wahnsinn und Gesellschaft*. Frankfurt a. M.: Suhrkamp.

Foucault, Michel. 2012. *Über den Willen zum Wissen*. Berlin: Suhrkamp.

Han, Byung-Chul. 2015. *Die Errettung des Schönen*. Frankfurt a. M.: Fischer.

Hey, Tony, Stewart Tansley, and Kristin Tolle. 2009. *The Fourth Paradigm: Data-Intensive Scientific Discovery*. Redmond, WA: Microsoft Research.

Humphreys, Paul. 2009. The philosophical novelty of computer simulation methods. *Synthese* 169 (3): 615–626.

Kaminski, Andreas, Uwe Küster, Michael Resch, and Björn Schembera. 2016. Simulation als List. In *List und Tod. Jahrbuch Technikphilosophie 2016*, ed. Gerhard Gamm, Petra Gehring, Christoph Hubig, Andreas Kaminski and Alfred Nordmann, 93–121. Zürich und Berlin: Diaphanes.

Luhmann, Niklas. 2005. *Einführung in die Theorie der Gesellschaft*. Heidelberg: Carl-Auer.

Luhmann, Niklas, 2012. *Macht im System*. Berlin: Suhrkamp.

Ortega y Gasset, José. 1988. *Der Aufstand der Massen*. Gütersloh: Bertelsmann.

Pentland, Alex. 2015. *Social Physics – How Social Networks Can Make Us Smarter*. United States: Penguin Books.

Pfister, Wally. 2014. *Transcendence*. DVD. Burbank, CA: Warner Home Video.

Popper, Karl. 1992. *The Logic of Scientific Discovery*. London and New York: Routledge.

Resch, Michael. 2013. What's the result? Thoughts of a Center Director on Simulation. In *Computer Simulation and the Changing Face of Scientific Experimentation*, ed. Juan M. Durán and Eckhardt Arnold, 233–246. Newcastle: Cambridge scholars Publishing.

Szabó, Barna. 2015. Simulation Governance: An Idea Whose Time Has Come. *IACM expressions* 37: 6–8.

Weaver, Warren, and Claude Elwood Shannon. 1963. *The Mathematical Theory of Communication*. Champaign, IL: University of Illinois Press.

Weber, Max. 1992. Vom inneren Beruf zur Wissenschaft. In *Max Weber. Soziologie – Universalgeschichtliche Analysen – Politik*, ed. Johannes F. Winckelmann, 311–339. Stuttgart: Kröner

Winsberg, Eric. 2010. *Science in the age of computer simulations*. Chicago: The University of Chicago Press.

The Art of Staging Simulations: Mise-en-scène, Social Impact, and Simulation Literacy

Bruno Gransche

Abstract Computer simulations have tremendous influence in a society that faces the irreducible complexity of an open future and that feels the urge to anticipatorily deal with possible future developments. The perspective proposed in this essay investigates the entire process of computer simulation as a *mimesis* operation that draws much of its social power from the staging decisions made in the process. Simulations are understood equally as composed *imitations* of something real and as *creations* of something fictitious or imaginary. The concept of mimesis—following Paul Ricœur—combines these two aspects of imitation and creation. It allows us to tackle important questions: To what extent must the persuasive power of simulations be accompanied by recipients' *simulation literacy?* How can this literacy be fostered? How can the science and art of simulation be embedded into a cultural context and how can the appropriate cultural skills that are needed in order to 'fluently read' and properly interpret simulations be provided? Another mimesis operation—theatrical *staging* or *mise-en-scène*—has developed unique composition techniques between imitation and creation. While seeking to investigate simulations' efficacy in society, it is rewarding to focus on the staging character of simulation, on the *mise-en-scène* aspects of this powerful 'computational *as if.*' The following article will discuss the insights to be gained by looking at computer simulations as a peculiarity of staging and theatricality. It positions the art of staging simulations as a starting point both for more socially compatible simulations and for a more simulation-literate society.

1 Introduction

Computer simulation is spreading as a phenomenon and already has a huge impact on science, society, and politics. It will increasingly affect everyday life and the very notion of what is and will become real. Yet, there is an irreconcilable gap

B. Gransche (✉)
Institute of Advanced Studies (FoKoS), University of Siegen, Weidenauerstr. 167,
57076 Siegen, Germany
e-mail: bruno.gransche@uni-siegen.de

© Springer International Publishing AG 2017
M.M. Resch et al. (eds.), *The Science and Art of Simulation I*,
DOI 10.1007/978-3-319-55762-5_4

between simulations and reality. Computer simulations may exert tremendous influence in a society that faces the irreducible complexity of an open future and that feels the urge to anticipatorily deal with possible future developments.

As computer simulation is a subtype of simulations more broadly, it possesses certain simulation-specific properties. Simulations can be seen as composed *imitations* of something real, and as *creations* of something fictitious or imaginary. In this perspective, to simulate means 'to act *as if*.' Simulation can be understood as an act of transforming the world into a composition that is configured in order to allow for specific insights. The science and art of simulation has reached an impressive performance level that can be overwhelmingly persuasive. Computer simulations artistically present their imitations or creations *as if* they were real. This can tempt recipients to forget about the constitutive gap between simulations and reality, and therefore to mistakenly understand what was simulated '*as if it were real*' as '*being real as a matter of fact.*' Simulations have a very powerful capacity to persuade, to present creations as apparently obvious and thereby to hide their composed nature. As such, they are a powerful tool for influencing social discourse and allocating resources—attention, support, and funds alike. The 2 °C target in climate policy, for instance, is derived from climate simulations and used to motivate all sorts of action, from individual energy-saving behavior to global emission limits.

This leads to the question of how simulations affect their recipients and to what extend their persuasive power has to be contained or accompanied by recipients' *simulation literacy*. This kind of literacy can be formed by embedding the science and art of simulation into a cultural context and by providing the appropriate cultural skills needed in order to properly interpret simulations. There is an analogous context in which the '*art of as if*' is performed and in which distinct cultural skills have been developed: the theatre. The unique theatrical composition technique between imitation and creation—that is: *staging* or *mise-en-scène*—is well known and meets well established interpretational skills.

The following article discusses the insights to be gained by looking at computer simulations as a peculiarity of staging and theatricality. Simulation cannot be equated to staging, but while seeking to investigate simulations' efficacy in society, it is rewarding to focus on the staging character of simulation, on the *mise-en-scène* aspects of this powerful 'computational *as if*.'

2   Poietic Simulation

In this article, computer simulation is understood as a method for studying systems, including "choosing a model; finding a way of implementing that model in a form that can be run on a computer; calculating the output of the algorithm; and visualizing and studying the resultant data" (Winsberg 2015). In addition to Winsberg's description, a special emphasis will be placed on the visualization of the output and on the entire *mise-en-scène* of the output presentation.[1] The perspective proposed here is to investigate the entire process of computer simulation as a special case of simulations in general and as a *mimesis* process that draws much of its social power from staging decisions, especially in the late phase of presenting and visualizing the results. The mimesis concept—to anticipate this much—does not prompt an emphasis on imitation; it rather combines the two aspects of imitation and creation, thus fitting the double character of simulation suggested above.

2.1 Mimesis One, Two, Three

The French philosopher Paul Ricœur developed a concept based on Aristotle's understanding of *mimesis* to analyze the interaction between the world, the author with his or her narrative compositions or stories, and the recipient with his or her interpretative sense-making. This threefold concept of mimesis can be used to shed light both on how simulations rely on their creators' worldviews and composing skills as well as how they affect their recipients, whether in science, society, or politics. Mimesis is at the very heart of simulations: "The most significant feature of a simulation is that it allows scientists to *imitate one process by another process*" (Hartmann 2005, p. 1)[2]; a simulation "accurately mimics a complex phenomenon" (Kaufmann and Smarr 1993, p. 4). The relation between mimesis and simulation has been discussed in theory as everything from contrary to complementary.[3] When described in contrary terms, mimesis has been rejected[4] as a valid characterization of simulation. Such a view supposedly emphasizes that simulating is more than just *imitating*; it is also *creating*. Although this emphasis is correct, the rejection of mimesis can be seen as premature, and might stem from a superficial understanding of the concept. Building on Ricœur's interpretation of Aristotle's concept, mimesis can be reconciled with simulation, since the latter is not just the mere imitation of something but rather the creation of something different, yet similar: different, for instance, in its structure and dynamics, yet similar in its performance and

---

[1]That is not to say that the social efficacy of simulations is entirely a matter of staging the output; on the contrary, it starts at the very beginning of choosing a model. Philine Warnke argues that the choice of a model in simulations already has a social dimension and changes such as, for example, the potential social acceptability of the technology that results from the simulations. The real-world environment where such technology is used has to be adjusted according to the simulation in order to make the technology work properly (Warnke 2002).

[2]Or simulations imitate one process, structure, dynamic, etc. by means of another. Hartmann adds: "In this definition, the term 'process' refers solely to some object or system whose state changes in time. If the simulation is run on a computer, it is called a *computer simulation*" Hartmann (2005, p. 5). The point here is to focus on *imitation*.

[3]For an overview, see Dotzler (2010).

[4]Dotzler describes a tendency to reject the mimesis category ["Tendenz zur Absage an die Mimesiskategorie" (Dotzler 1991, p. 12)].

appearance. Mimesis as explained by Aristotle is an inherently creative, *poetic* operation. Ricœur points out that the adjective *poetic* (deriving from the Aristotelian *poiesis*) indicates "production, construction and dynamism."[5] Mimesis in Aristotle's sense thus has to be understood as active processes, "as operations, not as structures."[6] Ricœur insists that mimesis has to be conceived of as a mimicking operation, as an active process of "imitation or representation."[7] Therefore, imitation or representation "must be understood in the dynamic sense of making a representation, of a transposition into representative works."[8] Simulation, seen as a mimetic operation, can consequently be thought of as an *active transposition into representative works*. In the case of computer simulation, this transposing agent is the simulating scientist with equipment such as a computer, (3D) screens, projectors, speakers, and "simulation theatres," the venues in which simulations are presented to audiences, such as the HLRS "Cave."[9]

What does Ricœur mean by his threefold concept of mimesis, and how can it help us to rethink computer simulations and their impact on various audiences? Ricœur developed his concept in order to explain the relationship between three elements of narration or storytelling: the world, the author, and the recipient (Ricœur 1984, pp. 52–90). He calls "mimesis II" the actual act of composing a narrative, the artistic *poiesis* of arranging heterogeneous elements (events, settings, persons, motifs, props, etc.) according to certain narrative rules and structures (beginning, ending, timing, relevance, etc.) and thus forming a story worth telling. The *creative* aspect of this mimesis can be emphasized: This narrative composition is a new work; it is a poetic creation that was not copied, nor merely imitated or retold unadulterated. Yet, the *imitation* aspect of this mimesis can also be highlighted: Neither the narrative nor any of its elements are entirely conceived *ex nihilo*; the writing process is an operation of composing, re-arranging, and sampling. So the art of *configuring* a narrative—that is, mimesis II—is an *imitative-creative*, *mimetic* act that represents a new creation, but at the same time strongly relies on the components, structures, and dynamics already found in the external world ("the world wherein real action occurs", Ricœur 1984, p. 71). Part of

---

[5]"[T]he adjective 'poetic' (with its implied noun, 'art'). It alone puts the mark of production, construction, dynamism on all the analyses, and first of all on the two terms muthos [mythos, BG] and mimesis, which have to be taken as operations, not as structures" (Ricœur 1984, pp. 32–33).

[6]See note 5.

[7]"The same mark has to be preserved in the translation of mimesis. Whether we say 'imitation' or 'representation' (as do the most recent French translators), what has to be understood is the mimetic activity, the active process of imitating or representing something. Imitation or representation, therefore, must be understood in the dynamic sense of making a representation, of a transposition into representative works" (Ricœur 1984, p. 33).

[8]See note 7.

[9]This high-end "simulation theatre" with black curtains, "ushers," five huge screens including floor and ceiling, ten 3D projectors, etc. is incredibly impressive and as close as it gets today to *Star Trek*'s holodeck. It allows users to manipulate interactive simulations in real time, thanks to high-performance computing as well as high-speed parallel rendering, 3D interfaces, and tracking systems (see HLRS 2016).

this mimesis II process is the selection of tellable, appropriate, and interesting elements of the external world, including direct perceptions as well as other already composed elements of the world, such as stories. For Ricœur, it is only possible to identify and choose these tellable elements of the world because they are always already perceived in a filtered, very specific, *prefigured* way. This narrative prefiguration of the world as seen by authors—and for Ricœur, every human is a potential author, if not of masterpieces then at least of everyday chatter—is called mimesis I. This first mimesis describes the encounter between the specifically perceived, *prefigured* elements of the world and the composer, who 'reads' the world as eligible for his or her composition. The second mimesis *configures* these elements and provides them with their own intelligibility and a new meaning so that the recipients who encounter the new creation interpret it through their own perspectives, schemata, concepts, experiences, and so on. Recipients—and this is mimesis III—*refigure* the configuration against the backdrop of their specifically prefigured worldview. This closes for Ricœur a non-vicious circle, because the prefiguration of our worldviews is strongly influenced by the sense-making perception (refiguration) of the imitative-creative compositions (configurations) we encounter; these encounters are influenced by previous ones and by the various prefigurations; finally, the configuring process itself is guided by the authors' prefigurations and the anticipated recipients' refigurations. The configuring operation (II) thus connects the world in its prefigured perceived shape (I) and the refiguration of the mimetic— imitative-creative—representations (III).[10]

Applied to the example of a novel, for instance, this concept means that an author writes about what he or she perceives in the world, while readers select and interpret specific aspects of the story as a result of what they know about the world. How the author sees the world is not how the reader sees it, and what was written never coincides with what is read. However, how the reader sees the world changes after every refigured story. If someone we meet resembles Captain Ahab, then it is because we once read *Moby-Dick* (or saw the film). What could be understood now by applying this heuristics of the threefold mimesis to simulations?

2.2 Composing Simulations

Computer simulations certainly select and configure specific elements of the world (depending on modelling decisions); they are created according to certain rules of

---

[10]For Ricœur, the importance of this connection can hardly be overestimated. He argues that the special structure of the configurations (in his case, narratives) both reflect and shape human worldviews, especially the concept and perception of time. His basic hypothesis in *Temps et Ré cit* is "that between the activity of narrating a story and the temporal character of human experience there exists a correlation that is not merely accidental but that presents a transcultural form of necessity. To put it another way, *time becomes human to the extent that it is articulated through a narrative mode, and narrative attains its full meaning when it becomes a condition of temporal existence*" (Ricœur 1984, p. 52).

composition and are presented to an audience (scientists, the public, etc.) in order to share insights or change worldviews. For instance, the mathematical understanding of fractals changed the perception and explanation of some natural, rugged, self-repeating structures as fractals or fractal-like. Especially in simulation and art, fractal structures have attracted an unusually high level of public attention for mathematical concepts, perhaps comparable to the Fibonacci sequence.

2.2.1 Simulation and Prefiguration

Concerning mimesis I in simulation: It is well known among simulation scientists how much depends on modelling decisions, on the respective selection of the elements of the world; that is, what parameters, thresholds, etc. are to be included. "Essentially, all models are wrong, but some are useful" (Box and Draper 1987, p. 424).[11] This essential wrongness consists in the fact that a perfectly comprehensive model would be the world itself again, and as such, as useless for modelling as the world itself; a model always focuses on selected elements of the world while necessarily ignoring other elements. Due to these ignored elements, every model is wrong, but that is precisely why they can become useful. Therefore, 'wrong' cannot be understood normatively here; rather, it simply describes the concept of models. The fact that simulation starts with selective modelling decisions in favor of some elements and against others, according to the simulation scientists' prefigured worldview, reveals how close this process is to mimesis I. The elements, parameters, and variables chosen and not chosen for a simulation are a result of the scientists' knowledge, skills, intuitions, epistemological interests, disciplinary backgrounds, institutional positions, interactions with peers, and so on. Their choices reflect the scientists' prefigurations of the world and determine the 'material' for the simulation, which is then configured and run in an operation of mimesis II.

2.2.2 Simulation Configuration

Mimesis II in simulation refers to the very operation of composing, the assembling of chosen elements in mimesis I and—in the case of computer simulations—their implementation on a computer. This configurative process mediates between mimesis I and III; it is an act of transforming (prefigured elements of) the world into a mimetic composition that is configured in order to allow for specific insights (refigurations). These same factors (knowledge, skills, interest, etc.), along with

---

[11]This nearly classic statement has received renewed attention in the context of big data technology: "Peter Norvig, Google's research director, offered an update to George Box's maxim: 'All models are wrong, and increasingly you can succeed without them'" (Anderson 2008). For a critical view on this renewal in high-performance computing, see Gransche (2016).

the results of mimesis I, determine the outcome of this process. What was not chosen as a relevant parameter cannot be included in the configuration now. In addition, the anticipated perception (III) of the simulation determines what guides the configuration process, which is dependent on the presentational purpose of the simulation: Is it addressed to scientists? If so, the configuration pursues the question the scientists want to answer. Is it addressed to a wider public audience or to policy-makers? In that case, it follows primarily instrumental and impact-based consider-ations. All sorts of anticipated perceptions come into play here. Is the simulation scientist the only one who is going to see this simulation (e.g., if the simulation is merely an exercise)? Will he or she present it to his or her close colleagues, to the entire scientific community, to his or her supervisors or funding staff, etc.? What does he or she wish to communicate when presenting the simulation: should it astonish, instruct, entertain, convince, pervade, raise awareness, shock, warn, motivate actions, allocate resources, etc.? Visualization choices, for instance, are guided by certain visual cultures; the interpreting customs develop reciprocally with visualizing standards within these cultures. The convention of coloring high temperatures in red and low ones in blue might be inspired by the observation that hot things emit red light. The convention of showing cold temperatures in blue is widely followed, although emitting blue light physically indicates even higher temperatures than red light. Coloring heat maps or elevation maps from blue or green for low to red for high is a common convention. Due to everyday exposure to this visual code—in weather forecasts, for instance—spectators understand it very well. Aiming at a refiguration in mimesis III that aligns with their intentions, scientists are well-advised to choose this color configuration for simulation, even when transferring it to other matters, such as flow patterns of aerodynamic drag in automotive design or density in crowd management applications. These visualiza-tion conventions are of restricted complexity and harbor the risk of assigning well-known interpretation patterns to unknown simulated matters. Avoiding inadequate refiguration reflexes, on the other hand—by introducing completely new color codes, for example—runs the risk of preventing intended interpretations. Simula-tion scientists must face the fact that there is no neutral coloring scheme when presenting in visualization cultures. The same holds for all their configuration decisions concerning refiguration cultures.

2.2.3 Refiguring Simulations

Mimesis III in the simulation context is the conception of simulations by any audience, be it in science, society, or politics. Just as the creation in mimesis II can only consider aspects that were included in mimesis I, the interpretation in mimesis III can only take into consideration what was included in mimesis II. However, what a spectator sees, understands, and conceives is highly heteroge-neous, depending on the spectator's knowledge, intuition, interests, and interpreta-tional skills, as well as the context of the presentation, and so on. The presentation of simulations is—no different from other presentations—an act of giving or offering. Releasing a composition—whether a novel or a simulation—frees the creation from the creator's configurational sovereignty and offers it to the interpretational sovereignties of a plethora of refigurations. To the giving character of presentations corresponds a taking character of spectatorship and vice versa; the audience gives and the presenter receives attention and approval. The taking, though, has a sense-making, *actively refiguring* character; it is not just *receiving*, but *conceiving*.

While simulation scientists might appreciate skillfully composed simulations, being fully aware of their selectiveness and artistry, less simulation-literate audiences might see them as a sort of direct disclosure. Depending on who is confronted with simulations how and where, the awareness of the determining wrongness or selectivity of mimesis I will differ greatly. The same holds for the awareness of the actual scope of composition and the artistic freedom of simulation scientists in mimesis II; the art and science of simulation—in all the splendor of today's grandiose possibilities for visualization—can easily be mistaken for a mere disclosure mechanism, a mirroring process or a sort of night-vision device that reveals certain things as they really are. The social impact of simulation already begins in mimesis I and II, and a major part of the meaning that will be seen in the simulations depends on choices in these phases. Nevertheless, the factors that influence mimesis III perception—to *whom*, *how*, *when*, and *where* the presentation is displayed—are major aspects of the societal impact of simulations. Once configured works have been released to variable refigurations, the perceptions of them cannot be controlled; the interpretational sovereignty belongs to the audience. However, the mode of presentation offers many possibilities for influencing the interpretations in one way or another; there is no strict control, but there is a certain shaping potential. The art that addresses the who, how, when, and where of presentations is that of *staging* or *mise-en-scène*.

3   Mise-en-scène and Presentation Impact

Presented simulations are deliberately staged. Their elements are arranged in order to achieve a certain impact; the simulation is 'brought before the public'—*mise-en-scène*. Although staging aspects are not the focus of either the simulations or their audiences, they are a key issue in the refiguration of the simulations, and that is what they were made for in the first place. Simulations mimic elements of the world not in their ontological order, but in their order of appearance. In other words: Simulations are produced in order to show something and without refiguration, without spectators, there is no showing. One major advantage of simulations is that they can render visible what cannot otherwise be seen.[12] No human eye has ever

---

[12]Other advantages are cost efficiency and safety when imitating something observable, but expensive or dangerous, e.g., nuclear chain reactions or the spread of an epidemic.

seen the wind; it can only be felt or deduced by an observed dynamic of leaves or other particles. Fog or smoke in a wind tunnel, however, or blue and red dots and lines can be observed. Simulations make wind observable, in the first case via an experimental simulation using water particles, in the latter via computer simulation using a conventional color visualization.

Mise-en-scène, staging, is the giving form to what refuses form. It comprises those practices that represent what otherwise could not become representational. Computer simulations share this capacity: They make use of stage effects to render the invisible visible. Because of this entanglement, simulation can learn from the performing arts, especially when it comes to the interdependencies between presenter and spectator, between configuration and refiguration. Unlike in the realm of simulation, staging is a central, widespread, and culturally embedded part of the theatre.

Staging covers those cultural skills and practices that can provide a visible form or appearance. Wolfgang Iser defined staging (*Inszenierung*) in *Das Fiktive und das Imaginäre* as a process that uses a specific selection, organization, and structuring of materials and persons to represent what is by nature not able to become representational (Iser 1991, p. 504). Staging refers to the physical place where all the elements are set on stage and the performance takes place. Staging means preparing a play for performance and arranging all relevant elements to that purpose. The phrase is derived from the French *mettre en scène*—hence *mise-en-scène*—which originally meant the *"transformation (d'un texte dramatique) en spectacle"* (Rey 2012, p. 1892). This reveals the character of mimesis (imitative-creative) and visualizing (representative): *mise-en-scène* is not just an imitation or a copy, but a creative production (*"schöpferische Hervorbringung"*[13]), a recomposing and transformation from a non-observable form (text or numbers) into a visible one (spectacle or simulation).

This understanding of staging as something creative evolved historically. Originally, *mise-en-scène* referred to an enacted version of a text, true to the writer's ideas, which simply visualized what was inherent in the script. In the nineteenth century, *mise-en-scène* was conceived of as a representation of the poet's work, but one which sought to complement the poet's intentions and to enhance the play's effect. Later, *mise-en-scène* was considered an artistic work equal to the writer's creation. Today, it is considered an art in its own right and, particularly in the staging of classical plays, the representation is often thought to outshine the text, such that the form (re)defines the content as art. This evolution of the meaning of *mise-en-scène* can be observed in the case of the theatre director, the *réalisateur* who composes the elements on stage (Fischer-Lichte 1998). The contemporary Academy Awards for best director are at least as prestigious as those for best

---

[13]The relationship between the concepts/terms staging and theatricality can be understood such that 'staging' means the aspect of theatricality which aims at creative production ("Das Verhältnis zwischen den Begriffen Inszenierung und Theatralität läßt sich also dahingehend beschreiben, daß 'Inszenierung' den Aspekt von Theatralität meint, der auf die schöpferische Hervorbringung zielt," Fischer-Lichte 1998, p. 86).

screenplay, if not even more so. Again, the French word for director is instructive: *réalisateur* carries the word "real," which indicates that the director *realizes* (notices) something in the world and then transforms it into another form; he or she *realizes* (makes real) an intelligible, imaginary, subjective entity by configuring exterior means into an intersubjectively observable performance (play or simulation). The actuality, the effect, and impact of this representation (its potential refigurations) lie primarily in the form of this transformation (the arranging of material, persons, etc.), that is, its staging. This raises the question of whether simulation needs specialized directors, *réalisateurs* who are experts in composing visual elements, in combining the cultural skills and practices of staging, and who are explicitly familiar with visual and spectator cultures. This could be carried even further: Expecting the simulation scientists to stage their potentially enormously powerful simulations single-handedly is like expecting writers to direct their own plays. In the performing arts, this would succeed only in very few cases. More often, it could let a great configurational potential go to waste, and sometimes—especially in the case of scientifically, socially, and politically exploited plays and/or simulations of broad appeal[14]—it could waste the influence that accurate staging can exert over potential refigurations.

The location where the presentation is staged is—along with materials, persons, and others—one of the elements that has to be arranged. The character of the 'place for viewing,' the kind of theatre where plays or simulations are staged, has a decisive role in guiding the spectators' views and thus in prompting the potential

---

[14]One might think of today's terror phenomena: Terror groups like ISIS (Islamic State of Iraq and Syria) stage themselves and their performed or threatened deeds in macabre media plays and simulate—that is, they create the impression of being something they are not, e.g., a state. Even the current spread of terror attacks across the world can be interpreted as the simulation of presence and power where there is little (because of massive recent losses in manpower, territory, and sources of funding). Worldwide suicide-bombing attacks are staged in order to recruit members; the less attractive terror groups become in terms of territory and money, the more these staging means are mobilized as a substitution. They attempt to create the appearance of something which has no essence—to simulate. It could be discussed what advanced computer simulation power in terrorist hands could cause, e.g., if as many millions could play *Call of Jihad* as now play *Call of Duty* (more than 20 million). How closely computer (game) simulations are linked to military and thus political decisions can be seen in the case of Dave Anthony, the writer, director, and producer of the *Call of Duty* series, the world's biggest first-person-shooter game. Anthony currently advises Washington on the future of warfare and "non-traditional threats" as a fellow at the Brent Scowcroft Center on International Security of the Atlantic Council, "where he focuses on the future of conflict and warfare, as well as the defense and security implications of global trends. Due to his expertise in visualizing the future of conflict, Anthony assists the Scowcroft Center in creatively thinking about what warfare will look like, how it will be fought, and what strategies will be required to deter and defeat enemies" (Atlantic Council 2016). That is one emblematic example of the power of a simulation artist whose "expertise in visualizing" is shaping war and politics. "[I]n video games the military is able to try out its theories, to simulate its strategies, to set a devastating domino run in motion and see where the pieces land, without consequence. Anthony believes that, for all their historical ties, perhaps games and war aren't close enough after all. 'I would like to see more collaboration with the military and game developers,' he says" (Parkin 2014). Parkin is wrong, or at least inaccurate, when he claims this is "without consequences."

refigurations. This can be emphasized by recalling the common etymology of *theatre* and *theory*. The theatre is the location where the scene takes place, the elements are brought on stage, and the audience gathers to see the presentation. *Theatre* is related to the Greek *theasthai* ('to view,' 'to behold') combining *thea* ('a view,' 'a seeing'; 'a seat in the theatre') and *-tron*, a suffix denoting 'place.' Thus *theatron* meant literally 'a room or place for viewing,' the 'theatre.' Closely related to theatre is the term *theory*, for it goes back to the same *thea*, this time combined with *horan* ('to see'). The combined verb *theorein* means 'to consider, speculate, and look at.' *Theoria* literally meant 'a looking at, viewing; a sight, show, spectacle, things looked at.'[15] This highlights that a spectator (in Greek: *theates, theoros*) does not just passively receive information, but always imposes his prefigurations on his observations, trying to make sense of what he or she sees. The gaze of the spectator is always somehow a theorizing and considering one, combining *theasthai* with *theorein*. Presentations, plays that are *given*, are actively *taken* into consideration—configurations are refigured. The location is one of the interpretation signals. It gives the spectators an idea of what kind of presentation to expect. It pre-tunes the refiguration and primes the theorizing and considering gazes. Unlike the home or the streets, a theatre is a place where something relevant is displayed; seeing something in a theatre comes with the expectation that whatever is shown is worthy of consideration. We look differently at a performance in a theatre, a museum, a scientific institute, or ministerial office than we do at what happens in the streets. Along with the simulation literacy of today's potential audience, these interpretation signals offer the opportunity to guide the uncontrollable refigurations of simulations.

In the following paragraphs, it will be asked how these insights (which are quite undisputed in the field of performing arts) about mimetic configuration, active refiguration, and the location of presentations could lead both to more socially compatible simulations and to a more simulation-literate society.

4 Staging of Simulations and Simulation Literacy

Many questions that arise in the field of simulation are more typically addressed in the performing arts, cultural sciences, or art history. Though these questions bear on simulation insofar as it relates to contemporary art, they have not been the focus in the creation, perception, and discussion of scientific simulations. Each phase of the triple mimesis—pre-, con-, and refiguration—requires careful designing when dealing with a phenomenon as increasingly widespread and as potentially powerful as simulation. Fortunately, philosophy, narratology, literature, and theatre studies, as well as science communication, science and technology studies, and philosophy of science are well equipped to grasp these three stages. Additionally, the

---

[15]*"Theatre, theory"* in Harper (2016).

performing arts offer a vast pool of mimesis experiences and best practices. Simulation arts could function as a link between scientific simulation and the arts. Simulation scientists can learn from these insights, cultural skills, and practices and adapt them to their specific demands. They already do so simply by being part of the cultural community that shares conventions and refiguration intuitions—this is why they color a heat or elevation map with blue, yellow, and red. Nevertheless, they could do so more explicitly by making active use of professionally and scientifically elaborated skills and knowledge.

4.1 Refiguration Signals

Two basic directions can be differentiated in order to guide or intentionally shape the refiguration processes. First, the interpretational skills of the audience could be raised to fully-fledged simulation literacy, building on the culturally diffused visual and performing arts literacies.[16] Second, the signaling possibilities of the staging of simulations could be further developed into an art of its own—just as happened historically with the theatre—or into an integral but decisive part of the science of simulation itself. These two directions are closely interconnected, as they describe different aspects of the same operation, namely the refiguration of the configuration, or the transition from mimesis II to III. The staging signals are part of the configuration process because the simulation scientist has to arrange them; but they are directed towards the spectator because their arrangement can only be decided by anticipating (or intelligibly simulating) the presumed spectators' refiguration skills and practices. Thus, a presumed (internal) spectator guides the choices and use of staging signals of the simulation director (*réalisateur*). The actual (external) spectator then inevitably differs from the presumed one, which is why all the guiding signals can still lead to completely different refigurations. In the arts, this is a widely desired effect; art often aims at an endlessly open refiguration cosmos, giving the artwork as many meanings as there are spectators and even single acts of viewing. In scientific or public simulations dealing with topics like climate change, lake pollution, the spread of epidemics, etc., this is not the case. A conscious staging, with a carefully considered offering of refiguration signals, has to be complemented by an interpretative ability on the part of the spectators. This is important, on the one hand, to make the staged signals more likely to be understood by the spectators. Fostering interpretative abilities brings the actual spectator closer

---

[16]Saying that some of these literacies might be better developed than simulation literacy is not to say that they are themselves sufficiently or equally developed, nor that they are equally distributed throughout society. Maybe—once simulation literacy is more common—many other literacies could benefit from the refiguration skills taught by ubiquitous simulations. If it has become common not to take even the most realistic-looking video footage as proof of real events, then this might nurture an adequate level of doubt concerning the direct representational character of pictures.

to the presumed one. If, for instance, your interlocutor does not speak any English, it makes no sense to choose more expressive—but still English—words in an attempt to be understood; instead, it would be much more expedient to teach this interlocutor some basic English. Ideally, both speakers share a common language and cultural symbolic background. On the other hand, it is important to establish adequate refiguration skills on the part of the spectators in order to enable them to distinguish between inveigling and convincing signals, to unmask deceitful staging, and to be able to evaluate the composer's intentions and/or honesty.

4.2   Irony or Lie? Simulation or Deceit?

Whether an interlocutor understands a statement as serious, ironic, or as a lie depends on the statement's location and situation, on the speaker's role and personality, as well as on the refiguration signals communicated. Rhetoric, the art of discourse, makes use of the staging strategies of *simulation* and *dissimulation*. In this context, simulating means pretending to be or know more than the speaker actually is or does, whereas dissimulating means pretending to be or know less.

Theatre employs these rhetorical strategies as personified prototypes, and a theatre audience is easily able to recognize them as such. In ancient Greek *theatra*, these two prototypes were famous as *Alazon*, who acts *as if* he were more than he actually is, and *Eiron*, who acts *as if* he were less than he actually is. Even if those names have been forgotten, the prototypes are still well known—simulators appear in characters like Felix Krull or Frank Abignale,[17] as do dissimulators like Odysseus as a beggar in Ithaca or Mephistopheles as he accompanies Faust. These prototypes are perfectly known in their respective recipient cultures. Therefore, staging subtle Eiron or Alazon signals reliably prompts Eiron or Alazon refigurations. The rhetorical technique of dissimulation, of feigned ignorance, is called—after the prototypical dissimulator Eiron—*eironeia*, in English: *irony*. There are many forms of irony, but they all bear an essential difference between a staged surface meaning and an intended underlying meaning. If it is not a prototypical Eiron speaking, then the interlocutor has to refigure a statement as (a) serious, (b) ironic, or (c) as a lie. The respective refigurations succeed if (a) no irony signals are communicated and the interlocutor believes the speaker, (b) irony signals are communicated and the interlocutor does not believe the speaker's words, or (c) no irony signals are communicated and the interlocutor does not believe the speaker. The interlocutor takes successful lies and successful direct statements seriously, whereas if ironic statements are taken seriously, they fail to be ironic. If the interlocutor does not believe the speaker, only the staged signals can distinguish an ironic statement from a deceitful one. Irony—in a way—is lying while

---

[17]The main character from the film *Catch Me If You Can*, played by Leonardo DiCaprio.

simultaneously indicating the lie. A lack of these indicating signals turns an effective rhetorical staging technique into a deceit.

In the case of Eiron and Alazon, the respective staging signals and refiguration literacy co-evolved historically. This is not the case when scientific simulations are presented to scientists, society, or politicians, however. The signal-configuring (staging) and refiguration-prompting connection in the realm of simulation is far less worked out; at the same time, their interconnection is socially very important. Computer simulations influence society and politics in the way that narrations do. Just as there is no data privacy debate without reference to Orwell's infamous Big Brother, there is no climate change debate without climate simulations. Yet— due to sheer exposure—our refiguration skills are far better adjusted to novels and narrations than to computer simulations. This will most likely change, and it will be a challenge to shape that change adequately.

One striking feature of today's computer simulations is their performed realness: For a long time, *looking real* was a fairly good indicator for *being real*. Hyper-realistic paintings confused that connection, looking as real as photographs or reality itself, and their painters even simulated photographic artefacts like shallow depth of field, lens flare, and noise. This impressive effect of looking so real without (sometimes obviously[18]) being real is astonishing. The *theatra* of art—museums and galleries—prompt specific refigurations of the exhibits, thus bestowing a photograph, which elsewhere could be considered kitsch or profane, with the aura of a masterpiece. Computer simulations, special effects, animation, as well as computer manipulation of pictures and videos, now cast doubt onto all kinds of visual and audio footage. Being familiar with these techniques and technologies that make things look *as if* they were real is the foundation of a visual literacy that encourages skepticism towards the realness of what is seen. Nevertheless, even if one knows in principle that these advanced editing techniques exist, photoshopped pictures and computer-generated images persuade the viewer to believe them, and spectators are used to reflecting on grades of realness to very different extents. Even today, what looks real is easily taken for real and the amount of phenomena that perfectly simulate realness has never been greater.

One example is the massively edited or computer-generated pictures used for advertising, such as those of super-slim bikini models with flawless skin, which influence beauty standards in society and trigger eating disorders, especially among adolescent women.[19] Advertising businesses have no interest in communicating simulation signals in their advertisements—they usually do not want to be ironic

---

[18]Gottfried Helnwein's painting *L.A. Confidential (Cops II),* for instance, simulates a blue-toned photograph showing two cops inspecting a body at a crime scene. It could be easily mistaken for a photograph if not for the victim—the murdered Donald Duck.

[19]"It was found that exposure to idealized commercials led to increased body dissatisfaction for girls but not for boys. Idealized commercials led to increased negative mood and appearance comparison for girls and boys, although the effect on appearance comparison was stronger for girls" (Hargreaves and Tiggemann 2004, p. 351); "Results indicated that relative to a control group, the exposure to thin-and-beautiful media images adversely influenced the state body image

about what their product promises. Artist Daniel Soares has critiqued these unrealistic and adverse beauty standards with a "street art criticism towards the fashion industry" by adding simulation signals to public advertisements (Soares 2016). He pasted Adobe Photoshop toolbars onto billboards, for example—so called *adbusting*—to re-embed the pictures into their computer-editing context, thus guiding refigurations of the models as artificial beauties and not actual persons and role models.

What kinds of signals are needed and should be legally required if the simulation presenter has no interest in revealing his or her techniques of persuasion? Should simulations have to be labeled as such by law, as was proposed for digitally altered images?[20] If those signals make the difference between a good presentation and a deception, and if 'adequate refiguration' cannot be expected, should irony signals not be obligatory? Besides, who is to judge on the adequacy of a refiguration? In other fields, mandatory signals guiding proper refiguration are common, like the 'serving suggestion' signal on packed food. The 'serving suggestion' is an indication of the essential difference—the reality gap—between the staged surfaces on any label and the actual content inside the packaging. For persuasion purposes, this gap is legal, but it has to be accompanied by a simultaneous signal that separates advertising from deception. The 'serving suggestion' is for products what tone or smiling is for ironic speaking: a simulation signal. Even though most people know the difference between the content and the label, the signal is considered (legally) indispensable, because even principally informed—but not specifically reflective—spectators are easily persuaded by powerful presentations. This shows that, as we attempt to integrate simulations and society, both measures have to be considered: educating audiences in simulation literacy in order to enable them to responsibly and individually deal with persuasive simulations, on the one hand, and politically and legally enforce—if necessary—staging signals that allow even less simulation-literate spectators to adequately refigure simulations, on the other. In short: What kind of 'serving suggestions' do we need for what kind of simulation presentations? Reconnecting these questions to the imitative-creative mimetic character of simulation, one might ask: How should the creation and imitation aspects in simulations be balanced so that they will still be validly accepted as not deceitful?[21] The answer to these questions is complex because it has to be worked out in an interplay of interdisciplinary sciences, politics, and public discourse. One starting point,

---

of participants with high internalization levels. Media-literacy psychoeducation prior to the media exposure prevented this adverse effect" (Yamamiya et al. 2005, p. 74).

[20]"The promotion of unrealistic body images in some advertisements and magazines is thought to have a role in triggering eating disorders, [. . .] and some countries, including the United Kingdom, France and Norway, are now considering legislation to require digitally altered images to be labelled as such" (Graham-Rowe 2011).

[21]How should these aspects be balanced in order to deliver new insights? An entirely and perfectly imitating simulation would be an "emperor's map," a map as detailed as the world, and as such of no use at all (see Borges 1975, p. 131).

certainly, is the staging perspective and a simulation-oriented revision of existing practices of *mise-en-scène*.

5 Conclusion

Simulations in a broader sense, as well as computer simulations specifically, are *poietic* operations; they are a creative production and, as processes of mimesis, combine creation with imitation. Simulation scientists are also artists who configure prefigured elements of the world so that various spectators can refigure them. They model, design, implement, run, and stage the simulation as an artist invents, writes, and stages a play. In the field of performing arts, these roles have been differentiated and professionalized and, given that the core of simulation science is the modeling and configuring of a simulation, there might come a call for specialized simulation directors, for *réalisateurs*. Will the *mise-en-scène* of simulations then undertake the same historical evolution from subservient realization into an art of its own? Will this process be quicker because of the path already paved by theatre? How popular is this artistic side of simulations? It is more likely that scientific simulations are believed to present accurate visualizations of real phenomenon, rather than artistic configurations and expressions of many compositional choices. Even if this belief is theoretically clarified, it is not probable that this insight will guide every single refiguration act among scientists, nor in politics or society. Irony signals have to guide refiguration processes and should perhaps be required. Additionally, most spectators need to be sensitized to those signals. The location of the simulation's presentation—its *theatra*—is hugely important in prompting the refiguration success and the 'tuning' of the spectator towards an appropriate interpretation. In general, computer simulations hardly ever stage their *theatra* explicitly. Even the *theatra* of pioneers like the HLRS cave in Stuttgart are presumably not consciously designed as an artistic simulation theatre, but rather as a place for scientific work. Nevertheless, the HLRS cave exhibits various theatre-like features like a golden ceiling entrance, black curtains, foyer exhibitions, ushers, and so on.

If simulations become an increasingly influential cultural, social, and political phenomenon, do we not need a set of cultural skills and practices similar to the ones we have for narrations, novels, theatre, and film? Would computer games—as a combination of scientific computer simulations (like physics engines) and performing arts and narration (featuring real-time interactivity)—be an apt mediator to bridge the conventions of the two fields? In order to work out the configuration-refiguration flow of simulations, the familiarity with, for example, heat-related coloring schemes, ought to be aspired to in more aspects of simulation staging. Simulation literacy in a society that is confronted with simulations on a daily basis promises to tie simulations more closely to their social impact. This literacy should consist of the needed cultural skills not only to 'read fluently,' but also to critically interpret and evaluate simulations. Simulation literacy should not be interpreted as hostility to simulations, nor as a wholesale condemnation of simulations just because they do not show reality 'as it is.' We do not condemn irony for that reason, after all. One of the great powers of simulation is to present possible worlds and alternative events, including their potential costs and risks, without having to actually realize them. Simulation literacy could promote the successful use of simulations in decision-making in politics, science, and society at large by supporting adequate refigurations and further connecting the configuration with the refiguration operations. Concrete steps to foster a simulation-literate society have to be discussed, as well as various institutions founded to educate spectator groups. Public awareness campaigns like Soares' Photoshop Adbusting could be one among many strategies.

Learning from theatre and rhetoric, where dissimulation is at least as present as simulation, part of such a simulation literacy would be to form a habit of questioning how computer simulations are actually *computer dissimulations* and where they tend to hide what some of them actually are: means of discourse, strategic instruments for shaping the future, tools of power and persuasion, toys, number magic, *l'art pour l'art*. The performing arts have developed sophisticated concepts and practices when it comes to creative-imitative representations, to active refiguration, to *mise-en-scène*, and to staging. Therefore, a creative entanglement between scientific simulations and the arts—as is nascent in video games, simulation arts, or at festivals like Ars Electronica[22]—could be used as a starting point. This could promote a simulation literacy as well as disseminate existing cultural skills to promote the arts further in general throughout the society. The science of simulation has much to gain from theatre, literature, and other arts, just as a simulation-literate society has much to gain from well-staged simulations. Staging as an art of its own awaits appropriation by the science and art of simulation.

References

Anderson, Chris. 2008. The End of Theory. The Data Deluge Makes the Scientific Method Obsolete. *Wired*, June 23. http://archive.wired.com/science/discoveries/magazine/16-07/pb_theory. Accessed 27 September 2015.

Ars Electronica. 2016. Ars Electronica. Festival für Kunst, Technologie und Gesellschaft. http://www.aec.at/news/. Accessed 9 July 2016.

Atlantic Council. 2016. Dave Anthony. http://www.atlanticcouncil.org/about/experts/list/dave-anthony. Accessed 4 July 2016.

Borges, Jorge Luis. 1975. *A Universal History of Infamy*. Penguin Books Ltd.

Box, George E.P., and Norman Richard Draper. 1987. *Empirical model-building and response surfaces*. New York: Wiley.

Dotzler, Bernhard J. 1991. *Der Hochstapler: Thomas Mann und die Simulakren der Literatur*. München: Fink.

---

[22] Ars Electronica (2016).

Dotzler, Bernhard J. 2010. Simulation. In *Ästhetische Grundbegriffe*, vol. 5, ed. Karlheinz Barck, Martin Fontius, Dieter Schlenstedt, Burkhart Steinwachs and Friedrich Wolfzettel, 509–534. Stuttgart, Weimar: Metzler.

Fischer-Lichte, Erika. 1998. Inszenierung und Theatralität. In *Inszenierungsgesellschaft. Ein einführendes Handbuch*, ed. Herbert Willems and Martin Jurga, 81–90. Opladen, Wiesbaden: Westdeutscher Verlag.

Graham-Rowe, Duncan. 2011. Computer model spots image fraud. Software measures extent of 'airbrushing' in digital images. *Nature*, November 28. http://www.nature.com/news/computer-model-spots-image-fraud-1.9502. Accessed 9 July 2016.

Gransche, Bruno. 2016. The Oracle of Big Data. Prophecies without Prophets. *IRIE* 24: 55–62.

Hargreaves, Duane A., and Marika Tiggemann. 2004. Idealized media images and adolescent body image: "comparing" boys and girls. *Body Image* 1 (4): 351–361.

Harper, Douglas. 2016. Online Etymology Dictionary. http://www.etymonline.com. Accessed 6 July 2016.

Hartmann, Stephan. 2005. The World as a Process: Simulations in the Natural and Social Sciences. PhilSci archive. http://philsci-archive.pitt.edu/id/eprint/2412. Accessed 4 July 2016.

HLRS. 2016. HLRS High Performance Computing Center Stuttgart - The CAVE. https://www.hlrs.de/en/solutions-services/service-portfolio/visualization/virtual-reality/the-cave/. Accessed 29 June 2016.

Iser, Wolfgang. 1991. *Das Fiktive und das Imaginäre: Perspektiven literarischer Anthropologie*. Frankfurt am Main: Suhrkamp.

Kaufmann, William J., and Larry L. Smarr. 1993. *Supercomputing and the transformation of science*. New York: Scientific American Library: Distributed by W.H. Freeman.

Parkin, Simon. 2014. Call of Duty: gaming's role in the military-entertainment complex. *The Guardian*, October 22. https://www.theguardian.com/technology/2014/oct/22/call-of-duty-gaming-role-military-entertainment-complex. Accessed 4 July 2016.

Rey, Alain, ed. 2012. *Dictionnaire historique de la langue française*. Rev. and exp. ed. 3 vols. Paris: Le Robert.

Ricoeur, Paul. 1984. *Time and Narrative*. Vol. 1. Chicago, IL: University of Chicago Press.

Soares, Daniel. 2016. Photoshop Adbusting. http://www.danielsoares.me/work/hm-photoshop-adbusting. Accessed 9 July 2016.

Warnke, Philine. 2002. *Computersimulation und Intervention. Eine Methode der Technikentwicklung als Vermittlungsinstrument soziotechnischer Umordnungen*. PhD diss., Technische Universität Darmstadt.

Winsberg, Eric. 2015. Computer Simulations in Science. In *Stanford Encyclopedia of Philosophy* (Summer 2015 Edition), ed. Edward N. Zalta. https://plato.stanford.edu/archives/sum2015/entries/simulations-science/. Accessed January 2017.

Yamamiya, Yuko, Thomas F. Cash, Susan E. Melnyk, Heidi D. Posavac, and Steven S. Posavac. 2005. Women's exposure to thin-and-beautiful media images: body image effects of media-ideal internalization and impact-reduction interventions. *Body Image* 2 (1): 74–80.

Myths of Simulation

Björn Schembera

Abstract Certain myths have emerged about computer technology in general, such as the almighty electronic brain that outperforms humans in every discipline or legends about the capability of artificial intelligence. Some of these myths find echoes in the field of computer simulation, like simulation being pure number-crunching on supercomputers. This article reflects on myths about computer simulation and tries to oppose them. At the beginning of the paper, simulation is defined. Then, some central myths about computer simulation will are identified from a general computer science perspective. The first central myth is that simulation is a virtual experiment. This view is contradicted by the argument, that computer simulation is located in between theory and experiment. Furthermore, access to reality is possible indirectly via representation. The second myth is that simulation is said to be exact. This myth can be falsified by examining technical and conceptual limitations of computer technology. Moreover, arguments are presented as to why ideal exactness is neither possible nor necessary. A third myth emerges from the general overstatement of computer technology: Everything can be simulated. It will be shown that simulation can only solve problems that can be formalized and calculated—and can only produce results that are within the scope of the models they are based on.

1 Introduction

In the movie *Terminator 3: Rise of the Machines*, the world's military systems and supercomputers are interconnected in an experiment when the software running on them, *Skynet*, gains self-awareness and becomes an artificial intelligence that eventually fights and enslaves mankind. Tales and myths are not to be found only in sci-fi pop-culture but also in science, where they can become hazardous. One example of a myth in computer science is Alan Turings prediction that artificial intelligence would be realized by the year 2000. This could be measured by the

---

B. Schembera (✉)
High Performance Computing Center Stuttgart (HLRS), University of Stuttgart, Nobelstr. 19, 70569 Stuttgart, Germany
e-mail: schembera@hlrs.de

© Springer International Publishing AG 2017   51
M.M. Resch et al. (eds.), *The Science and Art of Simulation I*,
DOI 10.1007/978-3-319-55762-5_5

"Turing Test": Computers would be able to have a discussion with a human and after 5 min, there would be a 70% probability that the human would not have found out that they were talking to a computer (Turing 1950). This hypothesis has not yet been proved. It is strongly related to the underestimation of the complexity of human intelligence, but it is still an ongoing story-telling that this step lies ahead of us and will result in artificial intelligence. Ray Kurzweil now speaks of artificial intelligence by 2029 (Pagliery and King 2016). This tale is repeatedly encouraged in pop-culture, such as in the 2015 movie *Ex Machina*, where an android passes the Turing Test and escapes into the wild.

However, this paper focuses on myths of computer simulation and not artificial intelligence.[1] An example of a common legend from this field is that computer simulation is just number-crunching, i.e. mere calculations immediately derived from the maths behind them. Another more technical myth is that the acceptance of Monte Carlo moves in stochastic simulation should be around 50%. This has not yet been justified anywhere, yet is still in use as a rule-of-thumb (Frenkel 2012). Another myth that also has implications for computer simulation was already discussed in 1978 by James Moor, who states in *Myths on Computation* that computer scientists do not distinguish carefully enough between models, theories, and their programs, and calls this the third myth of computation (Moor 1978). This is relevant for simulation as model building. As soon as there is a program for the computation of a problem, it seems that a theory behind the problem can be derived immediately.

In the following, the term *myth* is characterized by its form and functions as a narrative concept. Myths are not dogmas that can be falsified. They are focused on emotional coherence rather than logical arguments. Blumenberg (1979) states that myths refer to a concept of people's thought and behavior towards the world and of overcoming fears of the unknown. Naming is an important function of myths: As we name something indeterminate, we make it addressable and hence tellable, which should result in both distance from and trust in the opaque. The subject matter itself is transformed into a narrative about the subject matter. The opaque can therefore be banned or inflated, depending if it is a dystopian or a utopian scenario. Myths always remain on a narrative level and are not able to resolve the tension as scientific methods can, and they have always had a strained relation to logic and science. Whereas science aims to eliminate the unknown, myths tolerate it.[2] They are narratives with a historicity and function as a coping strategy towards unknown phenomena. As we are aware of the tension between myth and science, we can make productive use of myths, since they bear a creative potential that is not bound to logical reasoning (Honer 2011).

---

[1]For myths and critique on artificial intelligence, see Dreyfus (1992).

[2]It seems that nowadays, myths are no longer relevant, due to the technical and scientific progress. However, this does not mean that science and logic are protected from falling back into myths, when logic and science are set as the absolute methods to gain knowledge in an epistemological process. Moreover, this means that enlightenment does not necessarily imply progress. Horkheimer and Adorno discuss this in Horkheimer and Adorno (1972).

In the following, examples are presented that can be referred to as myths of computer simulation. Even though they have no dysoptian character, they name something indeterminate arising from prejudices, lack of knowledge, and rumors about new technologies and computer simulation. For example, the overestimation of the abilities of a computer results in the myth that computers can simulate anything.

The structure of this paper is as follows: In Sect. 2, computer simulation is defined, in order to provide a foundation for the following sections. Section 3 is the main part of this work, where three myths of computer simulation are discussed and interrogated. In Sect. 3.1, it is discussed why computer simulation may seem as a virtual experiment, but is in fact its own, third branch of science and does not operate in a closed virtual space. In Sect. 3.2, I discuss why computer simulation understands "exactness" as "approximate but usable results". Section 3.3 focuses on the common tale that computers can calculate and therefore simulate anything. This is related to a general overestimation of the capacity of a computer. Facts are presented to undermine this myth. In the last Sect. 4, a summary is presented, conclusions are drawn and future work is outlined.

2 What Is Simulation?

Hartmann offers the definition that simulation in general "imitates one process by another process. In this definition, the term 'process' refers solely to some object or system whose state changes in time" (Hartmann 1996, p. 83), which means that simulation is a system that imitates the dynamic behavior of another system. Simulation can be seen as a reproduction of the operation of a real-world phenomenon or system over time, which requires a model. This model represents some key characteristics and/or functions of the phenomenon/system.

The key terms are *system*, *model*, and *representation*. The *system* is the object of study and can be either a real-world system or an imaginary one. It is also called the *target system*. The *model* is the abstract mapping of this (target) system, having some isomorphism with (some parts of) the (target) system. This is done by *representation*, aiming to mimic the characteristics, functions and processes of the system. Margaret Morrison emphasizes the importance of representation by stating that it "will enable you to extend the problem in interesting ways. In that sense, scientific representation is about conceptualising something in a way that makes it amenable to a theoretical or mathematical formulation" (Morrison 2015, p. 129).

Computer simulation, then, is the provisioning of simulations on computers, being the focus of this paper. There are different types of computer simulation. *Equation-based simulations* rely on differential equations grounded in physical theory, which in turn have their representation in mathematics. *Agent-based simulations* represent a system by a number of individual agents, all with a certain set of (local) rules. Another type of simulation is called *Monte Carlo simulation*, where randomness is used even though it is not a feature of the system to be represented. The process of simulation is the same for all of these types and can be referred to as the *simulation pipeline* (Kaminski et al. 2016): First, the structure of a (real) system has to be described by a model with a formal representation. This has to be transferred to a mathematical model, which can, for example be a numerical one in the field of equation-based simulation. The mathematical model is then to be implemented as an algorithm. After this step, the algorithm is computed and the results may be visualized, verified, and validated later. I would like to point out that this is a process of translations, transformations, and mappings between various representations, which should preserve the structure of the modeled target system as much as possible.

Simulation can be understood as the above process itself, as well as the art and science of minimizing losses within this process. As the aim of simulation is to gain knowledge of and insight into problems of our daily lives, such as global warming, myths may emerge. These will be discussed and dispelled in the next section.

3 Myths of Simulation

3.1 Myth 1: Computer Simulation Is a Virtual Experiment

When we hear or read about simulation, we think of colorful flow patterns or see moving pictures of the climate and its possible change. Even though we can see supercomputers as the material basis and the perceptible surface of an experimental apparatus, it looks like computer simulation operates exclusively in cyberspace. This leads to the myth that simulation is a special form of experiment, taking place in a virtual space.

It seems that computer simulation is a thought experiment (Di Paolo et al. 2000), functionally equal (El Skaf and Imbert 2013) or epistemically related (Beisbart 2012) to them. In contrast, Johannes Lenhard (2011) points out that, although simulation and thought experiments have an apparent resemblance, there are fundamental differences between them. The author introduces the distinction by examining how the concepts handle iteration. In thought experiments, iteration aims to produce transparency in terms of an insight into both the problem and its solution. This can only be achieved by intuition, logic, and scanning of the structure, which will result in a convergence towards the solution. In contrast, simulation is based on another form of iteration. Here, iteration is the concept to produce a bandwidth of results and to exploit all (or at least most) solutions. It serves as an empirical method to build a set of solutions, allowing the best one to be chosen. This of course, leads to complex behavior, because the single steps of a simulation depend on each other.[3]

---

[3] As Paul Humphreys (2009) states, humans are not able to oversee and reproduce the simulation process (and especially the calculations on the lower levels of computation) since it is too complex and the processing speed is too high. Consequently, computer simulation must be seen as a black box with lots of abstraction that a human is not able to retrace.

According to Lenhard, simulation has to be considered as an opaque *sui generis* activity, and for him, it is evident that simulation is not another form of thought experiment, due to its distinct mode of iteration.

If computer simulations are not thought experiments, might they be closely related to classic experiments? This seems valid when we see that computer simulation is also practical work with many iterations, trial-and-error, as well as quantitative results involved. In that respect, the methodology is similar. However, one could argue that working with the phenomenon itself is characteristic of experiments whereas simulation only works with a representation of the system or phenomenon. But today's experiments like the LHC, rely on big intermediary apparatus (e.g., supercomputers used to post-process the data gathered) and hence do not work with the phenomenon itself. Eric Winsberg (2009) states that the main characteristic that distinguishes between simulation and experiment is neither materiality nor representation, since experiments are based on representation as well. The key differentiator is, rather, background knowledge. Background knowledge is not about the structure of relation between the target system and its model. Reasonable arguments have to be found, why some representation is either formally exploitable (simulation) or has a relevant material similarity (experiment). Very specific background knowledge has to justify the use of simulation. We have to check case-by-case whether simulation is appropriate. Two specific features are important in simulation: First, the simulationist has model-building principles for the target system of the simulations. Second, he or she has to find external reasons why the study is valid.[4]

Following Winsberg, simulation must be positioned between theory and experiment. Winsberg states that computer simulation is exclusively based neither on theory nor on experiment, but is located between the two (Winsberg 2003). He breaks up the dichotomy of theory and experiment and replaces it with a trichotomy: speculation, theory articulation and experiment. To be exact, it is theory that is further split into two parts. Speculation is the phase in which hypotheses are formulated and laws defined. The second part is where theory gets its articulation and expression, for example in a mathematical formalism or an algorithmic language. He also refers to the second part as model building which cannot be included in theory building, being typical for computer simulation. This model is derived from theory respectively the speculative part of his trichotomy, but is has to be a feasible model in terms of solutions. However, computer simulation leads a life of its own, since all model-building, that emerges from theory must also fulfill practical conditions. The life of the simulation is produced by the modeller and reproduced and refined from time to time by others; therefore the historicity plays a crucial role.

---

[4]The example Winsberg gives of a physicist studying "the interaction of a pair of fluids at supersonic speeds", relies on the following background knowledge: The theory of fluids and the physicist's intuition regarding the physical assumptions are arguments for the external validity of the study. As a third, the tricks physicists apply to make the simulations work, which are in turn derived from the historicity of the simulation process, stand for the specific model building principle.

According to Winsberg, computer simulation is its own third, but interdependent field between theory and experiment. The application of background knowledge is vital when it comes to distinguishing simulation from experiment.

We have now heard reasons why computer simulation is neither a thought experiment nor another form of classical experiment, but that it is instead grounded in both theory and experiment. But what about its relation to reality? Can we argue that it is detached from nature just because it runs on a computer in a virtual environment?

Since the methodology of simulation is derived from theory, and since its implementation is executed on a computer (as a virtual space), it cannot refer to nature directly. The epistemic value of computer simulation starts from a theoretical point of view: equations are solved that reflect the model, which represents a system such as a natural process. We now can argue that it is not nature answering here but its representation. Models and representation play the key role in simulation. With simulation as model-building and the observation of how this representation behaves under various conditions and multiple iterations, we can gain mediated access to a system of study. For Margaret Morrison (2015), this is an essential function of science: reconstructing nature in a specific form and the observing, how this reconstruction behaves. Model-building is simulations specific form of reconstructing nature and approaching it in a mediated way. Nevertheless, we can gain relevant insights into nature. Indirect access to nature based on representation is a worthwhile strategy for gaining knowledge in areas that make it impossible for nature to answer for herself, for example in climate modeling: As we are not able to look into the future directly, we must rely on computer simulations. If we are aware that we are working with representations, we are able to make reasonable predictions grounded in this third branch of scientific methods, that is, simulation.

3.2   Myth 2: Computer Simulation Is Exact

A problem regarding computer simulation is that people often overestimate the results derived from it. For example, a study (Hatton and Roberts 1994) points out, that nine independent implementations of the same earth-science simulation led to highly divergent results—even under the same conditions, including programming language and algorithms. Facts like these have to be clarified when results are presented to disposing stakeholders. Michael M. Resch addresses this issue when he discusses the public understanding of simulations and the problem how to judge whether a simulation is accurate (Resch 2013). One part of the problem is the supposed exactness of computers, that is, that computers deliver correct results and not approximations. This myth of exactness can be further divided into two parts: The first claims exactness in simulation is possible; The second stipulates that ideal exactness is an overall requirement. The truth is that computer simulation cannot be exact, due to both technical and conceptual limitations. However, it does not need to be exact.

From a technical point of view, the computer simulation of continuous phenomena cannot in general be exact. For example, the behavior of an air flow with an obstacle can be described mathematically by Navier-Stokes equations in a continuous space. This space is represented by real numbers $\mathbb{R}$, which can have infinite decimal places like the number $\sqrt{2}$. A computer can represent these only as integer numbers. This is due to the fact that computers are based on a limited amount of discrete states for representing information such as numbers, leading to a certain imprecision. Computers are designed to work with a ruse to manage real numbers: floating point numbers (Goldberg 1991). These numbers offer the possibility to map real numbers onto integer numbers by splitting a real number into three parts, representing the parts in a binary form and letting the point "float". A computer has a fixed number of bits reserved for storing floating point numbers, typically 32 or 64bits overall. Compared to a fixed-point representation, both very large and very small real numbers can be expressed with the same relative precision. Moreover, a floating point arithmetic has to be defined, which controls the arithmetic operations on floating point numbers. This results in some problems such as rounding errors and, absorption for additions and subtractions, where decimal places can get lost. Another effect called cancelation can lead to the loss of correct decimal places. The concept of floating point numbers is derived from the technical limitation fact that resources on a computer are limited. However, as we want to be able to use computers to solve not only discrete but also continuous problems, we need this trick. But we need be aware that results represented by floating point numbers can never be exact.

From the conceptual point of view, in the process of simulation, that is, in the simulation pipeline, abstraction plays a crucial role. Events or processes are modeled from a certain point of view and only certain aspects are interesting and mapped to a model. Others are skipped, simplified, or not taken into account. This abstraction process is sometimes conditioned technically (not all aspects can be modeled), and sometimes by the necessity of a focus (not all aspects have to be modeled). The point is that simulation with its models, even if derived from theory "modifies it [the model] with extensive approximations, idealizations, falsifications, auxiliary information, and the blood, sweat and tears of much trial and error" (Winsberg 2003, p. 109). However, this partial isomorphism of the model representation is nothing to worry about. Abstractions and idealizations fused to formal rules contain lots of information that allows us to capture how a target system works. Morrison explains that the "model, by nature, leaves out certain elements deemed to be inessential parts of the real system and in doing so offers us a mediated account of how the system is constituted." (Morrison 2015, p. 153) Abstraction is necessary to obtain knowledge.

I have presented some reasons why simulation can, in principle, not be exact. The myth that simulation is exact is backed by an incorrect notion of exactness. People tend to see exactness as an absolute or ideal criterion to be fulfilled. In contrast, Wittgenstein states that exactness is never absolute but always purposeful:

"Inexact" is really a reproach, and "exact" is praise. And that is to say that what is inexact attains its goal less perfectly than does what is more exact. So it all depends on what we call "the goal". (Wittgenstein 1997, p. 46^e)

That means that the notion of exactness makes sense only when it refers a goal. In fact, results just have to be exact enough to work with. Such results are identified by Wittgenstein as "usable". What must be denied is the notion of ideal exactness. With respect to simulation techniques, floating point numbers are exact enough to allow us to forecast the weather, model climate or simulate fluid dynamics with usable results. Models are created with abstraction and therefore lose some certain aspects, but Morrison (2015) argues that the "representational inaccuracy" within the model is even an advantage, because it lets you focus on the relevant details. Absolute exactness is neither possible nor necessary. Awareness of this fact has to be raised for stakeholders as well as the public.

3.3   Myth 3: Computers Can Simulate Anything

The third myth that I will examine is the view that there is nothing that cannot be simulated by a computer. As an example, the *Human Brain Project* (HBP) (Human Brain Project Website) is a large-scale project that began in 2013 and will run for 10 years. It aims to build up an infrastructure to simulate a human brain at large, in order to gain insight into several brain-related fields such as neurorobotics and neuroinformatics. This should be accomplished by reengineering the brain via its neurons by simulating 86 billon neurons and 100 trillion synapses on multiple supercomputers proclaiming the model may be capable of consciousness (Markram 2009). This in-silico neuroscience project is an interesting enterprise. However, the question remains as to what can be expressed and which kind of knowledge can be gained from such a simulation at all. This is strongly related to a general overestimation of computation capability.

One fact opposing this overestimation is the problem of time complexity. In computer science, the time complexity of a (formalized) problem is defined as the amount of steps a computer program performs to find a solution related to the size of the input. There are categories like constant, linear, polynomial or exponential time behavior, meaning that for the input length of n, the computer program takes c (constant, that is, always the same steps regardless of the problem size), $c*n$ (linear), n^c (polynomial), or c^n (exponential) steps to complete. Preferably, algorithms should have a low time complexity, but for some problems this is just not possible. Especially in the field of combinatorics, most algorithms have an exponential time complexity meaning that even for small problem sizes, computation takes years to complete.[5] These algorithms can be used to simulate logistics or production systems. In practice, and especially for numerical simulation, the pre-exponential factor plays an important role: It is highly relevant whether an

---

[5]Quantum computing could change all of this since it is able to break down complexity classes so that problems with an exponential time complexity could become feasible. However, this is out of the scope of this paper. Furthermore, if-then argumentations lead to speculative discussions that are no longer scientific or productive, such as in the discussions on nanotechnology (Nordmann 2007).

algorithm takes $2 * n^2$ or just $1.5 * n^2$ steps to complete. Space complexity is also relevant in practice. Each algorithm has a characteristic behavior in the (memory and disk) space it uses. However, time is the critical factor, since (memory and disk) space is continuously expanded due to technological progress.

Another objection to this myth is the general question of what, in principle, can be calculated by a computer. The accepted hypothesis of Alan Turing and Alonzo Church states that each function which can be calculated intuitively (i.e. mechanically by a human) can be calculated by a Turing Machine (Turing 1939), and hence by a computer as a universal machine. This implies that, if and only if an algorithmic expression of steps towards the problem's solution can be found, it is in principle computable. Nevertheless, the Church-Turing thesis has been criticized for not being able to map interactive computing, since it is derived from a mathematical worldview. Goldin and Wegner (2005) argue that nowadays computers cannot be modeled by Turing Machines any more. The authors miss a pragmatic engineering worldview in Turings conceptions. However, they do not deny the statement that only what can be formalized can be calculated by a computer and nothing more. Or, as formulated by Douglas R. Hofstadter:

> In arithmetic, the top level can be "skimmed off" and implemented equally well in many different sorts of hardware: mechanical adding machines, pocket calculators, large computers, people's brains, and so forth. This is what the Church-Turing Thesis is all about. But when it comes to real-world understanding, it seems that there is no simple way to skim off the top level, and program it. (Hofstadter 1980, p. 565)

I want to emphasize that algorithmization is a primary concept in computer science, and whatever cannot be formalized in a certain way, cannot be handled by a computer. With respect to simulation, this is an important statement. In technical disciplines, algorithmization is mostly noncritical because the theory behind it already has a strong (mathematical) formalism that can be transferred without big losses. But it can become crucial in social sciences where there is mostly no strong formalism emerging from the theory. For example, in 1971 Thomas C. Schelling introduced an agent-based model for segregation (Schelling 1971), showing how tendencies regarding neighbors may lead to segregation. This leads either to full integration (random-like distribution) or complete segregation. Eretz Hatna and Itzhak Benenson state that this dichotomy does not represent real behavior and extend the model to a pattern with a semi-integrated state (Hatna and Benenson 2012). It is also worth arguing that segregation may have nothing to do with spatial relation (Grim et al. 2013). Moreover, this model can only provide information on how segregation spreads throughout certain properties. What causality is behind segregation is out of the scope of this model. Regarding evolution of cooperation in social sciences, Eckhart Arnold gives examples of typical narratives that seem to justify models, but states that there has been no successful empirical application of these models so far (Arnold 2015).

In addition to the fact that not everything can be simulated, all the results are within the scope of the models they are based on. The steps in the simulation process are performed on the (formal) representation of the target system. All results emerge out of the model's assumptions and are in the scope of the algorithm and within a certain determined solution space.[6] It may just seem that there are new surprising results because we humans were not able to anticipate them. Computational power simply made them visible. However, there is nothing mystical about it. A computer just follows the instructions in the computer program—the algorithm. These instructions are then reduced to even simpler instructions down to the hardware level, where all complex instructions are realized by very simple binary additions, subtractions, and multiplications. On this level, a computer is a number-cruncher whose strength lies in its speed of processing, not in its creativity.

I would like to emphasize that no intelligent behavior emerges from the computer itself, but only from the way it is programmed and used (e.g., for simulation). But the way to the solution must be known already and sketched out by a human with the computer as his or her tool. And only things humans can formalize can be simulated by a computer.

4 Conclusions

In this paper, three myths of computer simulation have been presented and criticized. For some, it may seem that computers can do and hence simulate anything. The fact is, however, that a computer is a number-crunching machine that obtains its "intelligence" from human problem-solving capabilities condensed into an algorithm. Regarding the HBP, it is daring to proclaim that learning about consciousness, memory, or emotions is possible without models and insight into how these work, but only with a copy of the neuronal structure of the brain in a computer system. No arguments are presented why this should work out. As Winsberg puts it, you already "need to know something to learn something" (Winsberg 2009, p. 591) from computer simulation. It seems like the background knowledge of the HBP is rather meager regarding the HBP.

Another myth discussed is the believed exactness of simulation. Reasons have been presented why this is neither possible nor necessary: From a technical perspective, the design of computers leads to approximations and not exact results. From a conceptual point of view, simulation as model-building excludes certain details in order to focus on a particular aspect of a problem. The results are then good enough to gain knowledge, but without a critical awareness of these facts relying on simulation results may become hazardous.

Moreover it is crucial to mention that computer simulations are often mistaken for classic experiments being conducted in cyberspace. In fact, simulation is neither

---

[6]One could now argue that machine learning could change the whole picture. Nevertheless, in terms of the algorithms, there is still strong transparency: All the steps of a computer program are determined, but the opaqueness of the paths of the steps as well as of the results, is increased so that they become not traceable. However, a closer look at machine learning is beyond the scope of this paper.

theory nor experiment, but rather derived from both. It is inserted in-between and has a mediating role for theory and experiment leading a life of its own. This is essential to remember. When using simulation, we are working with representations derived from theory, but with experimental-like methods as iterations. Thus, though it seems we are investigating real world phenomenon, we must be aware that we are looking at representations, with all the inaccuracies they imply. However, these representations hold for an indirect access to reality. That does not mean one can "represent anything with anything. Links with theory, explanation, and prediction are crucial aspects of the process of representation" (Morrison 2015, p. 129).

One myth that could not be covered within this paper is that simulation is plain technical and scientific activity. This is related to a general misbelief of technology and science standing outside of society with only little human interaction. When we look back at the HBP, the major points of critique were—in addition to the epistemological reasons—organizational problems, bad management and poor decision-making processes that even made a mediation necessary (Theil 2015). Besides, the social implications of simulation project are not trivial—just remember the study of segregation by simulation mentioned in Sect. 3.3. These questions will be interesting to work with in the future.

Will mankind have a brain in a supercomputer in the future (Markram 2009)? Will a Terminator be capable of human-like intelligence? Will a computer be able to love, as some futurists claim (Pagliery and King 2016)? The answer is no, it won't, because only "(s)ome kinds of things which a brain can do can be vaguely approximated on a computer but not most, and certainly not the interesting ones. But anyway, even if they all could, that would still leave the soul to explain, and there is no way that computers have any bearing on that." (Hofstadter 1980, p. 570) When myths take over, science becomes a sci-fi spectacle. This must be prevented.

Acknowledgments I thank *Dr. Andreas Kaminski* for encouraging me to do this paper and philosophical advice. I'd also like to thank *Dr. Juan Manuel Durán* for helpful comments and remarks on the draft. Moreover I want to thank *Wanda Spahn* for proofreading.

References

Arnold, Eckhart. 2015. How Models Fail - A Critical Look at the History of Computer Simulations of the Evolution of Cooperation. In *Collective Agency and Cooperation in Natural and Artificial Systems. Explanation, Implementation and Simulation, Philosophical Studies Series*, ed. Catrin Misselhorn, 261–279. Springer. doi:10.1007/978-3-319-15515-9.

Beisbart, Claus. 2012. How can computer simulations produce new knowledge? *European Journal for Philosophy of Science* 2 (3): 395–434.

Blumenberg, Hans. 1979. *Arbeit am Mythos*. Suhrkamp: Frankfurt a. M.

Di Paolo, Ezequiel A., Jason Noble, and Seth Bullock. 2000. Simulation models as opaque thought experiments. In *The Seventh International Conference on Artificial Life*, ed. Mark A. Bedau, John S. McCaskill, Norman Packard, and Steen Rasmussen, 497–506. Cambridge, MA: MIT Press.

Dreyfus, Hubert L. 1992. *What Computers Still Can't Do: A Critique of Artificial Reason.* Cambridge, MA: MIT Press.

El Skaf, Rawad and Cyrille Imbert. 2013. Unfolding in the empirical sciences: experiments, thought experiments and computer simulations. *Synthese* 190:3451–3474.

Frenkel, Daan. 2012. Simulations: The dark side. *Proceedings of the International School of Physics "Enrico Fermi"* 184:195–227. doi:10.3254/978-1-61499-278-3-195.

Goldberg, David. 1991. What Every Computer Scientist Should Know About Floating-Point Arithmetic. *ACM Computing Surveys* 23 (1): 5–48. doi:10.1145/103162.103163.

Goldin, Dina, and Peter Wegner. 2005. The Church-Turing Thesis: Breaking the Myth. In *New Computational Paradigms. LNCS* 3526, ed. Barry Cooper, Benedikt Löwe, and Leen Torenvliet, 152–168. Berlin und Heidelberg: Springer.

Grim, Patrick, Robert Rosenberger, Adam Rosenfeld, Brian Anderson, and Robb E. Eason. 2013. How simulations fail. *Synthese*: 190 (12): 2367–2390.

Hartmann, Stephan. 1996. The World as a Process: Simulations in the Natural and Social Sciences. In *Modelling and Simulation in the Social Sciences from the Philosophy of Science Point of View*, ed. R. Hegselmann, Ulrich Mueller, and Klaus G. Troitzsch, 77–100. Dordrecht: Kluwer.

Hatna, Erez, and Itzhak Benenson. 2012. The Schelling Model of Ethnic Residential Dynamics: Beyond the Integrated - Segregated Dichotomy of Patterns. *Journal of Artificial Societies and Social Simulation* 15 (1): 6. doi:10.18564/jasss.1873.

Hatton, Les, and Andy Roberts. 1994. How accurate is scientific software? *IEEE Transactions on Software Engineering.* 20 (10): 785–797. doi:10.1109/32.328993.

Hofstadter, Douglas H. 1980. *Gödel, Escher, Bach: An Eternal Golden Braid. A Metaphoric Fugue on Minds and Machines in the Spirit of Lewis Carrol.* Harmondsworth: Penguin Books.

Honer, Oliver. 2011. Sind wir alle Sophisten? Überzeugen und Wahrheit im verwobenen Spiel von Mythos und Logos. In *Tagungsband der Nachwuchstagungen für Junge Philosophie in Darmstadt. Brüche, Brücken, Ambivalenzen (2009), Die Wiederverzauberung der Welt? (2010)*, ed. Suzana Alpsancar and Kai Denker, 239–264. Marburg: Tectum.

Horkheimer, Max, and Theodor W. Adorno. 1972. *Dialectic of enlightenment.* New York: Herder and Herder.

Human Brain Project. https://www.humanbrainproject.eu/. Accessed 18 Mar 2016.

Humphreys, Paul. 2009. The philosophical novelty of computer simulation methods. *Synthese* 169 (3): 615–626.

Kaminski, Andreas, Björn Schembera, Michael Resch, and Uwe Küster. 2016. Simulation als List. In *List und Tod. Jahrbuch Technikphilosophie*, ed. Alfred Nordmann, Andreas Kaminski, Christoph Hubig, Gerhard Gamm, and Petra Gehring, 93–121. Zürich und Berlin: Diaphanes.

Lenhard, Johannes. 2011. Epistemologie der Iteration. Gedankenexperimente und Simulationsexperimente. *Deutsche Zeitschrift für Philosophie*, 59 (1): 131–145.

Markram, Henry. 2009. A brain in a supercomputer. TED Talk 2009. https://www.ted.com/talks/ henry_markram_supercomputing_the_brain_s_secrets. Accessed 28 Apr 2016.

Moor, James H. 1978. Three Myths of Computer Science. *The British Journal for the Philosophy of Science* 29 (3): 213–222.

Morrison, Margaret. 2015. *Reconstructing Reality: Models, Mathematics, and Simulations.* Oxford: Oxford University Press.

Nordmann, Alfred. 2007. If and Then: A Critique of Speculative NanoEthics. *NanoEthics* 1 (1): 31–46.

Pagliery, Jose and Hope King. 2016. Computers will overtake us when they learn to love, says futurist Ray Kurzweil. *CNN Money*, March 8. http://money.cnn.com/2016/03/08/technology/ ray-kurzweil-artificial-intelligence/. Accessed 8 July 2016.

Michael Resch, (2013) What's the Result? - Thoughts of a Center Director on Simulation. In *Computer Simulations and the Changing Face of Scientific Experimentation*, ed. Juan M. Durán and Eckhart Arnold, 233–246. Newcastle: Cambridge Scholars Publishing.

Schelling, Thomas C. 1971. Dynamic Models of Segregation. *Journal of Mathematical Sociology* 1:143–186.

Theil, Stefan. 2015. Why the Human Brain Project Went Wrong–and How to Fix It. *Scientific American*.   http://www.scientificamerican.com/article/why-the-human-brain-project-went-wrong-and-how-to-fix-it/. Accessed 29 Apr 2016.

Turing, Alan M. 1939. *Systems of Logic Based on Ordinals*. PhD, diss., Princeton University.

Turing, Alan M. 1950. Computing Machinery and Intelligence. *Mind* LIX s(236): 433–460. doi:10.1093/mind/LIX.236.433.

Winsberg, Eric. 2003. Simulated Experiments: Methodology for a Virtual World. *Philosophy of Science* 70 (1): 105–125. doi:10.1086/367872.

Winsberg, Eric. 2009. A tale of two methods. *Synthese* 169 (3): 575–592. doi:10.1007/s11229-008-9437-0.

Wittgenstein, Ludwig. 1997. *Philosophical investigations*, ed. G. E. M. Anscombe and R. Rhees. Trans. G. E. M. Anscombe, P. M. S. Hacker and Joachim. Schulte. Oxford, UK: Blackwell.

Part II
The Art of Understanding Computer Simulations

Understanding Social Science Simulations: Distinguishing Two Categories of Simulations

Nicole J. Saam

Abstract How can we understand the results of a simulation study? In this article, I address this epistemic question for social science simulations. I argue that we can distinguish two categories of simulations: simulations S_{TE}, which possess key features that resemble the epistemology and methodology of thought experiments, and simulations S_E, which resemble the epistemology and methodology of experiments. Based on Woodward's theory of causal explanation, I put forward the hypothesis that S_{TE} provide more understanding and a different kind of knowledge than S_E because they give well-founded answers to what-if-things-had-been-different questions. Epistemic opacity is a persistent problem for simulations S_E, while for S_{TE} it need not necessarily be so.

1 Introduction

The question of how results from social science simulations[1] can be understood can be addressed from several points of view. From a broader, philosophy of science point of view, the focus is on understanding these results as some sort of simulation results. From a narrower, philosophy of the social sciences point of view, the focus is on understanding how these simulations explain emergent social phenomena: To what extent can emergent phenomena (on the collective level) be reduced to explanations based on their components (the individual actors)? This question is taken by Sawyer (2013) and leads to intense discussions on reductionist explanations of social systems, in particular on mechanistic explanations (Hedström 2005) and on theories of emergence in sociology and philosophy (Sawyer 2004).

---

[1] In this article, I avoid the term social simulation for the reason that this umbrella term also encompasses models employed by, for example, ecologists and computer scientists, who do not relate their work to social theory. Instead, I use the term social science simulation to indicate this difference.

N.J. Saam (✉)
Institute of Sociology, Friedrich-Alexander Universität Erlangen-Nürnberg, Kochstraße 4, 91054 Erlangen, Germany
e-mail: nicole.j.saam@fau.de

© Springer International Publishing AG 2017   67
M.M. Resch et al. (eds.), *The Science and Art of Simulation I*,
DOI 10.1007/978-3-319-55762-5_6

What the narrower, philosophy of the social sciences point of view ignores is the variety of simulation approaches, as well as the variety of purposes these approaches are used for. Sawyer (2013) considers two ways of interpreting agent-based modelling, identifying a "simulation as theory" and a "simulation as experiment" camp. The former group of scientists describes simulation as a form of theory construction (e.g. Conte et al. 2001), while the latter argue that a simulation is a virtual experiment (e.g. Carley and Gasser 1999). In this latter view, the simulation plays the role of a data-generating experiment. It does not provide an explanation; rather, it provides raw data to aid in theorizing. This study will take these views as a starting point and ask from a philosophy of science point of view whether and how the results of these diverse simulation models can be understood. The topic of emergence will be bracketed in the first part and briefly addressed in the second part.

This article makes two claims: (1) Some simulations have key features that resemble the epistemology and methodology of thought experiments (S_{TE}), and some others have features that resemble the epistemology and methodology of experiments (S_E); (2) The question whether and how the results of simulations can be understood can be evaluated differently for different sorts of simulations. S_{TE} can be shown to provide more understanding than S_E.

The argument of this article is developed in four steps: Sect. 2 differentiates social science simulations that resemble the epistemology and methodology of thought experiments (S_{TE}) from those that resemble the epistemology and methodology of experiments (S_E). The simulation study by Macy and Skvoretz (1998) on the evolution of trust and cooperation between strangers and the simulation study on population growth and collapse of the Kayenta Anasazi in Long House Valley (Dean et al. 2000; Axtell et al. 2002; Gumerman et al. 2003) are offered as model cases. In Sect. 3, I argue that S_{TE} provide more understanding and a different kind of knowledge than S_E. My argument is based on Woodward's (2003) theory of causal explanation. In particular, I make use of Woodward's concept of "what-if-things-had-been-different questions". I argue that simulations S_{TE} give well-founded answers to these questions, while simulations S_E do not. In Sect. 4, I show how the loss of understanding from opacity is relevant for social science simulations.

However, the discussion of issues in this article will be limited in two respects: (a) The scientific understanding of phenomena is one of the principal aims of science. If scientists use simulation models to explain phenomena, the distinction between understanding the model/simulation and understanding the phenomenon with the help of model/simulation is important. This article concentrates on the first question: How can we understand a simulation study's results? We bracket the epistemological question about whether the simulation is correct or not, as well as the issue of how we might come to know this. We also bracket the question of how a simulation study might provide understanding of the phenomenon; (b) In all sections, we refer to Hartmann's definition of a simulation model: "A simulation results when the equations of the underlying dynamic model are solved. This model is designed to imitate the time-evolution of a real system. To put it in another way, *a simulation imitates one process by another process*" (Hartmann 1996, p. 83, emphasis in original).[2] This definition excludes simulations of static objects, such as Monte Carlo simulations.[3] Although we use agent-based models to illustrate the argument of this article, the argument includes macroscopic social science simulations.

2 Two Types of Social Science Simulations

In this section, the categories of social science simulations that either resemble the epistemology and methodology of thought experiments (S_{TE}) or the epistemology and methodology of experiments (S_E) are developed. Both sorts of simulations are defined and two model cases are presented to illustrate the distinction.

A simulation study is regarded as resembling the epistemology and methodology of a thought experiment (or an experiment) if distinct characteristics of a thought experiment (or an experiment) apply to it. These characteristics are obtained from the philosophy of the thought experiment and the philosophy of the experiment.

Cooper's (2005) account of thought experiments will serve as a reference for defining S_{TE}. According to Cooper (2005, p. 336), a thought experiment attempts to construct models of possible worlds. This model either constructs or represents a possible world. Strictly speaking, the model will not produce a single possible world, but rather a template for an infinite number of possible worlds. During a thought experiment, a series of "what if" questions is asked, and the "thought experimenter is committed to rigorously considering all relevant consequences in answering the 'what if' questions" (Cooper 2005, p. 337). This involves a manipulation of the thought experimenter's worldview. The result of the manipulations is either a consistent model or a contradiction.

An experiment is a method of data collection under controlled and varied conditions. Experiments involve the manipulation of one or more independent variables and observing the effect(s) on a particular outcome—the dependent variable. Basic elements of this definition are the intervention and observation of changes in the behavior of the system which is interfered with. This definition has

---

[2]Hartmann's definition applies to non-computational simulations as well. However, they are not relevant for the argument presented here.

[3]It is not certain that the restrictive definition of "simulation" by Hartmann (1996) still applies to all examples of current computer simulation, even in the particular domain of social sciences: e.g., there have been simulations that do not imitate a phenomenon with a temporal dimension (see e.g. Winsberg 2009). From this viewpoint, the exclusion of Monte Carlo simulations may also seem excessive and unjustified. However, for our present purposes we prefer a restrictive definition for two reasons: First, the vast majority of simulations in the social sciences are included in this restrictive definition, and it is more transparent to develop the present argument in line with this restrictive definition. Second, the argument may be transferred later to a more comprehensive definition of simulation, including, e.g., Monte Carlo simulations. Consideration of further sorts of current computer simulation would exceed the space limitations of a journal article.

been characterized as the "old image of experiment" (Morgan 2003, p. 217), since Hacking (1983, p. 230) pointed out that "to experiment is to create, produce, refine and stabilize phenomena" and recognized that phenomena are hard to produce in any stable way—which also became the basic insight of New Experimentalism. Hacking (1983) has introduced the hypothesis that experiments have a life of their own: "I think of experiments as having a life: maturing, evolving, adapting, being not only recycled, but quite literally, being retooled" (Hacking 1992, p. 307). He argues that the results of experiments achieve stability and are self-vindicating when three elements are brought into mutual consistency and support. These are (1) ideas: questions, background knowledge, systematic theory, topical hypotheses, and modelling of the apparatus; (2) things: target, source of modification, detectors, tools, and data generators; and (3) marks and the manipulation of marks: data, data assessment, data reduction, data analysis, and interpretation. Experimenters invent devices that produce data and isolate or create phenomena. However, in the end, they count them only as phenomena when the data can be interpreted according to a theory (Hacking 1992, pp. 57–58). Following Winsberg (2003), my argument will be based on Hacking's account.

2.1 Simulations S_{TE}

What I am endeavoring to establish is that some social science simulations have key features that resemble the epistemology and methodology of thought experiments (S_{TE}). Bearing Cooper's (2005) definition of the thought experiment in mind, I will now define the first sort of simulations: simulations S_{TE} attempt to construct models of possible worlds. These models either construct or represent a possible world. Strictly speaking, the model will not produce a single possible world, but rather a template for an infinite number of possible worlds. During a simulation experiment a series of "what if" questions is asked and the simulating scientist is committed to rigorously considering all relevant consequences in answering the "what if" questions. S_{TE} make either deductive or inductive inferences from presumptions implicit in the description of the simulation model, preserving truth or preserving the probability of truth. The emphasis is on these inferences. Simulation scientists concentrate on understanding how the conclusions are obtained from the premises.

2.2 Simulations S_E

I also want to argue that some other social science simulations have key features that resemble the epistemology and methodology of experiments (S_E). I will now define the second sort of simulations: simulations S_E concentrate on (artificial) data generation. Barberousse et al. (2009) advance the hypothesis that some simulations share some epistemic functions with field experiments. The point of reference is observation and discovery as typical of (real) experiments which generate (empirical) data ($data_E$). Barberousse et al. (2009) argue that simulations can be used as experiments because they represent phenomena. Winsberg (2003) argues that simulations use many, if not all, common sense techniques that experiments also use to sanction their results. Winsberg (2003) and Lenhard (2011) support Hacking's (1983) notion of attributing a kind of life of their own to simulations. Morrison (2009) has even put forward a more nuanced hypothesis and placed it in the context of experiments. She argues that the results of some simulations may be characterized as measurements, not simply as calculations, and that simulations can attain an epistemic status comparable to laboratory experimentation. The main reason for this is that models play an important role in simulations and experiments. Models can function as measuring instruments. In opposition to this hypothesis, Beisbart (2011, pp. 65–72) has objected that the results of computer simulations are over-controlled—they are determined substantially by the computer program and the input—which would not be true in the same way for the results of experiments: "There is no space left for an answer by nature" (Beisbart 2011, p. 67). Winsberg (2009) emphasizes that simulations produce results that resemble the data generated in experiments.

What is being argued here is that S_E are run to provide new data (Carley and Gasser 1999). Computer simulations produce $data_C$ (about the computer) that must be distinguished from $data_E$ (of empirical origin) and $data_A$ (about a target system) which are produced in field experiments (Barberousse et al. 2009). From an epistemological perspective, the critical question is to understand how $data_C$, namely the results of a computation, can be transformed into $data_A$. S_E rigorously explore and/or optimize large parameter spaces.

2.3 Two Model Cases

Two famous models can illustrate this distinction and serve as model cases:

The simulation study by Macy and Skvoretz (1998) on the evolution of trust and cooperation between strangers by and large qualifies as a simulation S_{TE}. Macy and Skvoretz concentrate on answering "what if" questions. Their objective is to "test the possibility of emergent social order under conditions previously believed to preclude it" (ibid., p. 647). They make deductive inferences from presumptions, preserving the probability of truth. They place emphasis on making inferences as transparent as possible. For instance, they find and argue that it is not the prospect of re-encounter that helps conventions for trusting strangers to evolve, but the ability to coordinate effective trust conventions in local interaction.

In particular, this simulation study is both elaborate and sophisticated in presenting premises and their conclusions. Macy and Skvoretz repeatedly state that a theory, hypothesis, or argument is being tested (e.g., "test this theory", ibid., p. 642; "our first experiment tests the hypothesis that the evolution of trust depends on the exit payoff [. . .] relative to the payoff for mutual defection", ibid.,

p. 648; "our study formalizes and tests the internal validity of the evolutionary argument," ibid., p. 659). The inferences drawn from the presumptions serve to pose follow-up questions that are intended to make the obtained conclusions as transparent as possible (e.g., how can projection and detection rules eventually win out over rules for only trusting neighbors? Why don't co-operators quickly learn to defect, causing trust conventions to collapse? Ibid., p. 652).

The simulation study on population growth and collapse of the Kayenta Anasazi in Long House Valley (Dean et al. 2000; Axtell et al. 2002; Gumerman et al. 2003) can be regarded as a simulation S_E. This simulation study rigorously explores and optimizes an eight-dimensional space of parameters in order to reproduce important spatial and demographic features of the Anasazi in Long House Valley from about A.D. 800–1300. The authors concentrate on generating simulated data and fitting it to the historical data that is available from the Long House Valley database of the Southwestern Anthropological Research Group. They discover that, over an entire range of possible environments (e.g. with different sizes and spatial distributions of sites), the simulation model does not predict the complete abandonment of the Long House Valley that occurred after A.D. 1300.

In particular, this simulation study is elaborate and sophisticated in calibrating and estimating the input data (minimum/maximum death age of agents, minimum/maximum age, end of fertility, minimum/maximum fission probability, average harvest, harvest variance). Huge parameter spaces are systematically varied to optimize the fit between the simulated and historical output data (e.g. population size, size and spatial distribution of sites, patterns of land use in different environmental zones). The results are checked for robustness (which again produces huge amounts of data). Considering the large number of individual results, their presentation concentrates on their description and on comparison with the historical data. Dean and colleagues repeatedly state that their goal is to explain the settlement and farming dynamics. However, they are not interested in individual hypotheses. Instead, an overall assessment of the results is presented. This assessment focuses on how closely the model reproduces the record of the archaeological survey. In the course of their studies, they make two major discoveries: In the earlier study, even the best model predicts a total population that is much larger than expected (Dean et al. 2000, p. 190). Axtell et al. report that all attempts to reduce the population in that model by changing agent parameters resulted in premature population collapse (Axtell et al. 2002, p. 7277). The later study suggests that even the degraded environment of the 1270–1450 periods could have supported a reduced, but substantial, population. The simulated valley is not abandoned by its inhabitants. They draw a conclusion that goes beyond the model's assumptions: It is not the (modelled) environmental, but rather additional (not yet modelled) social determinants that are made responsible for the abandonment of the Long House Valley.

To summarize, simulations S_{TE} and S_E have different purposes. While the former are used to give in-depth answers to "what if" questions, the latter are used for a more general objective—altogether, S_E are run to provide new data. The purpose is reflected in the set-up of the simulation experiments, which is a methodological feature. The set-up of the simulation S_{TE} experiments follows the "what if" questions. The sequence of simulation runs has a narrow focus and is intended to make the inferences in the calculations as transparent as possible. The experimental set-up of simulations S_E follows a broader scheme. Huge parameter spaces are systematically varied, depending on the specific research question.

There may, however, be simulation studies which do not resemble either of these epistemologies or methodologies. To classify all social science simulations is beyond the scope of this article. The distinction between S_{TE} and S_E is meant to be gradual, not categorical. The distinction can not only be used for epistemic purposes. If diverse objectives of simulation studies can be differentiated on a more abstract level, and different epistemologies be related to these objectives, then the methodology of simulations may be further developed based on the epistemic differences.

3 Understanding the Results of Simulations

In this section, the following thesis is put forward:

T: S_{TE} provide more understanding and a different kind of knowledge than S_E because they give well-founded answers to what-if-things-had-been-different questions.

My argument is based on Woodward's (2003) theory of causal explanation. His account was chosen for two reasons: (1) It is well suited to the social sciences; (2) Although it addresses the scientific understanding of phenomena, it lends itself to use in the scientific understanding of simulation results.

Ad (1). Since Woodward's approach does not make special assumptions about causal mechanisms or require laws of nature, it applies not only to physics but to biomedical and social sciences as well—where mechanisms and laws are harder to find (Woodward 2003, p. 6). In particular, Woodward introduces the weaker idea of "invariance" as an alternative for the controversial notion of "law."

Ad (2). Essentially, Woodward addresses the scientific understanding of phenomena. Causal explanation provides such an understanding (Woodward 2003, p. 23). He puts forward a manipulationist conception of causal explanation. Woodward argues that the distinguishing feature of causal explanations is that they "furnish information that is potentially relevant to manipulation and control: they tell us how, if we were able to change the value of one or more variables, we could change the value of other variables" (Woodward 2003, p. 6).

I argue that his account can be transferred to the scientific understanding of results of simulation models (*transfer hypothesis*). Three important reasons justify my transfer hypothesis: First, Woodward's account relates causation to experimentation: causal relations are determined by manipulating a putative cause (by intervention) in order to see whether there are changes in the effect, a procedure that is tantamount to experimentation. This procedure is also typical of simulation studies. Second, Woodward claims that the information is *potentially* relevant to manipulation and control. This means that experiments do not have to be actual or real; they are typically hypothetical experiments that do not even have to be realizable in practice. In this way, computer simulations may substitute for real experiments. Third, Woodward's account relates causation to counterfactuals: his conception of causal explanation refers to what would happen in case of counterfactual interventions. Computer simulations typically implement large numbers of counterfactual interventions. More exactly, they execute manipulations that substitute for large numbers of counterfactual interventions.

3.1 What-If-Things-Had-Been-Different Questions as a Basis of Inferential Performance Constitutive of Understanding

In particular, my argument makes use of Woodward's (2003) concept of "what-if-things-had-been-different questions." His counterfactual theory of explanation asserts that a good (causal) explanation exhibits patterns of counterfactual dependence. Any successful explanation should be associated with a hypothetical or counterfactual experiment that shows whether and how manipulation of the factors mentioned in the *explanans* would be a way of manipulating or altering the *explanandum*. Woodward (2003, p. 203) has summarized his idea as follows:

> (**EXP**) Suppose that M is an explanandum consisting in the statement that some variable Y takes the particular value y. Then an explanans E for M will consist of (a) a generalization G relating changes in the value(s) of a variable X (where X may itself be a vector or a n-tuple of variables X_i) and changes in Y, and (b) a statement (of initial or boundary conditions) that the variable X takes the particular value x. A necessary and sufficient condition for E to be (minimally) explanatory with respect to M is that (i) E and M be true or approximately so; (ii) according to G, Y takes the value of y under an intervention in which X takes the value x; (iii) there is some intervention that changes the value of X from x to x' where $x \neq x'$, with G correctly describing the value y' that Y would assume under this intervention, where $y' \neq y$.

In short, any successful explanation should answer a what-if-things-had-been-different question:

> The explanation must enable us to see what sort of difference it would have made for the explanandum if the factors cited in the explanans had been different in various possible ways. We can also think of this as information about a pattern of counterfactual dependence between explanans and explanandum, provided the counterfactuals in question are understood appropriately. (Woodward 2003, p. 11)

The answers to what-if-things-had-been-different questions are the bases of inferential performance constitutive of understanding.

Transferring Woodward's account to the understanding of simulation results provides:

> (**EXP-S**) Suppose that M is an explanandum consisting in the statement that some variable Y takes the particular value y. Then an explanans E for M will consist of (a) a generalization G relating changes in the value(s) of a variable X (where X may ifself be a vector or a

n-tuple of variables X_i) and changes in Y, and (b) a statement (of initial or boundary conditions) that the variable X takes the particular value x. A necessary and sufficient condition for E to be (minimally) explanatory with respect to M is that (i) E and M be true or approximately so; (ii) according to G, Y takes the value of y under an intervention *executed in a simulation experiment* in which X takes the value x; (iii) there is some intervention *executed in a simulation experiment* that changes the value of X from x to x' where $x \neq x'$, with G correctly describing the value y' that Y would assume under this intervention, where $y' \neq y$.

3.2   Understanding the Results of Simulations S_{TE} and Simulations S_E

I argue that simulations S_{TE} provide more understanding than simulations S_E and a different kind of knowledge because they give *well-founded* answers to what-if-things-had-been-different questions. Simulations S_{TE} concentrate on giving in-depth answers. Thus, their answers to what-if-things-had-been-different questions are based on arguments.[4] In an *explorative* study, the argumentation focuses on reconstructing why a particular set of assumed premises has produced a particular outcome. The simulation scientist will go through all relevant consequences of the what-if-things-had-been-different questions. The *explanandum* or *explananda* that were derived from the simulations have to be made plausible. In an *anticipative* study, the argumentation focuses on the premises found to generate an outcome that more or less resembles a given *explanandum*. The simulation scientist will reconstruct those premises. They reflect different what-if-things-had-been-different questions. The simulation scientist will seek to understand why certain premises failed to generate the desired outcome, while others produced an outcome displaying some similarity to the *explanandum*. Irrespective of whether an explorative or an anticipative study is conducted, the argumentation will reconstruct the premises and the outcome in an *explanans-explanandum* style. This is considered to provide a well-founded answer to a what-if-things-had-been-different question. Numerous what-if-things-had-been-different questions are answered in this way, making the argumentation more transparent. The answers given to the what-if-things-had-been-different questions converge onto a limited number of paths.

As opposed to simulations S_{TE}, simulations S_E do *not* give well-founded answers to what-if-things-had-been-different questions. Even though from a formal point of view, simulations S_E might seem to ask what-if-things-had-been-different questions, their focus is on rigorously exploring and/or optimizing large parameter spaces. Simulations S_E do *not* reconstruct the premises and the outcome in an

---

[4]I remain neutral toward two theses that have established an argument view. I do not argue that each thought experiment can be reconstructed as an argument (Norton's thesis put forward in Norton 1996), nor do I argue that each computer simulation can be reconstructed as an argument (Beisbart's thesis put forward in Beisbart 2012).

explanans-explanandum style. The answers given to the what-if-things-had-been-different questions do *not* converge onto a limited number of paths.

3.3   Understanding the Results of the Model Cases

To illustrate this argument, see our first model case, which has been classified as a simulation S_{TE}, the simulation study by Macy and Skvoretz (1998) on the evolution of trust and cooperation between strangers. This study offers answers to sociological "what if" questions in an elaborate way. The analysis is structured as follows: (1) A what-if-things-had-been-different question ("*what* would happen *if* the prisoner's dilemma is structurally embedded in social networks *as opposed to* not being structurally embedded?") is derived from a sociological "what if" question ("what happens if the prisoner's dilemma is structurally embedded in social networks?"); (2) the what-if-things-had-been-different question is translated into a suitable experimental design with a set of, overall, two what-if-things-had-been-different questions (q_1, q_2), a set of 29 alternative premises ($p_{1\ 0}$–$p_{2\ 26}$) and a set of 5 scenarios (H_0–H_4; see Table 1); in the section on the experimental results, the argumentation focuses on reconstructing why a particular set of assumed premises has produced a particular outcome; (3) answers to what-if-things-had-been-different questions are related back to the sociological "what if" questions: the evolution of Protestant sects is revisited. Macy and Skvoretz refer to Weber's theory of Protestantism and trust in an emerging market society. Weber had tacitly assumed that the need to discern character led Americans to rely on church membership as a telltale sign.

Table 1 Experimental design (Macy and Skvoretz 1998)

Set of what-if-things-had-been-different questions (q_i)	Set of alternative premises (p_{ij})	Set of scenarios (H_k)
What would happen if the prisoner's dilemma is structurally embedded and . . .		
. . . the exit payoff changes? (q_1)	Exit payoff equals the cost of mutual defection ($p_{1\ 0}$). Exit payoff is preferable to the payoff from mutual defection but less attractive than the payoff from mutual cooperation ($p_{1\ 1}$).	Cost of exit-scenarios (H_0–H_1)
. . . the network structure changes? (q_2)	Undifferentiated population ($p_{2\ 0}$). Minimally differentiated population ($p_{2\ 1}$). Neighborhood size increases from 10 to 50 members (in steps of 10 members) and embeddedness of interaction with neighbors increases (from 0.5 to 0.9 in steps of .1; $p_{2\ 2}$–$p_{2\ 26}$).	Network structure-scenarios (H_2–H_4)

Macy and Skvoretz argue that their study formalizes and tests the internal validity of the evolutionary argument that underlies Weber's explanation. The sociological insight derived from the simulations suggests that Protestant church membership became associated with trustworthiness in local congregations characterized by highly embedded interactions. Macy and Skvoretz argue that the convention then spread through occasional contact with strangers (Macy and Skvoretz 1998, p. 658). Throughout their analysis, Macy and Skvoretz reconstruct the premises and the outcome in an *explanans-explanandum* style. Their answers to the what-if-things-had-been-different questions are well founded.

To further illustrate my argument, I refer to the second model case, the simulation study on population growth and collapse of the Kayenta Anasazi in Long House Valley (Dean et al. 2000; Axtell et al. 2002; Gumerman et al. 2003) which has been classified as a simulation S_E. In the course of their studies, Dean, Axtell, Gumerman et al. make two major discoveries: Recall that in the earlier study (Dean et al. 2000), even the best model predicts a total population that is much larger than expected, and recall that all attempts to reduce the population in that model by changing agent parameters resulted in premature population collapse. The later study (Axtell et al. 2002) suggests that even the degraded environment of the 1270–1450 periods could have supported a reduced, but substantial, population. The simulated valley is not abandoned by its inhabitants. Recall that Axtell and colleagues draw a conclusion that goes beyond the model's assumptions: It is not the (modelled) environmental, but rather additional (not yet modelled) social determinants that are made responsible for the abandonment of the Long House Valley. In all these studies, the authors do *not* concentrate on giving answers to what-if-things-had-been-different questions. They do *not* reconstruct the premises and the outcome in an explanans-explanandum style. Rather, the model provides raw data to aid in theorizing. Ultimately, Axtell and colleagues do not clarify why all interventions resulted in premature population collapse in the 2000 study. And, in the 2002 study, it remains unclear why the simulated valley is not abandoned by its inhabitants. The conclusion that social determinants are responsible for the abandonment of the Long House Valley cannot be made apparent by the model, since the related premises are not included in it.

4 The Challenge of Opacity

In recent years, the philosophy of simulation (Humphreys 2004, 2009) has acknowledged a loss of understanding that is based on the epistemic opacity of simulations. This has been recognized by simulating scientists in the social sciences (e.g. Elsenbroich and Gilbert 2014, p. 11). In this section, I show how the loss of understanding from opacity is relevant for social science simulations.

4.1 Opacity Versus Epistemic Transparency

In a straight forward argument, Humphreys (2004, pp. 147–151) holds that there are two sources of epistemic opacity: (1) Referring to Wolfram (1985) and Marr (1982), he argues that there are computationally irreducible processes. In this case, there are no mathematical "short cuts," no mathematical techniques, to deduce the future state of a system. The process has to be calculated step by step, replacing the mathematical insight; (2) Most steps in the process are not open to direct inspection and verification. Computational processes are too fast for scientists to follow in detail (for a profound discussion of these sources and the implications, see Kaminski 2017). Humphreys (2009, p. 618) has given a concise definition of the concept of opacity:

> A process is epistemically opaque relative to a cognitive agent X at time t just in case X does not know at t all the epistemically relevant elements of the process. A process is essentially epistemically opaque to X if and only if it is impossible, given the nature of X, for X to know all the epistemically relevant elements of the process.

As a consequence, two scientists, X and Y, may disagree on the epistemically relevant elements. While X may consider a particular step in the process to be relevant, Y may hold that this step is sufficiently trivial to be eliminated. Humphreys argues that a switch from an individualist to a social epistemology, within which the work is divided among groups of scientists, will not make a significant difference as the "computations involved in most simulations are so fast and so complex that no human or group of humans can in practice reproduce or understand the processes" (Humphreys 2009, p. 619).

A third source of epistemic opacity has been pointed out by Lenhard and Hasse (2017). They argue that the parameterization of simulation models covers errors as well as implausibilities of the model assumptions. Parameters are often "adapted"—Lenhard and Hasse prefer this term to the concepts of calibration and tuning—corresponding to the global behavior of the model. Neglected is the fact that they may represent several objects or relations in (physical) reality. A model parameter, in practice, combines several parameters into a bundle. Such bundled parameters often lack a theoretical (here: physical) interpretation, and they cannot be measured independently from other parameters that are hidden in the bundle. These bundles cannot even be decomposed *ex post*.

Opacity has been contrasted with epistemic transparency, which is attributed to analytic models. Humphreys ends with a daring conclusion: "Because these constraints cannot be circumvented by humans, we must abandon the insistence on epistemic transparency for computational science" (Humphreys 2004, p. 150). In computational science, opacity has already been discussed in the philosophy of computer-aided proofs, and the concept of surveyability has been introduced to account for their limited transparency. A proof counts as surveyable "if it can be looked over, reviewed, verified by a rational agent" (Tymoczko 1979, p. 59). Referring to this discourse, it has been pointed out that computer simulations are arguments that are not often surveyable (Beisbart 2012, p. 429).

It has also been argued, however, that simulations are in some sense transparent: they consist of a large number of simple steps, programmed into a computer (Beisbart 2012). Beisbart argues that a sufficiently patient monitor could trace the entire simulation step by step from start to finish. There is a transparency of the individual steps of simulations (Beisbart and Norton 2012, p. 411). This argument has been put forward in a similar way by Morgan (2003). She distinguishes between experiments on mathematical models—later, on computer models—of natural or social systems and experiments directly in the natural or social systems. If the results of both kinds of experiments surprise us, "we can go back through the model experiment and understand why such surprising results occurred," while that possibility may not be open to us with material experiments (Morgan 2003, p. 220). Lenhard (2011, p. 136) emphasizes that compiled computer programs are the most explicit descriptions that are used in the sciences. Practically, they do not tolerate any vagueness. This concept of transparency has been conceptualized as algorithmic transparency (e.g. Lenhard 2011, p. 137). However, it ignores the fact that while the program code (with several tens of thousands of lines of code) may be epistemically transparent, the compiled code is not (several million lines of code are possible). The compiled code also includes sequences from secondary and tertiary codes from the used libraries and auxiliary programs, which are not transparent to the scientist.

I suggest using the concept of explicitness of the model assumptions from Suppes (1968) to refer to that kind of transparency that is intended to indicate the availability of a formal representation of the scientist's modelled assumptions. Explicitness may involve epistemic opacity if the simulation model includes bundled parameters or parameters which lack a theoretical interpretation, if there are no mathematical "short cuts" to deduce the future state of a system, or if computational processes are too fast for scientists to follow in detail.

4.2 Loss of Understanding

The philosophy of simulation acknowledges a loss of understanding from opacity. In the philosophy of simulation, the concepts of transparency, surveyability, and opacity have been related to distinct epistemologies, in particular to the goals of explaining or understanding phenomena. On one hand, the concept of DN-explanation (Hempel 1965) has been used to evaluate opacity (e.g., Beisbart 2012). On the other hand, opacity has been re-evaluated based on a concept of scientific understanding (Humphreys 2004, 2009).

Humphreys (2004) stresses the methodological implications of opacity, arguing that opacity can result in a loss of understanding. He refers to Kitcher (1989), who has emphasized that in "most traditional static models our understanding is based upon the ability to decompose the process between model inputs and outputs into modular steps, each of which is methodologically acceptable both individually and in combination with the others" (Humphreys 2004, p. 148).

Beisbart (2012, p. 427ff.) compares computer simulations with computationally assisted proofs of theorems. Computer simulations are not often surveyable. He concludes that "the question is how much and what kind of understanding we can obtain in this way" (Beisbart 2012, p. 429).

4.3   Relevance for Social Science Simulations

Both types of social science simulations, simulations S_{TE} and S_E, are characterized by explicitness on the level of scientific computer codes.

Right from the beginning of a simulation study, both types of simulations will typically be characterized by epistemic opacity. Only for a minority of simple simulation models in the social sciences will we find mathematical shortcuts. Agent-based models, in particular, will hardly be epistemically transparent, as there typically exists no comprehensive model at the level of the system. Typically, parameters which lack a theoretical (here: sociological, political scientific, economic) interpretation are included in the model code. For the present, we may conclude that for *many* simulation models, we do not know all the epistemically relevant elements of the process, particularly for those that are not simple—and the special power of simulations is the ability to model complex phenomena, one of the main reasons why such models have been developed. These simulation models are not opaque because of sloppy modelling that is poorly understood. They are opaque because they are complex.

The course of the experimental investigation in simulations S_{TE} and S_E differs in such a way that this may have an effect on the epistemic opacity. In simulations S_{TE}, where scientists concentrate on giving in-depth answers to "what if" questions by way of understanding how the conclusions are obtained from the premises, the insight from the final simulation results may allow for a formulation of an analytic model for some selected interactions in the simulation model. Analytic treatment of this auxiliary model will help scientists to understand the simulation results. Mathematical "short cuts" may be found. There are, however, not only technical conditions for this, but also institutional ones. Social scientists running simulations would have to cooperate with analytic modellers—which can be observed in economics, but less often in sociology or political science. And there would have to be a continuous and cumulative quantitative research on the modelled social phenomenon. Again, this can be observed in economics, but less in sociology or political science. To summarize, only if mathematical "short cuts" can be found will the epistemic opacity be reduced. However, due to the parameters without a theoretical interpretation, we cannot expect that the epistemic opacity will be eliminated.

In simulations S_E, where scientists concentrate on generating data$_C$ and rigorously explore and/or optimize large parameter spaces, no such insight will arise from the final simulation results. From the experimental set-up, it cannot be expected that mathematical "short cuts" can be found. Therefore, epistemic opacity is a persistent problem for simulations S_E.

5 Conclusions

In recent decades, the human capacity for investigating complex systems of various scales has been greatly enhanced by computer simulation, even in the social sciences (Epstein 2008). This progress is not without a price, though: The very fact that simulation models do away with the idealizations and tractability assumptions of analytic models often makes the models themselves epistemically opaque. The understanding of simulation results and the treatment of epistemic opacity is a great challenge for simulation scientists, and not only the social scientists. Opacity endangers the explanation and scientific understanding of phenomena, which is, after all, one of the principal aims of science.

This article has argued that we can distinguish two categories of simulations: simulations S_{TE}, which possess key features that resemble the epistemology and methodology of thought experiments, and simulations S_E, which resemble the epistemology and methodology of experiments. Based on Woodward's (2003) theory of causal explanation, the hypothesis has been put forward that S_{TE} provide more understanding and a different kind of knowledge than S_E because they give well-founded answers to what-if-things-had-been-different questions. Epistemic opacity is a persistent problem for simulations S_E, while for S_{TE} it need not necessarily be so. However, even there, the requirements are difficult to fulfill. This makes the problem of opacity relevant for most social science simulations.

Outlook The proposed epistemology adds to the technical and philosophical literature on the understanding of social simulations (e.g., Evans et al. 2013; Izquierdo et al. 2013; Sawyer 2013). Based on the classification of model results, Evans et al. (2013) discuss pattern recognition techniques and visualization methods to promote understanding simulation results, while Izquierdo et al. (2013) concentrate on Markov chain analysis to move towards greater mathematical tractability. While these technical studies do not reflect their concept of understanding, Sawyer (2013) seems to identify his concept of understanding with the concept of scientific explanation. He discusses the alternatives between the deductive-nomological approach, the statistical relevance approach, and mechanistic approaches. The proposed epistemology of this article is based on Woodward (2003). The differences between these approaches encourage a broader discourse on what "understanding a simulation" means.

Computer simulation is a young method on the methodological map of the sciences and social sciences. This article argues that we are still involved in a learning process as far as understanding how to use simulations is concerned. There is an opportunity involved in making a distinction between simulations S_{TE} and simulations S_E. Simulation scientists can aim at different goals and adopt different epistemologies and methodologies. This offers alternative ways of dealing with opacity. In essence, the problem of opacity cannot be resolved. But some simulations will deal with this problem more than others. Those simulation scientists who want to promote an understanding of social phenomena by way of simulation should aim at developing simulations S_{TE}. Understanding the results of simulations is a prerequisite for understanding social phenomena investigated with the help of model/simulation. My intuition is that this will also facilitate communicating simulation results to the non-simulating mainstream in social science research.

Finally, from a general philosophy of science point of view, one might ask whether the distinction between simulations S_{TE} and simulations S_E can be fruitfully applied to discourses regarding the understanding of simulation results in other sciences as well.

Acknowledgments The author would like to thank Andreas Kaminski for his valuable comments.

References

Axtell, R. L., J. M. Epstein, J. S. Dean, G. J. Gumerman, A. C. Swedlund, J. Harburger, S. Chakravarty, R. Hammond, J. Parker, and M. Parker. 2002. Population Growth and Collapse in a Multi-Agent Model of the Kayenta Anasazi in Long House Valley. *Proceedings of the National Academy of Sciences* 99 (3): 7275–7279.

Barberousse, Anouk, Sara Franceschelli, and Cyrille Imbert. 2009. Computer Simulations as Experiments. *Synthese* 169: 557–574.

Beisbart, Claus. 2011. A Transformation of Normal Science. Computer Simulations From a Philosophical Perspective. Unpublished Habilitation Thesis, Technical University Dortmund.

Beisbart, Claus. 2012. How can Computer Simulations Produce New Knowledge? *European Journal for Philosophy of Science* 2: 395–434.

Beisbart, Claus, and John D. Norton. 2012. Why Monte Carlo Simulations Are Inferences and Not Experiments. *International Studies in the Philosophy of Science* 26: 403–422.

Carley, Kathleen M., and Les Gasser. 1999. Computational Organization Theory. In *Multiagent Systems. A Modern Approach to Distributed Artificial Intellgence*, ed. Gerhard Weiss, 299–330. Cambridge, MA: MIT Press.

Conte, Rosaria, Bruce Edmonds, Scott Moss, and R. Keith Sawyer. 2001. Sociology and Social Theory in Agent Based Social Simulation. A Symposium. *Computational Mathematical Organization Theory* 7: 183–205.

Cooper, Rachel. 2005. Thought Experiments. *Metaphilosophy* 36: 328–347.

Dean, J. S., G. J. Gumerman, J. M. Epstein, R. L. Axtell, A. C. Swedlund, M. T. Parker, and S. McCarroll. 2000. Understanding Anasazi Culture Change Through Agent Based Modeling. In *Dynamics in Human and Primate Societies: Agent Based Modeling of Social and Spatial Processes*, ed. T. Kohler and G. Gumerman. SFI Working Paper 1998-10-094. New York and London: Oxford University Press.

Elsenbroich, Corinna, and Nigel Gilbert. 2014. *Modelling Norms*. Berlin: Springer.

Epstein, Joshua M. 2008. Why Model? *Journal of Artificial Societies and Social Simulation* 11 (4) 12. http://jasss.soc.surrey.ac.uk/11/4/12.html.

Evans, Andrew, Alison Heppenstall, and Mark Birkin. 2013. Understanding Simulation Results. In *Simulating Social Complexity. A Handbook*, ed. Bruce Edmonds and Ruth Meyer, 173–195. Berlin: Springer.

Gumerman, G. J., A. C. Swedlund, J. S. Dean, and J. M. Epstein. 2003. The Evolution of Social Behavior in the Prehistoric American Southwest. *Artificial Life* 9: 435–444.

Hacking, Ian. 1983. *Representing and Intervening: Introductory Topics in the Philosophy of Science.* New York: Free Press.

Hacking, Ian. 1992. The Self-Vindication of the Laboratory Sciences. In *Science as Practice and Culture,* ed. A. Pickering, 29–64. Chicago: University of Chicago Press.

Hartmann, Stephan. 1996. The World as a Process: Simulation in the Natural and Social Sciences. In *Modelling and Simulation in the Social Sciences From the Philosophy of Science Point of View,* ed. Rainer Hegselmann, Ulrich Müller, and Klaus G. Troitzsch, 77–100. Dordrecht: Kluwer.

Hedström, Peter. 2005. *Dissecting the Social. On the Principles of Analytic Sociology.* Cambridge: Cambridge University Press.

Hempel, Carl Gustav. 1965. *Aspects of Scientific Explanation and Other Essays in the Philosophy of Science.* New York: Free Press.

Humphreys, Paul. 2004. *Extending Ourselves. Computational Science, Empiricism, and Scientific Method.* Oxford: Oxford University Press.

Humphreys, Paul. 2009. The Philosophical Novelty of Computer Simulation Methods. *Synthese* 169: 615–626.

Izquierdo, Luis R., Segismundo S. Izquierdo, José M. Galan, and José I. Santos. 2013. Combining Mathematical and Simulation Approaches to Understand the Dynamics of Computer Models. In *Simulating Social Complexity. A Handbook,* ed. Bruce Edmonds and Ruth Meyer, 235–271. Berlin: Springer.

Kaminski, Andreas. 2017. Der Erfolg der Modellierung und das Ende der Modelle. Epistemische Opazität in der Computersimulation. In *Technik - Macht - Raum. Das Topologische Manifest im Kontext interdisziplinärer Studien,* ed. Andreas Brenneis, Oliver Honer, Sina Keesser and Silke Vetter-Schultheiß, Wiesbaden: Springer.

Kitcher, Philip. 1989. Explanatory Unification and the Causal Structure of the World. In *Scientific Explanation,* ed. Philip Kitcher and W. Salmon, 410–506. Minneapolis: University of Minnesota Press.

Lenhard, Johannes. 2011. Epistemologie der Iteration. Gedankenexperimente und Simulationsexperimente. *Deutsche Zeitschrift für Philosophie* 59: 131–145.

Lenhard, Johannes, and Hans Hasse. 2017. Fluch und Segen: Die Rolle anpassbarer Parameter in Simulationsmodellen. In *Technisches Nichtwissen. Jahrbuch Technikphilosophie 2017,* ed. Alexander Friedrich, Petra Gehring, Christoph Hubig, Andreas Kaminski and Alfred Nordmann, 69–84. Baden-Baden: Nomos.

Macy, Michael, and John Skvoretz. 1998. The Evolution of Trust and Cooperation Between Strangers: A Computational Model. *American Sociological Review* 63: 638–660.

Marr, David. 1982. *Vision.* Cambridge, MA: MIT Press.

Morgan, Mary. 2003. Experiments Without Material Intervention. Model Experiments, Virtual Experiments, and Virtually Experiments. In *The Philosophy of Scientific Experimentation,* ed. Hans Radder, 216–235. Pittsburgh: University of Pittsburgh.

Morrison, Margaret. 2009. Models, Measurement, and Computer Simulation: The Changing Face of Experimentation. *Philosophical Studies* 143: 33–57.

Norton, John. 1996. Are Thought Experiments Just What You Thought? *Canadian Journal of Philosophy* 26: 333–366.

Sawyer, R. Keith. 2004. The Mechanisms of Emergence. *Philosophy of the Social Sciences* 34: 260–282.

Sawyer, R. Keith. 2013. Interpreting and Understanding Simulations. The Philosophy of Social Simulation. In *Simulating Social Complexity. A Handbook,* ed. Bruce Edmonds and Ruth Meyer, 273–289. Berlin: Springer.

Suppes, Patrick. 1968. The Desirability of Formalization in Science. *Journal of Philosophy* 65: 651–664.

Tymoczko, Thomas. 1979. The Four-Color Problem and its Philosophical Significance. *Journal of Philosophy* 76: 57–83.

Winsberg, Eric. 2003. Simulated Experiments: Methodology for a Virtual World. *Philosophy of Science* 70: 105–125.

Winsberg, Eric. 2009. A Tale of Two Methods. *Synthese* 169: 575–592.

Wolfram, Stephen. 1985. Undecidability and Intractability in Theoretical Physics. *Physical Review Letters* 54: 735–738.

Woodward, James. 2003. *Making Things Happen*. Oxford: Oxford University Press.

Seven Problems with Massive Simulation Models for Policy Decision-Making

Till Grüne-Yanoff

Abstract Policymakers increasingly draw on scientific methods, including simulation modeling, to justify their decisions. For these purposes, scientist and policymakers face an extensive choice of modeling strategies. This paper distinguishes two types of strategies: *Massive Simulation Models* (MSMs) and *Abstract Simulation Models* (ASMs), and discusses how to justify strategy choice with reference to the core characteristics of the respective strategies. In particular, I argue that MSMs might have more severe problems than ASMs in determining the accuracy of the model; that MSMs might have more severe problems than ASMs in dealing with inevitable uncertainty; and that MSMs might have more severe problems than ASMs with misinterpretation and misapplication due to their format. While this in no way excludes the prospect that some MSMs provide good justifications for policy decisions, my arguments caution against a general preference for MSM over ASMs for policy decision purposes.

1 Introduction

Policymakers and their advisors today face a bewildering array of models to choose from. Most obvious, perhaps, is their choice between different structural and causal features, as well as between different parameterizations for each. On another level, they also need to choose how much detail their models shall incorporate. Recent technological advances have rapidly expanded the amount of detail that can be processed when computing a model. Models whose detail is constrained largely by current computational capacities I call *Massive Simulation Models* (MSMs). Models whose detail is also constrained by other considerations (of simplicity, of transparency, etc.) I call *Abstract Simulation Models* (ASMs). Although simulation models can, of course, be distinguished further, this simple dichotomous distinction will suffice for the present argument.

It might seem an obvious and trivial claim that policymakers should prefer MSMs over ASMs for most if not all purposes: MSMs, because they contain

T. Grüne-Yanoff (✉)
KTH Stockholm, Royal Institute of Technology, Brinellvägen 32, 10044 Stockholm, Sweden
e-mail: gryne@kth.se

© Springer International Publishing AG 2017
M.M. Resch et al. (eds.), *The Science and Art of Simulation I*,
DOI 10.1007/978-3-319-55762-5_7

more detail, can be closer approximations to the real system; they can better represent complexity and population heterogeneity; and the policymaker can use them as holistic test-beds for potential policy interventions. ASMs, due to their additional constraints on detail, do not offer the same potential as MSMs in these regards—and therefore might be regarded as inferior for policy purposes.

Contrary to that claim, I will argue in this paper that for many policy purposes, ASMs are preferable to MSMs. Essentially, my argument is that, although MSMs have larger potentials than ASMs in various dimensions, they are also more likely to fail—and that in many cases, this probability of failing outweighs their higher potential. Because this argument is difficult to make in full generality, I will focus on one case here, that of smallpox vaccination policies. By comparing one specific MSM and one specific ASM, I show that for some policy purposes, the ASM is preferable to the MSM.

The paper is structured as follows: Sect. 2 gives a conceptual distinction between MSMs and ASMs; Sect. 3 illustrates this difference with a case from the smallpox vaccination literature; Sect. 4 discusses the seven problems with MSMs that make ASMs preferable for some policy purposes; and Sect. 5 concludes.

2 MSM vs. ASM

In this paper, I distinguish *Massive Simulation Models* (MSMs) from *Abstract Simulation Models* (ASMs). By simulation model, I mean any dynamic model that represents a target and that is solved through some temporal process (Humphreys 2004, p. 210). For most simulation models, these solution processes also have a representational function—they are interpreted as a representation of the dynamic processes or mechanisms operating in the target (Hartmann 1996, p. 83). Many such models, and in particular MSMs, are implemented on a computer, but this is not an essential property. Instead, some ASMs are also realized materially (like Schelling's checkerboard model, Schelling 1971) or as paper-and-pencil models.

MSMs differ from ASMs at first glance by their much higher level of detail, especially the number of variables and parameters they include, and the number of relation between these. In the case that I discuss below, for example, the MSM includes approximately 1.6 million vertices with maximally 1.5 million edges that might change 24 times a day; while the smaller ASM includes approximately 7900 vertices with maximally 6000 edges (and approximately 55,000 vertices for the larger one) that can change maximally 17 times a day.

Based on the richness in realistic detail, MSMs are often claimed to offer a highly accurate picture of the real system:

> Such models allow for the creating of a kind of virtual universe, in which many players can act in complex—and realistic—ways. (Farmer and Foley 2009, p. 686)

Understood in this way, MSMs are typically seen as *direct* representations of real systems: their structure allows for a mapping from the model to the target without having to take recourse to mediating models. ASMs, in contrast, can hardly ever claim to represent a real system directly—their level of detail is not sufficient. At best, they are able to represent *stylized facts* about or abstractions of a system, which have been prepared through an abstraction or idealization procedure from the real system.

That MSMs represent real systems directly is further supported by the practice of fitting or calibrating the model directly to real data. The MSM I discuss below, for example, bases the specification of edges and their hourly change on census data. The authors of the comparison ASM, in contrast, interpret certain edge changes as "being at home," "going to work," "being at the hospital," etc.—however, these interpretations are not based on data from actual target systems, but rather rely on plausibility intuitions. Alternatively, they could have been based on mediating models, which abstract stylized facts of "going to work" or "being at the hospital" from available data, and then allow the representation of these abstractions in the ASM.

Both MSMs and ASMs typically represent processes of their target systems. But even here, there is an important difference. MSMs typically represent a multitude of simultaneous processes or mechanisms, while ASMs typically represent only one or a small number of such processes. Take, for example, the following claim about the advantages of agent-based models in economics:

> A thorough attempt to understand the whole economy through agent-based modeling will require integrating models of financial interactions with those of industrial production, real estate, government spending, taxes, business investment, and with consumer behavior. (Farmer and Foley 2009, p. 686)

Presumably, many of these components will operate through different mechanisms. Consequently, putting them all together in a single MSM implies that many different processes will operate simultaneously when producing a model outcome. ASMs, in contrast, will typically focus on a small subset, or even just one instance of these processes.

So far, I have distinguished MSMs and ASMs only with respect to their different representational relations to a target. Now I also wish to distinguish them with respect to how these relations are interpreted and for what purposes they are used. Regarding interpretation, the greater amount of detail in their models is typically employed by MSM modelers in order to achieve a "realistic" interpretation of the model's representational function. "Realisticness" is a subjective psychological effect that might stem from an impression of familiarity and might lead to greater trust in the model and its conclusions:

> [D]ecision makers might be more willing to trust findings based on rather detailed simulation models where they see a lot of economic structure they are familiar with than in general insights obtained in rather abstract mathematical models. (Dawid and Fagiolo 2008, p. 354)

ASMs do not offer such a rich collection of familiar details, are therefore typically not considered as "realistic" as MSMs, and thus might not inspire the same amount of trust.

The differences discussed so far also imply an important difference in the use of these model types for policy decision-making. MSMs are often used as part of a "holistic approach": a "model of the whole economy" (Farmer and Foley 2009, p. 686) is used as a "virtual universe" (ibid.) to evaluate the effects of proposed interventions in the target system. That is, interventions are simulated in the model, and model results are interpreted as forecasts of the results of such interventions in the real system. ASMs cannot be used in this way, as they do not offer a representation of the whole system or of the combination of its many operating mechanisms. The holistic synthesis that the MSM promises as part of its package must be performed by the ASM user in some other way, for example through expert judgment.

To be clear, MSMs and ASMs have important similarities, despite the discussed differences between them. Both aim to represent non-linear and complex behavior, albeit on different levels of abstraction and idealization. Furthermore, both types of models abstract and idealize, but to different degrees, and for different reasons. MSMs abstract and idealize for tractability and computation reasons: they are mainly constrained by current computational capacities. ASMs, in contrast, are also constrained by other considerations (for example, of simplicity, of transparency, etc.), so that computability rarely becomes a relevant constraint for them.

Last, the distinction between MSM and ASM is itself a simplification. Many actual simulation models exhibit some properties of the one kind and some of the other, and thus do not clearly fall into either category. However, this does not pose a problem for my argument; my discussion in Sect. 4 addresses the relevant properties separately so that respective conclusions can be drawn for such "in-between models," too. While I am aware of the possibility of such cases, I have nevertheless decided to stick with the dichotomous distinction for ease of exposition.

3   The Case of Vaccination Policy Modeling

Vaccination is one of the most effective ways of fighting epidemics. However, many vaccines do not provide long-term protection, or have serious side effects, so that a preventive vaccination (e.g., to all children at age five) is not feasible. Instead, these vaccines should be applied only when the risk of an epidemic is sufficiently high. The policymaker then has to make a momentous decision: namely, how to apply vaccinations in a large population when an epidemic is imminent or has already broken out. The most relevant alternatives are a *tracing vaccination* (TV), where the potential recent contacts of an infected individual are traced and vaccinated; a *limited vaccination* (LV), where a random subset of the population is vaccinated; or a *mass vaccination* (MV), where the whole population is vaccinated. The choice is not trivial: MV is more likely to stop the spread of the disease, but is more costly and bears vaccination risks for a large population, while the effectiveness of LV and TV is less certain, but they are less costly, and do not expose a large number of people to vaccination risk. An instructive discussion in this regard is the evaluation of vaccine policies in the UK during the 2009 influenza pandemic, when an LV was implemented (Hine 2010).

Various modeling projects have sought to contribute to this policy decision (for an overview, see Grüne-Yanoff 2011). Early attempts tried to model the epidemic dynamics as an aggregate equation. For example, Kaplan et al. (2002) simulate an attack of 1000 initial smallpox cases on a population of 10 million. The population is assumed to mix homogeneously—i.e., to consist of identical individuals who have an equal chance of interacting with any other member of the population. R_0, the rate of infections a single infectious agent generates among susceptibles, is assumed to be uniform throughout the simulation. $R_0 = 3$ is derived from historical data. An infected agent undergoes four stages. Only in the first is she vaccine-sensitive; only in the third and fourth is she infectious; in the fourth, however, she shows symptoms (scabs) and is automatically isolated. Additionally, the administration of vaccinations is modeled under logistical constraints: MV of the whole population is achieved in 10 days. Tracking *and* vaccinating an infected person in TV, however, takes four times as many nurse-hours as a simple vaccination.

Kaplan et al. (2002) thus offer an example of an equation-based simulation study. By assuming homogeneous mixing, the infection rate R_0 becomes a parameter characterizing the population. Policy effects are then modeled directly on this population parameter, and the main question is whether vaccine administration can outpace the random spread in the population. Unsurprisingly, perhaps, the results heavily favor MV over TV. Initiated on day 5 after the initial attack, MV leads to 560 deaths, while TV leads to 110,000 deaths. Sensitivity analysis shows that TV is more sensitive than MV to the size of initial attack and changes in R_0, further supporting the strong results in favor of MV. The time to identify and then vaccinate the exposed is simply too long for the specified R_0 and for the assumed period in which the exposed are still sensitive to the vaccine.

Models like Kaplan et al. (2002) have been criticized for their homogeneity assumption. For smallpox infection, extended close contact between infected and healthy agents is required. In a population of 10 million, it is highly implausible that an infected agent has the same probability of having contact with any non-infected member. Furthermore, how the infected agents move through the population—i.e., with whom and with how many healthy agents they have contact—might influence the effects of different vaccination policies. To model this contact pattern was the main motivation behind the developments of various agent-based models. I will discuss two instances here, one ASM and one MSM.

My example of an ASM, Burke et al. (2006), simulates a single initial infected person attack on a town network of either 6000 or 50,000 people. Town networks either consist of one town (uniform), a ring of six towns, or a 'hub' with four 'spokes.' Each town consists of households of up to seven persons, one workplace, and one school. All towns share a hospital. Each space is represented as a grid, so that each cell in the grid has eight neighbors. Agents are distinguished by type (child, health care worker [5% of adult population], commuter [10%], and non-commuter [90%]) by family ID and by infectious status. Each 'day,' agents visit spaces according to their type, and then return home. On the first 'day' of the simulation, the position in schools and workplaces is randomly assigned, but after that, agents remember their positions. During the 'day,' agents interact with all of their immediate neighbors: 10 times at home, 7 times at work, and 15 times in the hospital. After each interaction, they move positions to the first free cell in their neighborhood. Homogeneous mixing is thus completely eschewed; instead, agents interact in a number of dynamic neighborhoods.

Transmission occurs at a certain rate in each of the agents' interactions. It can infect both contactor and contacted. Transmission rates depend on the stage the infectious person is in, the type of disease he has, and whether the susceptible agent has partial immunity.

Burke et al. (2006) assessed only TV as a first policy intervention, and LVs of varying degrees only as 'add-on' measures. Results for all three town networks showed substantial concordance. Contrasted with a 'no response' scenario, TV in combination with hospital isolation was sufficient to limit the epidemic to a mean of fewer than 48 cases and a mean duration of less than 77 days. Post-release LV of either 40% or 80% of the total population added some additional protection, reducing the mean of infected people to 33 and shortening the mean duration to less than 60 days.

My example of a MSM, Eubank et al. (2004), simulates an attack of 1000 infected agents on the population of Portland, OR, of 1.5 million. Portland is represented by approximately 181,000 locations, each associated with a specific activity, like work, shopping, or school, as well as maximal occupancies. Each agent is characterized by a list of the entrance and exit times into and from a location for all locations that person visited during the day. This huge database was developed by the traffic simulation tool TRANSIMS, which in turn is based on US census data.

Smallpox is modeled by a single parameter, disease 'load' (analogous to a viral titer). Agents have individual thresholds, above which their load leads to infection (and load growth at individual growth rates), symptoms, infectiousness, and death. Every hour, infectious agents shed a fixed fraction of their load to the local environment. Locations thus get contaminated with load, which is distributed equally among those present. Shedding and absorption fractions differ individually. Infected individuals withdraw to their homes 24 h after becoming infectious.

In the Eubank et al. (2004) model, MV with a 4-day delay resulted in 0.39 deaths per initially infected person; TV with the same delay in 0.54 deaths. Varying delays, the modellers found that delay in response is the most important factor in limiting deaths, yielding similar results for TV and MV.

Both papers give more or less unconditional policy advice. To quote just two examples: "[C]ontact tracing and vaccination of household, workplace and school contacts, along with effective isolation of diagnosed cases, can control epidemics of smallpox" (Burke et al. 2006, p. 1148); and "[O]utbreaks can be contained by a strategy of targeted vaccination combined with early detection without resorting to mass vaccination of a population" (Eubank et al. 2004, p. 180).

I classify Eubank et al. (2004) as a MSM and Burke et al. (2006) as an ASM. The former incorporates much more detail than the latter and is widely considered to be more realistic. The former is also proclaimed as a direct representation of a real system, namely the city of Portland, and it is based on and calibrated with census data from that target system. The latter is not claimed to represent any concrete system, nor does it make use of any data. Instead, it explicitly claims to represent an "artificial city" that shares some properties with real cities, but is different other-wise (Burke et al. 2006, p. 1142). Furthermore, the former includes many more simultaneous mechanisms than the latter: it distinguishes several activities at each location, each of which yields different contact rates; it also includes the effects of demographic factors (age in particular) on mixing; it distinguishes different forms of smallpox; and it tries to incorporate at least some rudimentary effects of infection on behavior. The latter model included a lesser number of locations and did not distinguish activities or demographics, nor did it include infection effects on behavior. Finally, while the Eubank et al. (2004) model at least implies a holistic approach, the Burke et al. (2006) has no such aspirations. One could therefore conclude, *prima facie*, that the former is a more powerful tool for deciding vaccine policies than the latter. In the following section, I will argue that this is not necessarily so.

4 Seven Problems with MSMs for Policy Purposes

This section discusses seven problems that show why, in some situations, an ASM might be preferable to a MSM for policy purposes. These problems are conceptu-ally separate, although in practice they often overlap.

4.1 What Is the Target?

Prima facie, MSMs like Eubank et al. (2004) have a particular target: for example, the town of Portland, OR. ASMs like Burke et al. (2006), in contrast, do not appear to have such a particular target; rather, they represent an abstracted type, like "a town" or "an urban population network." Consequently, MSMs are often judged to be more *realistic* than ASMs, as model users can more easily trace the MSM features to the properties of a particular target. This realisticness judgment, in turn, as the above quote from Dawid and Fagiolo (2008) shows, often induces policymakers to place more trust in the reliability and usefulness of the model in question. For this reason, MSMs often seem preferable to ASMs for policy purposes.

But is the inference from realisticness to reliability and usefulness justified? Presumably, the argument is that (1) judging a model to be realistic indicates that it is a highly accurate representation of the target, and that (2) highly accurate representation of the target is a necessary condition for the model to give reliable and useful information about possible policy interventions in the target.

While I do not dispute these claims individually here, I argue that their conjunction does *not* constitute a valid argument *if* the meaning of "target" changes between them. This is precisely what happens in the smallpox simulation studies. The target *of the policy question* is the city environment generally, as the introductory sentence of Eubank et al. (2004, p. 180) shows:

> The dense social-contact networks characteristic of urban areas form a perfect fabric for fast, uncontrolled disease propagation. [...] How can an outbreak be contained before it becomes an epidemic, and what disease surveillance strategies should be implemented?

Furthermore, because epidemic policies are typically the responsibility of national or international institutions, the targets of the policy question are all cities within the governing domain of that institution (e.g., all US cities, all cities in industrialized countries, all cities of the world, etc.). The target of such a policy question thus is an abstract entity: the network characteristics of all urban areas within the relevant domain.

The *model's target* in the MSM case, in contrast, is a particular: the city of Portland, OR. The authors of this model suggest that it is just an instance of the network characteristics in urban areas.[1] But by choosing a particular target, they allow for a possible divergence between the meaning of "target" in step (1) and (2) in the above argument. In particular, the judgment that their model is realistic might now be based on relational features of their model and the city of Portland that are wholly irrelevant for the relational features of their model and network characteristics of *all* urban areas within the relevant domain. For example, inclusion of the Columbia riverbed, of the locations of Portland's universities, as well as Portland's public transport system, might increase the realisticness of the model. However, these might be features that are either *irrelevant* for the path of an epidemic through an urban network, or they might not be representative of urban networks in the US more generally. Both of these cases might sever the relation between realisticness, reliability, and usefulness: a MSM with these features might be more realistic than an ASM, while the ASM is more accurate representation of the general network characteristics of all urban areas within the relevant domain. In such cases, the ASM would be a more powerful policy tool than the MSM.

---

[1]"We view the social networks created by TRANSIMS as a single instance of a stochastic process defined in an enormous space of possibilities" (Eubank et al. 2004, Supplement, 3).

4.2   How to Measure Parameters

MSMs differ from ASMs in their much higher level of detail, especially the number of variables and parameters they include, and the number of relation between these. Assuming that both models have the same target (so that problem 4.1 does not arise), a higher number of variables and parameters gives MSMs more potential than ASMs to accurately represent the target system. *Prima facie*, this gives MSMs an advantage over ASMs for policy purposes.

However, this argument assumes that the additional variables and parameters that give MSMs an advantage over ASMs can be measured or estimated with sufficient accuracy. Both of these assumptions are problematic. I will discuss measurement problems in this subsection and estimation problems in the next.

The measured variables and parameters of the smallpox MSM are those whose value is directly obtained from some external data source. For example, properties like age, occupation, health, and home location are obtained from census data for all of the 1.5 million agents in the model. Properties of the urban transport network and of land occupation and use are obtained from urban planning organizations (Eubank et al. 2004, Supplement, 3). These examples of massive data intake seem indeed to support the comparative detail richness of MSMs over ASMs.

However, a closer reading of the article and its supplementary material reveals that many of the parameters and variables could not be accurately measured (or even measured at all). Instead, they are determined by *ad hoc* assumptions, best guesses, or the use of reasonable ranges. I describe three instances here for illustrative purposes. The first concerns the disease-relevant contacts of agents within a location, which cannot be found in census data:

> We do not have data for proximity of people, other than that they are in the same (possibly very large) location. [...] It seems as though the dependence on distance is very coarse: one mode of transmission occurs at close ranges (< 6 feet) and another for large ranges. We have developed an *ad hoc* model that takes advantage of this coarseness. (Eubank et al. 2004, Supplement, 9)

This *ad hoc* model makes uniform assumptions about the occupancy rate of locations within a city block that are, the authors admit, "nothing more than reasonable guesses" (Eubank et al. 2004, Supplement, 11). Location occupancy rates, however, crucially influence the number of possible contacts—and hence may be relevant for the spread of disease.

Another example concerns the parameterization of the disease model:

> There is not yet a consensus model of smallpox. We have designed a model that captures many features on which there is widespread agreement and allow us to vary poorly understood properties through reasonable ranges. (Eubank et al. 2004, p. 183)

What "reasonable" means in this context, and how much it is related to available data, remains unclear. Finally, here is an example concerning the parameterization of the TV intervention:

> Every simulated day, if contact tracing is in effect, a subset of the people on the list
> [of people showing symptoms] is chosen for contact tracing. [...] In the experiment
> reported here, we use the fraction 0.8 and set the absolute threshold at either 10,000 or
> 1000. These are probably unrealistic numbers, but they allow us to estimate the best case
> results of a targeted vaccination strategy. (Eubank et al. 2004, Supplement, 11)

In all of these examples, the large set of parameters and variables poses the
question of how to fill them with content. By default, one might assume that they
are filled with empirical data. But it turns out that for these examples, empirical data
is not available, or of too low a quality. So the modelers instead resorted to *ad hoc*
assumptions, best guesses, or reasonable ranges.

I do not intend these observations as criticisms of the particular smallpox model,
or of MSMs more generally. It seems perfectly reasonable to improvise on some
parameters of one's model. But when discussing model choice, and in particular
how to choose the resolution of detail of one's model, one should be mindful of how
this choice affects the need to improvise. Imagine an extreme case, where a simple
model with only a few parameters that all can be determined from high-quality data
can be developed into a detail-rich model, whose parameters can be filled only by *ad
hoc* assumptions, best guesses, or use of reasonable ranges. Because these impro-
visations carry a large chance of error, the simple model is likely more accurate and
therefore preferable for policy purposes than the detail-rich model. My MSM
vs. ASM case is much less clear-cut than this extreme case, firstly because the
parameters of the ASM are typically determined in a haphazard way, too, and
secondly because the MSM does include a lot of certified data. However, there is
a similar trade-off as in the extreme case, and that trade-off might in some cases lead
to the conclusions that the ASM is a more powerful policy tool than the MSM.

4.3   Number of Parameters

Assume that the measurement of parameters was not a problem, so that 4.2 would
not impose any constraints on the amount of detail incorporated in a MSM. In that
case, another argument against such unchecked increase of detail arises from the
comparative performance of such models in parameter estimation or calibration.

Disregarding technical detail, estimation and calibration both aim to determine
values of unobservable model parameters by fitting the model to observable data. In
the smallpox case, many parameters of the underlying TRANSIMS and EpiSims
models are thus determined. To put it simply, the model takes census data, transport
network data, land use data, etc. as inputs, and gives as output contact incidences,
duration, and locations between individual agents. In accordance with the generative program in simulation studies (Epstein 1999), model parameters are then
adjusted so as to generate that model result that fits best with observational data.
Once a close enough fit to such data has been achieved, the model is considered
validated, and counterfactual policy interventions are introduced.

At first sight, MSMs appear to be better equipped to perform well in estimation
or calibration exercises. If the target is of high complexity (which, in the case of

vaccination policies, it undoubtedly is), then the more constraints one imposes on the model (in terms of the nature and number of its parameters), the less well such a model can fit the target. Conversely, the fewer constraints are imposed on a model, the better it can fit its target. Thus, it seems that MSMs can achieve a better fit to their targets than ASMs, and therefore appears as the more powerful policy tool.

The above intuition, although correct, misses an important trade-off that is well known in the model-selection literature. Although models with more free parameters have a larger *potential* to fit the target well, the larger number of free parameters *in practice* often yields a lesser fit than the one achieved by a model with fewer parameters.

This trade-off becomes clearer by distinguishing two steps in the process of fitting a model to data. The first step consists in selecting a model—i.e., in specifying the number of parameters. Here, increasing the number of parameters indeed increases the model's *potential* to accurately represent the target.

The second step consists in calibrating or estimating the parameters based on a data *sample* drawn from the population. Increasing the number of parameters increases the model's fit to the sample—but this is not the ultimate goal. Rather, increasing the model's fit *to the target* is. Fitting the model "too closely" (i.e., by including too many parameters) to the sample will pick up on the inevitable random error in the sample, and thus leads to an increase in the divergence between model and target. This phenomenon is well known as "overfitting" in the statistics and machine-learning literature, and it applies to simulation modeling as well (Myung 2000).[2]

Selecting the right number of free parameters thus is the problem of "finding an appropriate compromise between these two opposing properties, *potential* and *propensity to underperform*" (Zucchini 2000, p. 45). As various studies have shown, if the sample size is large, adding more parameters above a certain threshold will not substantially increase fit to target; if sample size is medium or small, adding more parameters even decreases fit to target (Zucchini 2000; Gigerenzer and Brighton 2009).

This general finding also applies to the choice between MSM and ASM. In Sect. 2, I defined MSMs as containing many more parameters than ASMs. Consequently, MSMs are more subject to the danger of overfitting, and therefore more likely to fit the underlying target badly. Of course, whether in a particular case of comparing a MSM and an ASM the trade-off will favor one or the other is an open question (in particular, this is also the case for the two smallpox models, as a numerical study of their respective fit is beyond the scope of this paper). However, this general tendency makes it implausible to generally prefer MSMs over ASMs for policy purposes.

---

[2]This issue further compounds the problem of particular model targets when policy targets are more abstract, discussed in Sect. 4.1. A close fit to the particular *model target*—even without the problem of overfitting—might not improve the model's usefulness for questions about the abstract *policy target*.

4.4 Number of Mechanisms

One of the important features of the simulation models discussed here is that they explicitly aim to represent *mechanisms*. In the smallpox case, both the MSM and the ASM were introduced as improvements over Kaplan's et al. (2002) macro model, because they explicitly modeled the population mixing mechanism instead of simply assuming homogeneous mixing. Nevertheless, the MSM and the ASM differ substantially in how they introduce such additional mechanisms. The small-pox ASM seeks to introduce a small number of simple mechanisms, while the MSM introduces a multitude of detail-rich mechanisms that are assumed to operate simultaneously.

In particular, the MSM distinguishes several activities at each location, each of which yields different contact rates; it also includes the effects of demographic factors (age in particular) on mixing; it distinguishes different forms of smallpox; and it tries to incorporate at least some rudimentary effects of infection on behavior. The ASM, in contrast, includes a lesser number of locations and does not distinguish activities or demographics; nor does it include infection effects on behavior.

Most observers seem to see the inclusion of additional mechanisms in comparison to the Kaplan et al. (2002) model as beneficial. It then also seems *prima facie* plausible to prefer the MSM to the ASM, as the former includes even more mechanisms and mechanistic detail than the latter.

Countering this intuition, I will use an argument made against the purported higher explanatory power of realistic simulation models. This argument has been put forward by Lenhard and Winsberg (2010), amongst others, with a specific focus on climate models. In short, they argue that with increasing complexity, models get more and more *opaque*; and this opacity prevents or at least reduces understanding the model components' contributions towards the model outcome.

More specifically, Lenhard and Winsberg argue that, with increasing complexity, the "fuzzy modularity" of a model increases. The more complex a model, the more subcomponents it has. Furthermore, when running a simulation on a complex model, these model components are run together and in parallel. But they do not all independently contribute to the model result. Rather, the components, in the course of a simulation, often exchange results of intermediary calculations among one another—so that the contribution of each component to the model result in turn is influenced by all those components that interacted with it.

> The results of these modules are not first gathered independently and then only after that synthesized. [...] The overall dynamics of one global climate model is the complex result of the interaction of the modules—not the interaction of the results of the modules [... D]ue to interactivity, modularity does not break down a complex system into separately manageable pieces. (Lenhard and Winsberg 2010, p. 258)

To put it differently, the effect of the multiple mechanisms is underdetermined more in a MSM than an ASM: first, due to the larger number of mechanisms included in a MSM, but also due to the increased interaction—the "fuzzy modularity"—of the mechanisms in the MSM. Clearly, there is more fuzzy modularity in a MSM like Eubank et al. (2004) than in an ASM like Burke et al. (2006). In the first place, this is a problem for the explanatory power of MSMs. Although MSMs might generate the *explanandum* quite closely, because of the higher degree underdetermination, it is more difficult in MSMs than in ASMs to infer from this fit which of the modeled mechanisms contributed to the generated result. If understanding consists in identifying the mechanisms that produced the *explanandum*, then a model's fuzzy modularity undermines improvements in our understanding.

This concern also applies to policy uses of MSMs. The model and simulation are supposed to help policymakers identify interventions that reliably produce desired outcomes in the relevant contexts. If we simulate such an intervention on a model that is severely underdetermined, then we don't know on which mechanisms (or interaction between mechanisms) the effect of the intervention was based. Something like this is the case in Eubank et al. (2004): their results might depend on some or all of the mechanisms in the model, or on their specific interaction, but it is impossible for the modelers to pry these influences apart. Such analyses are easier with ASMs, and for this reason they might be preferable for policy purposes.

4.5   Counterfactual Questions

By their nature, simulation studies for policy purposes involve counterfactual scenarios. In the models discussed here, this is the case at least in two instances: First, at the moment when the smallpox infection is introduced, and second, when the respective vaccination policies are implemented. For neither of these modeling steps can the modeler point to actual data: there hasn't been a smallpox epidemic in an industrialized city in the twentieth century (that was not caught at the very early stage), nor have the different vaccination policies been tested in such environments. So even if the overfitting (4.3) and underdetermination (4.4) problems could be solved, modeling such counterfactual mechanisms cannot be validated by data fitting, because such data is not available.

Instead, parameters are set at some plausible values. Take, for example, the question of what fraction of identified people the TV intervention will likely be able to contact, and what the maximal capacity for such a program will be per day. Eubanks et al. cannot provide exact numbers, but instead suggest plausible values (see quote in Sect. 4.3). They then admit that "these are probably unrealistic numbers, but they allow us to estimate the best case results of a targeted vaccination strategy" (Eubank et al. 2004, Supplement, 11).

This poses the same problem for both MSMs and ASMs. However, in ASMs, this uncertainty about counterfactual mechanisms matches the uncertainty about the other components of the abstract model. Consequently, the policymaker is more likely to interpret the ASM model results as *possible outcomes* that are affected by the uncertainty surrounding the mechanisms, variables, and parameters included in the model. The appearance of MSMs, in contrast, might propose a different interpretation: the uncertainty might appear to *dissipate* in the computational process, as multiple mechanisms and parameters that are interpreted as realistic interact with the uncertain components. Yet for reasons discussed in 4.4, it is typically not possible to discern by which components a model result was driven. Therefore, such a dissipation claim can typically not be sustained. Due to this opaque treatment of the uncertainty surrounding the counterfactual mechanisms, an ASM might often be preferable to a MSM for policy purposes.

4.6 Structural Uncertainty

From the discussion so far (as well as from common sense), it follows that uncertainty in model specification can never be fully eliminated, however little or much detail one might want to include in one's model. Some sources of uncertainty affect MSMs more than ASMs, as discussed in Sects. 4.2 and 4.3. But other inevitable uncertainties just stem from the general fallibility of human knowledge, and thus affect MSMs and ASMs equally. In this section, I will ignore the former differential problems and assume that MSMs and ASMs face the same degree of uncertainty. The question then is whether MSM and ASM offer different strategies for dealing with such inevitable uncertainty, and which of these strategies is better.

Consider the following example from Eubank et al. (2004). The contact data on which the simulation is based gives a detailed account of social interaction. The model lacks any account of how these social contacts may change under external shocks. The arrival of a threatening epidemic is, arguably, such a shock: it may well have important influence on how often people appear in public, go to work, or go to the hospital. The authors deal with this uncertainty as follows.

> One of the most important assumptions in any smallpox model is whether infectious people are mixing normally in the population. [...] We undertook to model two (probably unrealistic) extreme cases: one in which no one who is infectious is mixing with the general population and another in which no one's behavior is affected at all by the disease. In addition, we modeled one more realistic case between these two extremes. (Eubank et al. 2004, Supplement, 11)

The model results strongly depend on the different assumptions. In particular, if people withdraw to the home, then all vaccination policies yield similar results, particularly if there is a delay in the vaccination procedure. However, if people do not withdraw, then LV is substantially less effective than either MV or TV (Eubank et al. 2004, p. 182, Figure 4).

Note that the MSM here only allows a qualitative distinction: depending on whether withdrawal occurs "early," "late," or "never," the simulation results in a different cumulative number of deaths. Such an analysis is similarly feasible with ASMs. The MSM authors do not assess the uncertainty included in these qualitative results beyond displaying them. While I agree that this seems the correct procedure in this case—as not enough evidence is available to provide a quantified assessment of the behavioral changes under shocks—the question is why one would go through the additional effort and cost of creating a MSM, if similar results could have been obtained with an ASM.

What MSMs often aspire to achieve instead is an overall quantification of the uncertainty involved. Although Eubanks et al. do not do this (correctly, I believe), they could have tried to specify a probability distribution over the different behavioral mechanisms and then represent the model outcome as expected cumulative deaths. Such one-size-fits-all approaches in MSMs have been justly criticized for providing *false precision*:

> [I]f uncertainty is represented and reported in terms of precise probabilities, while the scientist conducting the analysis believes that uncertainty is actually 'deeper' than this— e.g. believes that available information only warrants assigning wide interval probabilities or considering an outcome to be plausible—then the uncertainty report will fail to meet the faithfulness requirement; it will have false precision. (Parker and Risbey 2015, p. 4)

My argument here is that, in most applications of MSMs for policy purposes, non-quantifiable uncertainties arise. These should not be patched over by false precision, as described in the quote above. Alternatively, MSMs are used for providing different qualitative results, like the Eubanks et al. example above— which also could have been provide by an ASM. Defenders of MSMs here might reply that the advantage of such qualitative results from MSMs are more accurate than the comparative results from ASMs. However, my earlier arguments in Sects. 4.2–4.4 question whether this is necessarily the case. Consequently, the uncertainty quantification strategies facilitated by MSMs are not necessarily better than the strategy of ASMs.

4.7   Match with Decision Tools

MSMs, because they offer quantitative outcomes even when dealing with uncertainty, can easily be combined with standard quantified risk approaches to decision-making. For example, a MSM that gives possible outcomes of interventions (e.g., pairs of cost and cumulative deaths) at different probabilities can easily be combined with an expected value or an expected utility approach to decision-making. For this purpose, the outcome pairs are either monetized or their utility is determined, and this evaluation is weighted by the probability of this outcome. The policymaker chooses that intervention which yields the highest expected value or expected utility. ASMs, because they typically do not provide probabilities over uncertain outcomes, do not offer such a convenient procedure to the policymaker. For this reason, they might *at first* be considered inferior for policy purposes.

However, the combination of MSMs with quantified risk approaches is based on mere appearances, and lacks a justification. For reasons given in Sects. 4.4 and 4.6, most models include inevitable uncertainty, which typically cannot be quantified. Furthermore, for reasons given in Sects. 4.2 and 4.3, MSMs often include higher uncertainty than ASMs. Probabilistic quantifications of the uncertainty of MSMs, therefore, often represent claims that lack sufficient evidential support.

This raises the question of whether MSMs could provide better support for qualitative decision approaches, which take uncertainties into consideration without quantifying them. These approaches include *structured qualitative decision-making*, which assumes that all relevant possible outcomes of an act can be identified, but that outcome uncertainty cannot be quantified; and *argumentative approaches* that identify only some of the relevant consequences (typically without being able to quantify their evaluation or their probability of occurring), while acknowledging that others are possible, too. Examples of the former include Maximin, Minimax regret and the O-P rule. Examples of the latter include pro-and-con tables and ordered checklists.

How would a MSM contribute in a better way to such approaches than an ASM? One answer is that we might be more confident in the possible outcomes that a MSM produces than in those of the ASM, since the former includes more relevant detail both in terms of parameters and mechanisms. While I do not deny that this might be the case, such a conclusion is by no means necessary, as the MSM's outcomes are affected more by overfitting and underdetermination than the ASM's. Consequently, while both types of models typically support qualitative decision approaches, ASMs might occasionally better suited than MSMs, contrary to first appearances.

5   Conclusions

In this paper, I caution against an overly optimistic assessment of MSMs for policy purposes. In particular, I argued that MSMs might have more severe problems than ASMs in determining the accuracy of the model (4.2, 4.3); that MSMs might have more severe problems than ASMs in dealing with inevitable uncertainty (4.4, 4.6); and that MSMs might have more severe problems than ASMs with misinterpretation and misapplication due to their format (4.1, 4.5, 4.7). This of course does not exclude that some MSMs provide good justifications for policy decisions (and even better justifications than some ASMs); but it should caution against a general preference for MSM over ASMs for policy decision purposes.

References

Burke, Donald S., Joshua M. Epstein, Derek A. Cummings, Jon I. Parker, Kenneth C. Cline, Ramesh M. Singa, and Shubah Chakravarty. 2006. Individual-Based Computational Modeling Of Smallpox Epidemic Control Strategies. *Academic Emergency Medicine* 13 (11): 1142–1149.

Dawid, Herbert, and Giorgio Fagiolo. 2008. Editorial. Agent-based models for economic policy design: Introduction to the special issue. *Journal of Economic Behaviour & Organization* 67 (2): 351–354.

Epstein, Joshua M. 1999. Agent-based computational models and generative social science. *Complexity* 4 (5): 41–57.

Eubank, Stephen, Hasan Guclu, V. S. Anil Kumar, Madhav V. Marathe, Aravind Srinivasan, Zoltán Toroczkai, and Nan Wang. 2004. Modelling Disease Outbreaks In Realistic Urban Social Networks. *Nature* 429 (6988): 180–184. See supplement at http://www.nature.com/nature/journal/v429/n6988/extref/nature02541-s1.htm. Accessed 15 March 2016.

Farmer, J. Doyne, and Duncan Foley. 2009. The Economy Needs Agent-Based Modelling. *Nature* 460 (7256): 685–686.

Gigerenzer, Gerd, and Henry Brighton. 2009. Homo Heuristicus: Why Biased Minds Make Better Inferences. *Topics in Cognitive Science* 1 (1): 107–143.

Grüne-Yanoff, Till. 2011. Agent-Based Models as Policy Decision Tools: The Case of Smallpox Vaccination. *Simulation and Gaming: An Interdisciplinary Journal* 42 (2): 219–236.

Hartmann, Stephan. 1996. The World as a Process: Simulations in the Natural and Social Sciences. In *Modelling and Simulation in the Social Sciences from the Philosophy of Science Point of View*, ed. Rainer Hegselmann, Ulrich Mueller, and Klaus Troitzsch, 77–100. Dordrecht: Kluwer.

Hine, Dame Deirdre. 2010. *The 2009 Influenza Pandemic: An independent review of the UK response to the 2009 influenza pandemic*. Available at https://www.gov.uk/government/uploads/system/uploads/attachment_data/file/61252/the2009influenzapandemic-review.pdf. Accessed 02 May 2016.

Humphreys, Paul. 2004. *Extending Ourselves: Computational Science, Empiricism, and Scientific Method*. New York: Oxford University Press.

Kaplan, Edward H., David L. Craft, and Lawrence M. Wein. 2002. Emergency response to a smallpox attack: The case for mass vaccination. *Proceedings of the National Academy of Sciences* 99 (16): 10935–10940.

Lenhard, Johannes, and Eric Winsberg. 2010. Holism, entrenchment, and the future of climate model pluralism. *Studies in History and Philosophy of Science Part B: Studies in History and Philosophy of Modern Physics* 41 (3): 253–262.

Myung, In Jae. 2000. The importance of complexity in model selection. *Journal of Mathematical Psychology* 44 (1): 190–204.

Parker, Wendy S., and James S. Risbey. 2015. False Precision, Surprise and Improved Uncertainty Assessment. *Philosophical Transactions of the Royal Society A: Mathematical, Physical and Engineering Sciences* 373 (2055): 20140453.

Schelling, Thomas. 1971. Dynamic models of segregation. *Journal of Mathematical Sociology* 1: 143–186.

Zucchini, Walter. 2000. An introduction to model selection. *Journal of Mathematical Psychology* 44 (1): 41–61.

Between Knowledge and Action: Conceptualizing Scientific Simulation and Policy-Making

Dirk Scheer

Abstract This chapter conceptualizes computer simulation and policy-making at the science-policy interface exploring boundaries between scientific knowledge production and political action orientation. The conceptualization entails four layers. First, compatibilities of scientific simulations with the policy-making system rely on key characteristics of modelling meeting policy's reasoning, forward-looking and decision oriented needs. Simulations meets these needs with their capability to reduce complexity, compare options, analyse intervention effects, deliver results in numbers, and carry out trial without error. Second, from a systemic perspective, simulations serve as a knowledge instrument contributing to secure and uncertain knowledge and the known unknowns. Simulations also enable, amplify and feedback communication. Third, taking an impact perspective, the policy use of simulations differentiates in instrumental, conceptual, strategic and procedural use patterns. Finally, evaluation and assessment of simulations by decision-makers follows several simulation-inherent and simulation-contextual criteria.

1 Introduction

Computer simulations are a crucial innovation in the field of information and communication technologies and have established as an important tool with a wide variety of applications in science, business and industry. It is primarily in basic and applied science where simulations play a significant role as an additional epistemic method approach besides theory and experimentation. To name just some examples: simulations are used in genetics, gravitation physics, molecular modeling, earth system and geo-sciences, energy system modelling, various fields of engineering sciences and last but not least, climate change and technology assessment studies. As such, computer simulations have well established and will even further gain more importance on the whole range of science disciplines.

D. Scheer (✉)
Institute for Technology Assessment and Systems Analysis (ITAS), Karlsruhe Institute of
Technology (KIT), Karlstraße 11, 76133 Karlsruhe, Germany
e-mail: dirk.scheer@kit.edu

© Springer International Publishing AG 2017   103
M.M. Resch et al. (eds.), *The Science and Art of Simulation I*,
DOI 10.1007/978-3-319-55762-5_8

However, knowledge gained from computer simulations is not limited to the scientific community itself but impacts other domains of society such as politics, business and industry, and the public at large. Production of simulation-based knowledge and its communication towards political decision-makers have become a crucial factor within policy-making. Impacting societal domains, simulations meet two principal functions: they serve as both a knowledge and a communication instrument at the science-policy interface. Nonetheless, so far science did not consider in depth how processes and circumstances of simulations-based knowledge transfer at the science-policy interface works in detail. This chapter conceptualizes epistemic simulation and policy-making at the science-policy interface exploring boundaries between scientific knowledge production and political action orientation. Initial thoughts and preliminary ideas of the conceptualization have been disseminated in dispersed publications (cf. Scheer 2011, 2013, 2015; Kissinger et al. 2014; Scheer et al. 2015). However, with this chapter I intend to synthesise and further detail and develop a coherent framework of simulations impacting policy.

The chapter is structured in the following way. Section 2 elaborates on principal compatibilities of scientific simulations and policy-making processes. Section 3 conceptualizes from a systemic perspective simulation modes of knowledge and communication. Section 4 differentiates categories of simulation research use by policy taking an impact perspective into account. Finally, Sect. 5 introduces a set of quality assessment criteria indicating how decision-makers perceive and judge on simulation quality representing an evaluation perspective. The chapter ends with drawing some conclusions.

2 Scientific Simulations and Policy-Making Compatibilities

Policy-making in modern pluralistic societies is forward-looking, decision-oriented, and obliged to state evidence-based reasons. Policies result from a process where problems to be solved are identified and articulated, policy objectives and solutions are formulated, alternative policy options are developed, and binding agreements are finally decided (Scharpf 1973, p. 15). Problem identification, alternative courses of action, and solution-orientated interventions are thus key aspects of a decision-based understanding of policy-making. First, the forward-looking aspect is an inherent feature of policy-making: with deciding on specific policies policy-makers intend to solve an identified problem in the future. While doing so, policy-makers meet the challenge to develop, evaluate and decide on policy options to become effective in the future with analysing a current problem situation. Second, political decision-making in modern democracies requires reasoning and justification provided by policy-makers to secure popular legitimacy and acceptance. Legitimacy resources are, for instance, institutionalized decision-making procedures, sufficient consent and acceptance from the public and stakeholders, and scientific knowledge. Scientific expertise and findings are a legitimacy resource for policy-making due to its assigned features of objectivity, independency and objective evidence. The use of science in policy-making thus ideally may have a share in debate objectification and delivering an evidence-based background for policy decisions. In addition, the use of science is also binding in institutionalized decision-making procedures. The German Supreme Court, for instance, urged the legislator to carry out impact assessments in order to pre-evaluate impacts and effectiveness of intended policy laws. Regulatory impact assessment studies need to consider the scientific state of knowledge and technology. Against that background the vague legal concepts of "Stand der Wissenschaft" and "Stand der Technik" ("state-of-the-art science and technology") have been introduced as legal terms (von Beyme 1997).

Thus, a key task of modern policy-making is making general binding decisions based on both evidence-based knowledge, and on societal legitimacy. This leads to three fundamental "policy needs" science has to contribute: enhance understanding and knowledge, support decision-making and provide legitimacy. Understanding and knowledge relates to the knowledge base of policy-makers that is to understand well in advance relevant problems and their cause-effect relationship. Scientific policy advice may contribute to optimize the knowledge base among policy-makers in delivering the state-of-the-art knowledge in order to guarantee robust policies. Moreover, science should contribute with delivering reflexive knowledge (i.e. meta knowledge), which allows an assessment of the existing knowledge base considering uncertainty, risks and ambiguity (Grunwald 2009). Decisions are at the core of modern policy-making. In a broad sense, decisions relate not only on decision-making but include preparation of upcoming decisions (e.g., opinion-building and political debate). Scientific expertise may have a share in debate objectification, contribute to "social robust" decision-making, and give an evidence-based background for decisions. Finally, legitimacy is a central component of democratic political systems. Political action requires a minimum of legitimacy in order to implement generic binding decisions. Research input in order to encourage legitimacy relies on contributing objective and evidence-based knowledge to opinion-building and decision-making. Scientific expertise is a resource of legitimacy on its own, based on its attributes of objectivity and independence. Research input, therefore, may justify decisions and is a support for finding acceptance.

Scientific computer simulations are to a great extent compatible with these three policy-making features. In the following, I will illustrate and specify in which way simulations support future, decision and legitimacy orientation as inherent features of modern policy-making. Key characteristics of computer simulations can be synthesized into the following specific capabilities:

- Reduction of complexity: simulations have the capability of reducing, representing and visualizing real world system complexities and statuses.
- Comparison of options: simulations have the capability of representing and, hence communicating comparatively various problem dimensions and courses of action.

- Intervention effects: simulations have the capability of representing and, hence communicating impact and effects of different political steering interventions.
- Formats of results: simulations have the capability of aggregating and transforming time-depended system states into easy accessible formats of pictures, diagrams and numbers.
- Trial without error: simulations have the capability to use trial and error to find optimal solutions without serious real-world consequences.

Using computer simulations, complex real-world systems are reduced to its relevant structural system functions, are replicated in a simplified system "copy", and are visible through various visualization techniques. Running a computer simulation allows to reproduce dynamic system processes over time, and identify and image various system statuses at specific points of (future) time. Against this background, scientific simulations can be judged a future research or foresight knowledge instrument able to virtually analyse and visualize several system states over time. Unlike experimentation which base future statements on extrapolating its results, computer simulations are already able to extrapolate the object of investigation into the future, and thus pretend to be future observing which meets the forward looking aspect of policy-making.

In addition, when applying different scenarios and statuses of the system considered, modellers are able to analyse the bandwidth of possible system developments. With modifications of influencing factors (e.g., parameter and parameter values) modellers are able to analyse impact and effect of specific (policy) interventions with a trial and error method—using a virtual environment without serious real-world damage. Variable system configurations and interventions to be used in simulations meets the policy needs of developing different policy options and find best intervention solutions to solve a problem. Thus, simulations combine the abilities run through several alternatives, and find the objectively optimal solution. Aggregating and visualizing simulation results into tangible numbers and diagrams also suggest an accuracy which meets the expectation of policy and decision-makers.

While simulations are by know well established in many scientific disciplines, they also transfer scientific reputation and legitimacy. Therewith they contribute to policy-making science-legitimized future knowledge.

However, the compatibility and acceptance of scientific simulations with policy-making is not guaranteed. Simulation-based policy decisions are vulnerable and eventually become under attack by political opponents or competing experts. Complexity reduction, option comparison and intervention effects are frequently based on oversimplified system functions, starting point assumptions and cause-impact relationships which insufficiently meet real-world phenomena. On the other side, computed quantitative results in pictures and numbers tend to obscure underlying uncertainties and suggest a level of accuracy which is often not adequate to reality. Having said this, the production and reliability of simulation results is often only understandable by the modeller him/herself and is not traceable from the outside. Production of simulation knowledge is sometimes an opaque endeavour only accessible to modelling experts—provided the computer code is open access. It is not surprising to see computer simulation as a basis of or information resource for political decision-making being heavily criticised: lack of trust in models and modellers, spurious accuracy of simulation results, and inadequacy of the computing process itself are only some points of criticism raised (cf. Hellström 1996; Brugnach et al. 2007; Ivanović and Freer 2009; Fisher et al. 2010; Wagner et al. 2010).

3 A Systemic Perspective: Simulations Modes of Knowledge and Communication

Scientific simulation at the science-policy interface fulfil a twofold task. On one hand, they serve as a knowledge instrument generating scientific expertise and know-how. On the other side, they serve as a communication instrument transferring knowledge messages and contents from the science to the policy community. Based on this fundamental observation of a dual function of simulation in policy-making, one may further differentiate their corresponding modes of knowledge and communication. To my knowledge, a systemic view on simulations in policy-making focusing on its knowledge and communication role has not yet been developed in simulation based impact assessment literature. Hence, the following thoughts represent some first conceptual and explorative ideas on functionalities of scientific simulations at the science-policy interface. The main distinctions and features are summarized in Table 1.

Scientific simulations serve as a knowledge production instrument and complement the well-established scientific methods of theory and experimentation. Epistemological studies in the area of philosophy of science have laid much emphasis on discussing the epistemic features of simulations towards its truth claim.

Table 1 Types of knowledge and communication

Modes of knowledge		
Secure knowledge	*Unsecure knowledge*	*Recognized non-knowledge*
Full target system knowledge Transferability of target system on computer Successful verification and validation	Nature of uncertainty Range of uncertainty Methodological unreliability Value diversity	Hinting to knowledge deficits Serve as early warning tool But limited to point on outside phenomena
Modes of communication		
Enabling communication	*Amplifying communication*	*Feedback on communication*
Specify and visualize foresight knowledge Methodical and thematic interface for communicators	Modelers act as political voices Simulations as dialogue and communication platform	Simulation results shape the way we think the world New visual components enter our cognitive patterns

Source: Own elaboration

However, no agreement and consensus has been reached whether simulations contribute to an objective and solid scientific knowledge base. The dividing line runs between emphasizing simulations to be a mere numerical continuation of mathematical models and/or experimenting, and stressing simulations to be an independent and original knowledge instrument apart from theory and experimentation (Duran and Arnold 2013). Nevertheless, what is indisputable is the fact that scientific computer simulations generate results containing scientific evidence and therefore contribute to establish a scientific knowledge-base. But what might be exactly their contribution?

Sociology and philosophy of science differentiates four different ideal-types of scientific knowledge. One may differentiate between secure/solid and unsecure/uncertain knowledge, and recognized and un-recognized non-knowledge. While the first three types are accessible to scientific analysis and specification, the type of unrecognised non-knowledge remains in the field of theoretical constructs and is not accessible to further scientific—and other—specification due to its unknown-unknown characteristic.

First, secure and solid knowledge in modern understanding of science is of temporal nature and remains valid as long as it is not falsified by repeated validity tests. Scientific solid knowledge in a sense of Popper's understanding of rationality approximates an objective truth claim the longer it is not falsified although it never will reach the ideal of absolute and perpetual knowledge. Thus, solid knowledge is relative. Simulations and their results contribute to solid knowledge in case several types of uncertainties along the production process remain as low as possible and reliability towards the target system is guaranteed. Ideally, initial and boundary conditions as well as cause-impact relationships of the target system are well known and can be transformed congruently into a virtual computer environment. This is in particular true for technology-oriented simulations with cause-effect relationships following simple deterministic laws, and initial conditions and system boundaries are easy to be defined. Using methods of verification and validation, computer simulations can be easily tested towards reliability.

Second, uncertain knowledge covers the large area where evidence and knowledge is in fact produced but the range of (quantifiable) uncertainty remains considerable. Thus, the validity of scientific results is backed and restricted by particular ranges of uncertainty. Several techniques of uncertainty statements exist such as probability statements via quantifiable confidence intervals. Simulation experts have laid much emphasis on specifying the range of uncertainty when doing simulations. One may differentiate between objective and subjective specifications of uncertainty modelling. The objective specification quantifies ranges of uncertainty via a frequentistic approach. The subjective specification uses Bayesian statistics to make probability statements. However, sorts of uncertainty along the modelling exercise is manifold and—as Petersen (2006) has shown—may refer to the nature of uncertainty (epistemic, ontic), the range of uncertainty (statistical, scenario), methodological unreliability and value diversity.

Third, simulations may contribute to the area of recognised non-knowledge in case they hint to existing knowledge deficits and risks and thus demonstrate and evidence known unknowns. While doing so, they serve as an important early warning tool for the policy system with early indicating emerging problems and policy issues. However, the early warning potential of simulation is limited since simulations have difficulties to discover new and completely unknown issues which are not already implemented in the cause-effect relation of the model itself. Simulation are able to specify phenomena with, for instance, detailing specific time-dependent system states. But they have difficulties in pointing out and specifying phenomena which are outside their conceptual frame. Thus, in that case simulations are different from experimentation since experimentation results have the capability to refer to phenomena which are not necessarily embedded into the experimental design.

Scientific simulations at the science-policy interface may also be considered from a communication perspective. From this view, the simulation contents and results do not lead the analytical focus but rather the impact of simulation instruments on the communication process itself. One may distinguish three types of communication modes: scientific simulations may enable communication, amplify communication, and feedback on communication and communicators respectively in the policy arena.

First, simulation modelling may enable communication in particular through their projection and prognostic future orientation. They are able to specify and materialize future states of the world as a virtual representation. With specifying foresight knowledge, simulations may initiate and enable prospective discourses among decision-makers and within the society as whole on available options to shape, design and decide the future. Political decision-making in modern pluralistic societies always implies communication on various alternative courses of action while on the other side concrete policy output is always a result of a (political) communication process. Scientific simulations enable communication with providing a methodical and thematic interface for communicators in order to frame, localize and focus on distinct topics and messages. Future-oriented simulations are an important foresight tool to estimate possible future pathways which are, for instance, not accessible to empirics (since still undone). Hence, 'editing' the future via simulation studies serves as an important communication object to stimulate reflections and deliberations on future developments.

Second, simulation as a communication object may reactivate the communication process itself—thus, simulations may amplify communication with the increasing number of corresponding modellers and simulations scientists. With establishing, institutionalizing and networking a scientific simulation community the communication potential increases. In case policy relevant topics are covered by simulations, they serve as a dialogue and communication platform stimulating actors to pick up the topics. In competition with other communication arenas, where other actors and topics compete for ensuring political attention, simulation-based communication is an additional resource in the political discourse. The simulation content (e.g., energy scenarios, carbon capture and storage) indirectly receives a louder voice and increasing significance compared to competing communication arenas and issues. Thus, simulations serve for political agenda setting with raising attention for specific topics, increasing its significance compared to competing issues, and acting as a selection mechanism for topic choices.

Third, simulations may also feedback on how the communication evolves and communicators think and act. Scientific simulations with their inherent number- and solution-oriented characteristics may influence cognitive thinking patterns and conceptual worlds of communicators—thus, they might impact on how we think issues. Taking simulation results as an example, their primary formats are numbers and number-based pictures. How may this impact our mental models and the way we think issues? Warnke (2002) argues it is obvious that the increasing significance of computer simulation as a method of technology-oriented knowledge production and the corresponding need to analyse simulation-based visualisations will bring in new visual components which inevitably shapes the way how engineers think issues. Porter (1995) argued that numbers serve as a communication medium disguising their content with objectivity and universality, and are particularly important in a communication process in case other procedures of consensus fail. Quantitative, number-based statements seek to reduce complexity while simulta- neously finding a high potential of consensus and acceptance. Science has been successful in using formalization measurements, for instance, the strongly formal- ized mathematical language, in order to attribute objectivity to numbers (Heintz 2007). As such numbers act as a decisive (scientific) source for ways of worldmaking. However, simulations feedbacking on communication and commu- nicators likewise have so far not been systematically researched both conceptually and empirically.

4 An Impact Perspective: Simulation Use by Policy

Scientific simulations at the science-policy interface raise the question of how the political system and corresponding decision-makers use provided research. From a policy perspective it is necessary to look for impact categories which indicate the use of simulations taking the rationale of the political system into account. Follow- ing policy advice and research impact literature (cf. Weiss 1979; Renn 1995; Williams et al. 1997; Nutley et al. 2007), I propose four research use categories: First the instrumental use embeds science in acts, rules and laws. Simulations can be used in rule making for technology support programs, regulation, and assessment serving for evaluation and control measures. Secondly, the conceptual use of simulation research yields to a better understanding and knowledge among decision makers. Thus, simulations contribute to early problem perception (e.g., climate modeling), delivering an evidence base (e.g., life cycle assessment) or illustrating the consequences of future policy options. Thirdly, the tactical/strategic use of simulation data may be stimulated by party competition seeking office during election campaigns, by justifying action in political windows of opportunities, or by strategies in playing for time. Fourth, the procedural use of simulation considers networking activities with encouraging technology development and acceptance (e.g., technology procurement, encouraging collaborative research). However, what should be stressed is the fact that these categories are of analytical value since these types are sometimes difficult to apply empirically and the boundaries between different types are often blurred (Nutley et al. 2007). In the following I will illustrate and exemplify how computer simulations specifically contribute to the four research use types and their specifications provided in Table 2.

The instrumental use of simulations by policy comprises identification and evaluation of policy options, design and implementation of policy decisions, and policy impact assessment and monitoring. A good example for simulations backing policy options is the use of energy system modelling in German nuclear lifetime policy decisions. In 2010, the German government commissioned a study to calculate three different energy scenarios considering varying nuclear lifetime periods in order to specify detailed policy options. One day after the study's publication the Federal government decided to extend nuclear operational lifetime on average 12 years meaning, for instance, the last nuclear power plant in Germany will be switched off in 2036. While in 2010 policy-makers explicitly referred to energy scenarios as backbone for extending German nuclear lifetime, the policy turn-around with reducing nuclear lifetime in response to the Fukushima event in 2011 completely waived references to energy scenarios. As a consequence, energy scenarios were never mentioned in Post-Fukushima energy policy-making. The example illustrates, policy-makers refer to simulation results as an evidence-backed basis for decision, provided a political window of opportunity is given—and do not in case the window is closed.

Concerning policy implementation and monitoring one may refer to the European Directive on Carbon Capture and Storage (CCS). Within the EU CCS directive, (EU 2009/31/EC) geo-scientific simulations are fundamental to serve as a characterization, control and monitoring instrument. The German CCS legislation replicated the EU annexes I and II bringing it into force in 2012. Hence, both the EU and the German CCS regulation specify in detail requirements for the

Table 2   Types of research use by policy

Research use by policy	
Instrumental use	Identification and evaluation of policy options Design and implementation of policy decisions Impact assessment and monitoring
Conceptual use	Problem identification and understanding Coded knowledge archive Early warning tool
Strategic and tactical use	Legitimacy base for normative positions Scientific façade for interests and values Technical manipulation of simulations
Procedural use	Knowledge communication towards lay people an non-experts Conflict avoidance and consensus making Networking and actor integration

Source: Adapted from Scheer (2013)

characterization and assessment of the potential storage complex and surrounding area (annex I), and for establishing and updating the monitoring plan and for post-closure monitoring (annex II) requiring multiple simulations for storage dynamic behaviour, sensitivity characterization and risk assessment. Predictive simulation results need continuously be compared with empirical data collection in order to update the monitoring plan. Similar modelling approaches imbedded in detailed policies are used in the European Water Framework Directive (EU 2000/60/EC). As such, simulations are widely embedded in existing policy regulations.

The conceptual use of simulations by policy refers to mere problem identification and understanding while modelling also serves as coded knowledge archive and early warning tool. Environmental and climate policy issues again serve as good examples. The famous World3-Model used in the ground-breaking analysis of "The Limits of Growth" by Denis Meadows et al. (1972) serves for illustration. With using a system dynamic approach for indicating trade-offs between population, growth, foodstuff and ecosystem boundaries the report had considerable impact on environmental problem perception both among decision-makers and the public at large. The study showed that ecosystem capacities are limited and exponential growth of the population will spoil capacity limits. The World3-Model, thus, served as an early warning tool for upcoming environmental problems and helped to set environmental issues on the political agenda.

Taking earth system and geo-science modelling as a further example, again the conceptual use of scientific simulation can be considered huge. Simulations in the field of CCS serve as an indispensable knowledge instrument able to reduce complexity, overcome in situ time and spatial constraints, and exemplify several future policy options. In addition, simulations provide a knowledge base to pre-assess technology potentials before stepping into the implementation of pilot and demonstrations stages. In that sense, modelling serves as an 'eye-opener' both for scientists and policy-maker alike to better understand real-world phenomena.

Strategic and tactical use of simulations puts emphasis on the communication role of modelling and its visualization respectively at the science-policy interface. The use of science is motivated due to its reputation and power of persuasion rather than its evidence and factual claim. Its reputation is used to legitimize singular normative positions and may serve as a scientific façade for interests and values. As such, decision-makers reinterpret and frame scientific results according to their own interests. According to Wagner et al. (2010, p. 336) strategic use of simulations appears in three intimately related but distinguishable strategies that a devious regulatory participant can deploy to reap benefits from models. The first strategy builds on the widespread false expectation that models are fact-generating machines. Regulators tend to portray simulations as answering machines in order to sidestep some unpleasant accountability controversies with statements that "the model made me do it". Such a strategy may prevent further scrutiny by institutional authorities and stakeholder. A second strategy finds it beneficial to be opaque about assumptions and uncertainties incorporated into the model. This opacity helps insulate the agency's many assumptions and modeling decisions from critical review, particularly by adversarial stakeholders. Finally, a third strategy to be observed demands an unobtainable level of empirical certainty. As a consequence of strategic demanded unfulfillability both use of model and corresponding policy options may be blocked. Demanding perfection for running the model intends to delegitimize the model and political and scientific proponents behind it.

Finally, procedural use of simulation puts emphasis on the process of modelling rather than the use of its final results. On one hand, the simulation process serves science communication towards lay people and non-experts based on their capability of complexity reduction and visualisation. On the other hand, simulations may be used as vehicle for conflict avoidance and consensus making. Van Daalen et al. (2002) quotes as a corresponding example the RAINS-Modell (Regional Acidification Information and Simulation). The RAINS-model was centre stage for the integrated assessment of acid rain and became a central element in negotiations towards the Second Sulphur Protocol of the UN-ECE Convention on Long-Range Transboundary Air Pollution. Grünfeld (1999) assumes that the agreed emission reduction targets fixed in the protocol are largely based on results obtained from scenario calculations using the RAINS-model. As such, the model waved and eased the path to establish international political consensus. Another procedural use of simulation represents the case of participatory modelling. The approach is a field of application for integrating experts and lay-people into science development at early stages. Participatory modelling can be defined as integrating experts and stakeholders into the production and/or usage phase of conceptual and computer-based models (Hare et al. 2003; Bots and van Daalen 2008; Dreyer et al. 2015; Scheer et al. 2015). Hence, participatory modeling opens up the modeling process for external actors who do not dispose of simulation and modeling expertise. In that sense, participatory modelling is a generic term for a large variety of experimenting with expert involvement in science development.

5 An Evaluation Perspective: Quality Assessment of Simulations

Scientific simulation expertise used by policy includes quality evaluation of simulation instrument, processes and results. Policy-makers, stakeholders and at times the public at large reflect and question the excellence of simulations when relevant for policy issues. In case simulations were judged reliable, they may have considerable impact in the policy-making process. Thus, a key question is how involved policy-making actors evaluate and assess the reliability of scientific simulations. Based on interviews with decision-makers in a case study on geo-science modelling in the field of Carbon Capture and Storage, I deduced a set of assessment criteria how people evaluate scientific simulations (Scheer 2015). Within this chapter I do not further specify on how decision-makers process simulation-based information. For further details on information processing one may refer to the analytical framework for assessing simulations impacting policies provided in Scheer (2013, 2015).

The interviews revealed a broad variety of quality variables which can be roughly summarized in the following interview quotation: "The crucial questions always are: who did the simulation, who participated in it, what about the used methodology, and were all currently known facts considered in setting up the simulation". The single evaluation criteria elicited from the interviews cover two different areas, namely simulation-inherent and simulation-contextual assessment criteria. While simulation-inherent variables are predominately used by decision-makers and experts with a genuine geo-scientific and simulation background, contextual criteria assessment are notably applied by experts lacking geo-scientific and simulation expertise. Table 3 summarizes the set of evaluation criteria for assessing scientific simulations.

Simulation-inherent aspects cover a broad range of specific simulation components, namely data input, setting of boundary conditions and underlying assumptions, parameters and their corresponding values, the model and algorithms used, considered natural laws and causalities, and finally balancing the model versus reality. Thus, evaluating simulation quality is done from an inside perspective. According to the interviews excellent quality of simulations rely on availability of empirical data with small range of error assessment, and on well-defined boundary conditions and underlying main assumptions. Used parameters and impact variables should be tested with corresponding quality tests (e.g., sensitivity and uncertainty analysis) in order to only use high impact parameters for simulations runs. The model itself should rather be simple without conflicting with reality while the software needs to be validated (e.g., model benchmarking and comparison). Moreover, the underlying laws of the target system should be well understood and adequately transformed into computer language and environment. Balancing simulations with reality and real-world phenomena is another important criterion. Empirical validation of model results is a key quality aspect to assess its scientific evidence. In the words of an expert: "Simulation results are only reliable when they were compared with reality. A model without empirical validation is an animated cartoon". Thus, decision-makers tend to cognitively correlate modelling results with empirical real-world phenomena within their boundaries of perceived reality.

Table 3 Evaluation criteria for assessing simulations

Quality of simulation process and results	
Model-inherent evaluation	Model contextual evaluation
Data	Source (author, institution)
Boundary conditions	Discourse among experts
Assumptions	Study comparison
Parameter	Level of disciplinary knowledge
Model	Integration and participation of experts
Causality	
Balancing model vs. reality	

Source: Adapted from Scheer (2015)

When taking simulation-contextual criteria into account decision-makers do not focus on simulation specifics in detail but rely on what might be called 'mediated' criteria. The interviews revealed in total five contextual quality criteria, namely the source of the simulation, the reception discourse within the scientific community, comparison of simulations results with similar studies, the level of knowledge in the corresponding discipline, and the degree of stakeholder participation in the simulation process. Assessing the source of a simulation is seen as a crucial quality aspect. Credibility and trust, reputation, independency and neutrality are essential quality aspects for source assessment. Trust in researchers and their corresponding science institutions are key aspects for quality assessment. A scientific background alone, however, is not sufficient to create high trust, as illustrated with the following quotation by a Member of Parliament: "is this a professor who has been foreseen as a forthcoming minister for economic affairs by our political opponent, than we would not rely on him in political controversial topics". A second reliability criterion focusses on the reception discourse. Decision-makers observe and evaluate whether and how other experts and researchers position themselves against newly published simulations data. The less disagreement among researchers and expert dilemma in general are observed, the more reliable simulation results are rated by decision makers. A similar evaluation pattern relates to assessing the bandwidth of competing results on the same research topic. In case the state of the art of research in one discipline is perceived very heterogeneous, than simulations results are interpreted less reliable—and *vice versa*. Interviewees also emphasized the general level of discipline knowledge where the simulation relates to. The more consolidated a discipline is the more reliable simulation data are judged—and *vice versa*. The final contextual criterion relates to the level of expert participation within the simulation exercise. Involving critical observers and opposing stakeholders in the process of running simulations is seen as a key factor for getting reliable and social robust simulation data. In the words of an interviewee: "one may present the most beautiful models and simulations studies which are all totally correct. But as far as these simulations are not checked and understood by the opposite party, mistrust prevails".

The simulation-inherent and contextual criteria deduced from the interviews revealed a broad range of quality aspects taken into account by decision-makers. However, in case decision-makers are confronted with evaluating a specific simulation study they selectively focus on some criteria disregarding others. This became clear when researching the reception of a specific simulation study, the so-called Regional Pressure Study simulating underground pressure dispersion when injecting CO_2 in the field of carbon capture and storage (Schäfer et al. 2010). When asked how quality evaluation of the regional pressure simulation data is done, interviews indicated to the fact that some quality criteria are obviously more important than others. Balancing the model results versus reality has been a decisive criterion for quality assessment. Relating the model with reality seems to be a generic evaluation approach to better understand the (non-)evidence of a simulation exercise. This is done with the help of evaluating the reliability of main assumptions, the boundary conditions, and parameters used. Interviewees also reflected the underground causality and mechanisms when injecting CO_2. The quality of data input (i.e. parameter values) and the model itself, in contrast, were not considered at all. Within the area of contextual quality aspects assessing the reliability of the source proved to be very important. Many experts brought up the role of the Federal Institute of Geosciences and Resources as main author of the study reflecting on its scientific status and reputation. Other contextual criteria such as comparing simulations results with similar studies and assessing the level of discipline knowledge had a lower impact while involvement of stakeholders and the reception discourse were not considered at all.

6 Conclusions

The chapter detailed conceptually the role of scientific simulation at the science-policy interface. By means of analytical and empirical backed type formation and categorisation the concept entails four layers. Compatibilities of scientific simulations with the policy-making system relies on key characteristics of modelling meeting policy's reasoning, forward-looking and decision oriented needs, namely the capability to: reduce complexity, compare options, analyse intervention effects, deliver results in numbers and pictures, and carry out trial without error. From a systemic perspective, simulations serve as a knowledge instrument contributing to secure and uncertain knowledge—and to a lesser degree to recognised non-knowledge. As a communication instrument simulations enable, amplify and feedback communication. Taking an impact perspective, the use of simulations differentiates in instrumental, conceptual, strategic and procedural use patterns. Finally, evaluation and assessment of simulations by decision-makers and stake-holders follows simulation-inherent and simulation-contextual criteria.

What becomes clear from the analysis is the high relevance of simulations for policy-making. It showed that decision-makers have to deal with scientific simulation when it is available and perceived against the great variety of competing information. The truth claim of science statements inherent in simulations cannot be neglected in modern policy-making which is based on a concept of rationality and evidence base. Scientific results may be contested and disputed by policy-makers and stakeholders, but they cannot be ignored. Scientific results are an essential legitimacy resource for policy-making and hence serve as a key point of reference and orientation.

References

Bots, Pieter W. G., and C. Els van Daalen. 2008. Participatory model construction and model use in natural resource management: A framework for reflection. *Systemic Practice and Action Research* 21 (6): 389–407.

Brugnach, Marcela, Andrew Tagg, Florian Keil, and Wim J. de Lange. 2007. Uncertainty Matters: Computer Models at the Science-Policy Interface. *Water Resources Management* 21 (7): 1075–1090.

von Beyme, Klaus. 1997. *Der Gesetzgeber: der Bundestag als Entscheidungszentrum*. Opladen: Westdeutscher Verlag.

van Daalen, C. Els, Leen Dresen, and Marco A. Janssen. 2002. The roles of computer models in the environmental policy life cycle. *Environmental Science and Policy* 5 (3): 221–231.

Dreyer, Marion, Wilfried Konrad, and Dirk Scheer. 2015. Partizipative Modellierung: Erkenntnisse und Erfahrungen aus einer Methodengenese. In *Methoden der Experten- und Stakeholdereinbindung in der sozialwissenschaftlichen Forschung*, ed. Marlen Niederberger and Sandra Wassermann, 261–285. Wiesbaden: Springer VS.

Duran, Juan M., and Eckhart Arnold. 2013. *Computer Simulations and the Changing Face of Scientific Experimentation*. Cambridge: Cambridge Scholars Publishing.

Fisher, Elizabeth C., Pasky Pascual, and Wendy E. Wagner. 2010. Understanding Environmental Models in Their Legal and Regulatory Context. *Journal of Environmental Law* 22 (2): 251–283.

Grünfeld, Hans. 1999. Creating Favorable Conditions for International Environmental Change through Knowledge and Negotiation. PhD diss., TU Delft. Delft, Netherlands: Delft University Press.

Grunwald, Armin. 2009. Technikfolgenabschätzung als wissenschaftliche Politikberatung am Deutschen Bundestag. *Denkströme. Journal der Sächsischen Akademie der Wissenschaften* 2:64–82.

Hare, Matt, Rebecca A. Letcher, and Anthony J. Jakeman. 2003. Participatory modelling in natural resource management: a comparison of four case studies. *Integrated Assessment* 4 (2): 62–72.

Heintz, Bettina. 2007. Zahlen, Wissen, Objektivität: Wissenschaftssoziologische Perspektiven. In *Zahlenwerk: Kalkulation, Organisation und Gesellschaft*, ed. Andrea Mennicken and Hendrik Vollmer, 65–86. Berlin and Heidelberg: Springer, Springer VS.

Hellström, Tomas. 1996. The Science-Policy Dialogue in Transformation: Model Uncertainty and Environmental Policy. *Science and Public Policy* 23 (2): 91–97.

Ivanović, Ruža F., Jim E. Freer. 2009. Science versus politics: truth and uncertainty in predictive modeling. *Hydrological Processes* 23 (17): 2549–2554.

Kissinger, Alexander, Vera Noack, Stefan Knopf, Dirk Scheer, Wilfried Konrad, and Holger Class. 2014. Characterization of reservoir conditions for CO_2 storage using a dimensionless gravitational number applied to the North German Basin. *Sustainable Energy Technologies and Assessments* 7:209–220.

Meadows, Donella H., Dennis L. Meadows, Jørgen Randers, and William W. Behrens. 1972. *The Limits to Growth: a report for the Club of Rome's project on the predicament of mankind*. New York: Universe Books.

Nutley, Sandra M., Isabel Walter, and Huw T. O. Davies. 2007. *Using evidence: How research can inform public services*. Bristol: The Policy Press.

Petersen, Arthur C. 2006. *Simulating Nature: A Philosophical Study of Computer Simulation Uncertainties and Their Role in Climate Science and Policy Advice*. Apeldoorn and Antwerpen: Het Spinhuis.

Porter, Theodore M. 1995. *Trust in Numbers: The Pursuit of Objectivity in Science and Public Life*. Princeton: Princeton University Press.

Renn, Ortwin. 1995. Style of using scientific expertise: a comparative framework. *Science and Public Policy* 22 (3): 147–156.

Schäfer, Frauke, Lena Walter, Holger Class, and Christian Müller. 2010. *Regionale Druckentwicklung bei der Injektion von CO2 in salinare Aquifere*. Hannover: BGR.

Scharpf, Fritz W. 1973. Verwaltungswissenschaft als Teil der Politikwissenschaft. In *Planung als politischer Prozess. Aufsätze zur Theorie der planenden Demokratie*, 9–40. Frankfurt a. M.: Suhrkamp.

Scheer, Dirk. 2015. In silico science for climate policy: How policy-makers process and use carbon storage simulation data. *Environmental Science and Policy* 47: 148–156.

Scheer, Dirk. 2013. *Computersimulationen in politischen Entscheidungsprozessen: Zur Politikrelevanz von Simulationswissen am Beispiel der CO2-Speicherung.* Berlin and Heidelberg: Springer, Springer VS.

Scheer, Dirk. 2011. Computer simulation at the science-policy interface: assessing the policy relevance of CCS simulations. *Energy Procedia* 4: 5770–5777.

Scheer, Dirk, Wilfried Konrad, Alexander Kissinger, Holger Class, Vera Noack, and Stefan Knopf. 2015. Expert involvement in science development: (re-)evaluation of an early screening tool for carbon storage site characterization. *International Journal of Greenhouse Gas Control* 37: 228–236.

Wagner, Wendy, Elizabeth Fisher, and Pasky Pascual. 2010. Misunderstanding models in environmental and public health regulation. *Environmental Law Journal* 18 (2): 293–356.

Warnke, Philine. 2002. Computersimulation und Intervention. Eine Methode der Technikentwicklung als Vermittlungsinstrument soziotechnischer Umordnungen. PhD diss., TU Darmstadt. http://tuprints.ulb.tu-darmstadt.de/epda/000277/DissWarnke_LHB.pdf. Accessed 20 April 2016.

Weiss, Carol H. 1979. The Many Meanings of Research Utilization. *Public Administration Review* 39 (5): 426–431.

Williams, Dorothy A., Michael McConnell, and Kay Wilson. 1997. *Is there any knowledge out there? The impact of research information on practitioners.* Boston Spa: British Library Research and Innovation Report RIC/G/321.

Part III
The Art of Knowing Through Computer Simulations

Outlines of a Pragmatic Theory of Truth and Error in Computer Simulation

Christoph Hubig and Andreas Kaminski

Abstract The highly dynamic development of simulation technologies is pro-pelled by the expectation that increasingly high-performing forecasting instruments can and will be employed. In current discussions, reference to "high-performing forecasting instruments" combines two perspectives that stand in an unresolved relationship to one another, which is philosophically revealing: forecasts as true, as in adequate, representations versus performance measured by the success of the technical practice. While the first perspective presupposes a theory of truth based on realism (adequate representations), the second orients itself towards pragmatic representations of truth. Once this is made explicit, a shortcoming in the existing philosophy of simulation becomes evident. An intense debate on the verification and validation of simulations has failed to address the theory of truth. This article undertakes a discussion on a theory of truth suitable for computer simulation that is not only based on a theoretical interest, but also on a practical one.

The highly dynamic development of simulation technologies is propelled by the expectation that increasingly high-performing forecasting instruments can and will be employed. In current discussions, reference to "high-performing forecasting instruments" combines two perspectives that stand in an unresolved relationship to one another, which is philosophically revealing:

1. "Forecasts"[1] refer to facts that should provide a true, as in *adequate*, representation. The performance of a forecasting instrument is measured by the existence of corresponding facts (for example: results with one quality or another; given relationships between state variables) which serve as truth-makers of the forecasts ex post facto.

---

[1]This includes intentional retrodictions in the history of nature or culture.

C. Hubig (✉)
TU Darmstadt, Institute of Philosophy, Karolinenplatz 5, 64289 Darmstadt, Germany
e-mail: hubig@phil.tu-darmstadt.de

A. Kaminski
High Performance Computing Center Stuttgart (HLRS), University of Stuttgart, Nobelstr. 19, 70569 Stuttgart, Germany
e-mail: kaminski@hlrs.de

© Springer International Publishing AG 2017
M.M. Resch et al. (eds.), *The Science and Art of Simulation I*,
DOI 10.1007/978-3-319-55762-5_9

2. "Performance" is also measured by the *success* of the technical practice. Here, the realization of practical purposes is considered a truth-maker within the plans of action of the assumed fact. Its goal is directed towards a successful exertion of influence over the conditions within the scope of the matter.

These two perspectives stand in mutual tension. Where does this tension emanate from? Although the answer may not seem obvious, it leads to a philosophically interesting question. The divergence emanates from the implicitly hypotheses that are adequate for a theory of truth in computer simulation. While the first perspective presupposes a theory of truth based on *realism* (adequate representations), the second orients itself towards *pragmatic* representations of truth.

Once this is made explicit, a shortcoming in the existing philosophy of simulation becomes evident. An intense debate on the verification and validation of simulations[2] (cf. Roache 1998; Oberkampf and Trucano 2002; Oberkampf and Roy 2010) exists; however, the philosophy of simulation has thus far failed to address the theory of truth. In other words: One speaks of verification and validation without an explicit[3] theoretical framework of truth. It is often discussed what conditions must be met for a simulation to be true, but not what truth is.

What we would like to explicitly undertake here is a discussion of a theory of truth suitable for computer simulation. This is not only based on a theoretical interest, but also on a practical one. That the question is of *theoretical* interest hardly requires explanation. The question regarding the theory of truth corresponds exactly to epistemological debates. Furthermore, it is relevant for the technological-philosophical engagement with computer simulation since pragmatic and realistic theories of truth rely on varying assumptions on the role of technology. From a realistic point of view, they are outlined by technical representation of facts. From a pragmatic perspective, they are the technical securement of standard conditions from which a fact can be acquired.

That this question is furthermore of practical *interest* becomes evident based on the strikingly varying assessments of what computer simulation yields. Both perspectives mentioned above return in form of the assessments contingent on the 'harvest' generated by simulation processes. We intend to show that conceptions—which encompass downright overly eager trust in the yields of simulation studies, as well as critical-relativizing views—clearly lack sufficient complexity in their assessments. Both perspectives tend to assume that it is merely possible to compare the forecasts and their corresponding truth and falsehood in order to evaluate the performance of simulations. This idea lacks sufficient complexity and, accordingly, leads to an assessment deficient in complexity. In order to arrive at a more appropriate analysis, the criteria for evaluating the performance of the forecasting

---

[2]Also, discussions concerning whether *new* problems of validation and verifications exist take place without specifying the scope within the theory of truth. (Cf. Winsberg 2010, pp. 32–38).

[3]This doesn't mean that there are no background assumptions based on a theory of truth, but that these are not made explicit and are therefore more comprehensible in terms of their limitations and consequences.

instruments need to be discussed. This leads to the following questions: First, how to handle possible errors; second, what are proper criteria to assess "truth" and "success"? The discussion takes us from a pragmatic theory of truth to a pragmatic theory of error.

1   Models *of* . . . and Models *for* . . .

To understand why the idea of a mere comparison of forecasts and their corresponding trueness and falseness lacks complexity, it is necessary to look at the methodology of simulation studies. Here it becomes evident that models are applied in two ways: as models *of* . . . and as models *for*. . . .

This will be outlined using a recent publicly discussed example. It deals with the forecasting performance of simulations within the scope of personalized medicine. The simulation responds to the following issue: Medical procedures do not have the same effect on all people. To improve the forecast on the effectiveness of a treatment, the simulation models include customizable parameters. Since patients differ in, for instance, the speed at which their livers can break down medication, patients with a "slow metabolism" may be in danger of a fatal overdose, while patients with a "fast metabolism" require higher doses of medication. A network of 70 research teams took this occasion to study responses in the flow of blood and metabolic processes of medication (von der Weiden 2015, p. 15). A number of simplifications were needed in order to manage the complexity of the processes within the human body. The simulation concentrated on the hub of exchange processes: a "virtual liver." Another measure for simplification (in modelling and computing efforts) was that a mouse's liver was used instead of a human's.

Exemplary of this approach is the alteration of two modelling levels: models *of* . . . and models *for* . . . The distinction is based on the relationship between the model and the modelled. Models for . . . tap into a(n) (unknown) modelling range by transferring a model from another range. Models of . . . represent a known modelling range. Both models can be instantiated and/or schematically abstracted. This means that a VW Beetle is a model of the model range (as an instantiation or exemplification), while a city plan is a model of one city or another (as its schematic abstraction). By contrast, a VW Beetle in a wind tunnel is a model for flow properties of the automobile in road traffic; and, as such a model, it is simultaneously an instantiation and schematic abstraction. One and the same object can, therefore, depending on what it refers to, serve as a model of or a model for. This can be likened to Kant's hand mill analogy, which represents a model of a deterministic system (as an instantiation) and reveals itself schematically as a model for a despotic government and how it is constituted (cf. Hubig 2006, pp. 198–200, 2015, p. 151).

In this sense, a complex alteration and intertwined cooperation between models of . . . and models for . . . in the simulation of pharmaceutical effects can be observed. The mouse liver is a model *for* the human liver. But for the mouse liver, a model *of* its blood flow and metabolic responses is created. For this model, a simulation was subsequently used based on 50,000 virtual cubes for each 3000 cells. The actual mouse liver is recognized as the validation instance of the forecasts, while also being a model *for* the simulation of personalized doses for humans. This, in turn, becomes a model *for* the actual doses within the scope of a medical procedure.

The paradigmatic idea that guides these development processes assumes that all processing steps in a "simulation pipeline" can be structured as a sequence that results in a technical course of action. The steps of these processes are important for the assessment and evaluation of a simulation. Before pragmatic criteria of truth are examined, the process within the scope of the "simulation pipeline" needs to be explored in a more precise manner.

2 The Application of Simulation

Due to the wide and often vague range of meanings of the word "simulation" and, consequently, "simulation pipeline", we recommend the following working definition: "Simulation is the *aggregate* of *transfers* of elements and their relation from one *representation* in another for the purpose of expansion, revision, and alteration of our theoretical and practical references to the world." By *aggregate*, we understand an assembly of categorically inhomogeneous elements under a joint interest (here following Husserl, who asserted this for the concept of the "number", Husserl 1970, p. 74). This common interest is provided in the definition for the purpose of the transfers (expansion, revision, etc. of references). We understand the term *medium* as a structured space of opportunity to identify and realize effects. And we understand the term *representation* in a Kantian sense: as a set of references, beliefs, forms of intuition, (technically mediated) sensual experiences/sensory data, concepts, categories, schemata, experiences, rules, principles, ideas, impressions, and so on; not, however, for names of strategies encompassing any reference to "concepts of reflection" (Kant CpR, A 320). This notion of "simulation" is directed against an interpretation in which "parallel worlds" are created in simulations (Frigg and Reiss 2009, pp. 597–598).

This definition allows for a broad understanding of simulation in both its poetic and scientific use. To speak of computer simulation more specifically, all *current practices* of transfers and each *current medium of representation* between these transfers must be considered. This is achieved if we take the so-called simulation pipeline into account (cf. Bungartz et al. 2013, pp. 1–4).

The "simulation pipeline" is a methodological reconstruction of simulation processes. It describes the sequence of such transfers (Kaminski et al. (2016) speak of translation in this regard) in a posteriori mediums of representation, namely, proceeding from a supposed real system, (1) the physical-qualitative modelling, (2) the mathematical modelling, (3) the subsequent numerical modelling/schematization, (4) the realization of the algorithms in a code/implementation, (5) the computing/"running" to temporalize the calculated results, (6) its implementation in a visualization that exemplifies the dynamics and is the basis of (7) a forecast of facts and situations that culminate in appropriate action plans. More precisely: (1) a physical model for... (e.g., graphical illustrations, reaction equations, base equations, etc.) simulates a segment of reality ("what the case is"); (2) the physical model is simulated in a mathematical model (partially counterfactual, e.g., density functional theory; see also Lenhard 2015, pp. 180–181); (3) the unattainable exact solution is simulated through a numeric approximation; (4) a computer code simulates the algorithms, in part extremely simplifying them; (5) the calculated results (for meshed boxes) simulate the model behavior; (6) the visualization simulates the calculated dynamic; (7) forecasts simulate the expected system states. The generated predications of the simulation (1–7) are ideally somehow measured against reality. In the meantime, however, simulations are virtually checked against other simulations (ensemble simulations) more and more in order to examine the degree of stability of the simulation on the basis of alternative simulations in the course of convergence tests (Wissenschaftsrat 2014, p. 12, with emphasis on IPCC FAR WG 1, 9; see also Gramelsberger 2007, p. 59 ff).

With regard to this imposing sequence of transfers, the question then arises of how to ensure that the transfers (2–7) simulate the target system—and not something else. This question is commonly (quite correctly) treated as a validation and verification problem. However, an aspect of the problem is thereby effectively ignored. It consists of the question as to which theory of truth in (current) computer simulation is suitable. Approaching this problem within the scope of validation and verification problems suggests that it would be sufficient to perform a formal comparison. However, according to our thesis, the justification for when a sufficiently large and sufficiently certain correspondence between each simulation and the simulated system/model is present cannot be dealt with without considerations of a theory of truth.

3 Which Theory of Truth Is Appropriate for Computer Simulation?

At first sight, it appears as if realistic or coherence theories of truth are predestined for computer simulation. We previously spoke of transfers in the simulation pipeline. The justification of the transfers can be thought of in terms of criteria of consistency; this means that the justification of the simulation would be understood as a question regarding its adequacy and therefore theoretic congruency par excellence. A realistic theory of truth as it applies to computer simulation would avoid the deficiency that concerns the realistic theory fundamentally, but not completely.

This deficiency has been termed a category mistake (cf. Schlaudt 2014, p. 45). It occurs when the examination cannot compare a representation to reality, but only to another representation. The latter would, however, be applicable for most transfer steps in the simulation pipeline (since here, representations in one medium are compared with representations in another medium). It seems as if nothing, in principle, speaks against examining any correspondences (between 2–3, 3–4, etc.)—unlike the case of the necessary but impossible comparison between reality and representation (hence, 1–2, or 1–7). For the time being, we will factor out this fundamental problem and will adhere to the following transfer steps (2 ff.).

The idea to assess consistency (adequacy, congruency) seems to be self-evident—as long as one does not ask how such an assessment can take place. What becomes evident then is that (a) such a comparison can only take place partially, and (b) consistency cannot be fully ascertained, but rather the degrees of consistency based on the practical interests can be sufficiently assessed. Regarding (a): The consistency of the results of simulation studies and empirical data can generally be assessed only partially. If comprehensive data sets existed, there would be no need for simulation. Even if partial consistency is ascertained, this does not mean that it persists in other, unknown areas and would therefore be complete. Precisely because simulation models are adjusted to empirical data in the course of parameter fitting (cf. Lenhard and Hasse 2017), the danger of overfitting arises for unknown (unassessed) areas. Consistency between the mathematical model and its transfer in a numerical model cannot be simply proven either. The mathematical model is not analytically solvable, and requires numerical mathematics, among other methods. Here, a further problem becomes evident, which leads to (b): The numerical model approximates the mathematical model. In doing so, the binary question of consistency is transformed into the question of when one thing is sufficiently similar to another. Determining the similarity, however, takes place according to practical considerations. In other words: The numeric solution should approximate the mathematical model with sufficient accuracy. The question of when something is sufficiently exact cannot be answered absolutely, but rather, as Wittgenstein convincingly demonstrates in his *Philosophical Investigations*, only against the backdrop of achieving objectives with means that are, or are not, sufficiently exact (cf. Wittgenstein 1972, §§ 68, 88 et passim).

The latter argument also argues against theoretical coherence models of truth. The question of when a chain of transfers is sufficiently consistent and coherent and when it isn't cannot be answered in formally logical terms, but only in practical terms as soon as approximations are involved.

In view of the objections that have been laid out here in detail, we now turn to a pragmatic conceptualization of computer simulation. We assume that this will entail higher performance—and, at the same time, that it poses serious issues (which we will respond to in later sections).

4   Why a Pragmatic Theory of Truth?

The idea is the following: Reliability tests of simulation (1–8) are in many different ways *pragmatically* motivated. According to these reliability tests, iteration loops occur between the simulation levels, which renders questionable the metaphor of a simulation *pipeline*. Iteration loops serve as the matching of simulation steps according to the leading particular interest: Because when, how, and why do we deem each step of every partial simulation successful, and procedures based on general experiences reliable? An assessment that is considered "reliable" is dependent on each respective interest.

The first step of simulation follows our general interest of casualization (Husserl 1962, p. 52, 184, 334, 499) and the associated technical interest regarding the reproducibility and plannability of effects (as is the case with causality concepts of interventionism and constructivism, which are also problematic for astrophysics). For one thing, this means that the models need to be experimentally accessible. It also deals with *controllable* experimental systems that cancel out disturbances; this is the only path towards any successful control (Ashby 1974, p. 290). The second simulation step of a possibly counterfactual mathematical model (cf. - Morrison 2015, especially Sect. 1) connects an interest with an environment of complexity (e.g., interactions on a molecular level, Lenhard 2015) with a functional of sufficient accuracy, including the corresponding adaptation of the performance. Already here, the first step in an iteration loop can be performed when the counterfactual degree of qualitative modelling/idealization adjustment is optimized. The discretization (cell size, polynomial degree) undertaken in the third step is dominated by the burden of an interest-led adjustment to an expected behavior. Thereby, the following approaches are not, or not primarily, self-determined by the conditions of the subject matter. Firstly, this leads to the "art" (Blechmann, cit. in Gramelsberger 2007, p. 52) of selecting parameters (right through to guessing), which can lead to parameter inflation when handling small subject areas (the "dark side of the science"). This takes place within the scope of differentiated result modelling, where cause and effect cannot be distinguished, which again leads to the problem of the dismissal of causality (Russell 1912). Secondly, the issue of specifying the filter size becomes apparent, which is accompanied by an assessment or any estimation effort, and can therefore result in phenomena getting lost (if the filters are too large or too coarse), or when computing power is taken into account (if the filters are too constrained). The fourth simulation step is primarily an interest of practicability. Hereby, the degree of simplification of the computer code that is matched during the "verification" with the interests of the third simulation step lies between the criteria of effectiveness ("doing the right thing regarding precision," etc.) and efficiency ("doing it right" relative to computing power, etc.). In the fifth step, oriented around the "veracity" (in a strict sense) of the simulated model behavior, iterative and explorative studies for setting the parameters (calibration, adjustment) exhibit iteration loops in all previous steps (and their conductive interests; Lenhard and Hasse 2017). Within the course of "validation" (in a strict sense) carried out herein, the total of all previous proceedings is reviewed. The sixth simulation step, encompassing the implementation in a visualization, is subject to the conductive interest of sufficient performance representation based on the disposability and requirements of an interaction in real-time ("velocity"). Then, the decisive interests for the seventh simulation step reach their connecting point, primarily those regarding the optimization of real systems on the basis of forecasts concerning future developments (e.g., for adaptation) and the development of solution spaces of a system (e.g., for mitigation). If, in the eighth step, the task arises to develop successful action plans, then the central interest at hand is that of "security" ("veracity" in a broad sense) regarding the successful outcomes of the actions, whereby its criteria are attributed to the success of a "validation" (in a broad sense) for all previous steps. Convergence and stability of simulations are in many cases only virtual indicators conceptualized for virtual action schemes when real models for technical-operative tests are not available, or when they are not suitable due to moral concerns.

As an interim summary: It becomes apparent that the direct adequation of simulations and facts does not entail the conductive objective, but that of a functional—subtly normatively justified—*equivalence* of the classical and simulated theory in its performance (cf. Kaminski et al. 2016, p. 102). Even if initially the normative justification for "action success" is set back, then at least a theoretical mode of justification for the iteratively performed modifications of each simulation step is made internally evident within the matching process. These are neither deductive nor inductive justifications, but abductions (Hubig 2006, pp. 198–213) of each result as "satisfactory" or "unsatisfactory" regarding (1) assumed causes (the success or the disturbance) within the course of an "abductive induction," or (2) the validity of assumed laws of nature ("rules") within a "hypostatical abstraction," or (3) the assumption of the validity of explanatory patterns, or rather, their assigned domains on the basis of "creative abduction," as well as (4) the reliability of explanatory strategies in general (see the considerations below of Winsberg 2006), and lastly, (5) assumptions regarding the performance of changes of the scientific conception itself. These modes of reasoning encompass all exceptionally uncertain "conclusions" and are dealt with as a kind of "bricolage," in the sense of being executed in a sudokoesque way with adopted rules, or serving the purpose of finding rules in a rather playful manner of testing. Here we find the general issue of the dialectics of rules and rule compliance that leads to the fabrication of "deliberation balances" (Goodman 1983).

When interests are known, the decisive question of what holds these interests together, what their content covers, and on what basis they are justifiable is still apparent. This problem will be dealt in the following section.

5   Features of a Pragmatic Theory of Truth

This is not the appropriate setting to present a comprehensive pragmatic theory of truth. Only several features can be outlined and obvious misconceptions can be excluded in order to proceed to asking how a pragmatic theory of truth can be a paradigm for simulation research (for an unsurpassable pragmatic theory of truth, see Schlaudt 2014, which informs the following summary in essential respects, although in a slightly modified form).

The following modern allegory, "Typus logicae," offers a hermeneutic anticipation. Taken from Gregor Reisch's *Margarita Philosophica*, which was published in one of the first scientific encyclopedias in 1513, the allegory was developed within the context of re-establishing the scientific agenda in humanism (Fig. 1).

Following Francis Bacon, the scientist appears as a hunter who, by means of his weapons, hunts down a problem, and by coping with it, receives many obvious benefits. He is supported during the hunt by two hands, one of which, the *veritas*, is portrayed as an eager support, while the other, the *falsitas*, is a weak failure. Truth and falsehood are no longer understood as an idea of illumination within the order of being and nature, polemically caricatured as "*silva opinionum*," or in other words, as a forest of opinions (following Parmenides), but instead subjected to a problem-solving capacity. Hereto, further weapons serve as "*vexatio naturae artis*" (Bacon 1963, p. 23), or effective instruments, such as the "*argumenta*," the arrows shot out of a bow, and the "*quaesetio*," the correctly formulated question. The sword of "syllogism" conclusively opens the internal structure of prey and offers, assembled in the "*conclusiones*," the conclusions, as a breastplate, or reliable safety in light of new challenges. The hunter, as a pragmatically-oriented nominalist, recognizable by the purely communicative, composed functionality of his statements (*sonus vox*) and the corresponding premises produced (not found), moves within a "laboratory" (which Feichter also characterized as a model system, cit. Gramelsberger 2007, p. 44), while unspoiled nature presents itself as an impenetrable forest and web of unsolvable problems ("*insolubilia*"). The theoretically-shaped knowledge does not appear as a representation and the adequacy of an *ordo naturae*, but as know-how, as technology enabling knowledge, and in this sense it goes against an image of computer simulation that does not appear as a simulation of a reality, but as a simulation of a theory that is evaluated based on its performance.

Such technology-enabling knowledge needs to be differentiated from a reduction of "pragmatism" to subjective utility. In the version proposed here, standards that are secured through the realization of specific performances are dealt with. In doing so, an objectivation is reached because the standards (and thus, the standardization of effects) override the mere subjective utility or pleasure. In their objectivation—standardization through mechanization—they allow the intersubjective verifiability of claims. Rather, the rule for the predication of a preposition as true is that empirical knowledge is generally verifi*able* or generally verification-lacking knowledge of effects, thus considering it in accordance with its

Fig. 1 "Typus logicae" (Source: Reisch 1503)

applic*ability*. The criterion is then an ability to act where taking action had previously been blocked. To precess x to something is therefore equivalent to a predication of what can be done with this x, as long as the technically experimental and technically applicable assembly is *correctly* executed. Rules that are, for their part, justified pragmatically are a precondition in the correctness of this execution. Therefore, a "true" predication refers on a higher level to reaching an "ability to get something done" in accordance with the general notion of technology. In contrast to a definition of truth as a rule of truth-*predication*, a pragmatic *criterion* of truth is a rule of truth-*performation*, which is a criterion of evaluation of the effect of a truth-*predication*. However, as Kant already emphasized, a general criterion is impossible to state, since it doesn't deal with a formal evaluation (Kant CpR, B83), but instead with every material evaluation. These refer—out of a pragmatic view—to the characterization of means regarding their service to given ends, which as such (in contrast to any desires or visions) are prioritized based on an assumed precipitat*ability*, hence, being subjected to the according means. Thereby, a correlation between possible means and possible ends can be exemplified (Hubig 2015, p. 50), which accounts for person- and situation-dependent disposable knowledge. To this extent, this is not about the validation of subjective convictions based on their utility of something to be held true, but about means in their objective condition with regard to which role they play for the establishment of facts. Rules regarding the confirmation of facts are based on the recognition that we never refer to things directly, but always only to somehow identifiable things that, in turn, become items. The "thing-ness" thwarts, irritates, and blocks our identification of items. Things articulate themselves as obstacles that are never exposed absolutely, but are only and always relative to the interests under which we perform our identifications of them as items ("performation" of truth or error).

6 Balance of a Pragmatic Theory of Truth in Simulation Research

To what extent can such a pragmatic theory of truth be a paradigm for simulation research? What would be the challenge inherent in such a paradigm? Essentially, the challenge is that no clear and simple answer emerges. The performance of a pragmatic theory of truth is highly ambivalent. There are prominent and frequently quoted cases that would justify applied simulation procedures intended to ensure the reliability of prognoses and the stable success of actions based on simulation results. A case in point is the so-called toy simulation. Modelling toy simulations is based explicitly on counterfactual assumptions; that is, the simulated qualities are not reflective of the real characteristics. Instead, the focus is on an equivalence of the temporalized results. For example, it is reported that medical simulations can model body tissue as "water plus damping factor" in the planning phase of a lithotripsy, optimizing the applied strategy (Weinberg 2008). The same applies for real-time simulations using robots for operations on hip joints (Caetano da Rosa 2013) or the prostate. Much the same is true for multi-agent simulations of segregation habits prevalent in metropolitan areas, which, when based on explicitly counterfactual assumptions, still yield a highly accurate prognosis/performance (see Gottschalk-Mazouz 2012, p. 21ff). In fluid mechanics, the counterfactual assumption that the viscosity of the medium located near a shockwave spreading at supersonic velocity is raised precipitously ("artificial viscosity," cf. Caramana et al. 1998) has been used in construction for more than 50 years. The success of this method of construction has *ipso facto* justified the use of models based on method and on comparable results. The construction process is a showcase for the success of using these simulation models (Winsberg 2006).

Previously, reference has been made to the relative stability of a successful outcome when all conditions are stable. The reliable simulation results are a required condition for pragmatically relevant system qualities (e.g., tipping points). Even a reference to the instability of certain specific types of systems does not conflict with this goal.

Contrary to the related view that a stable success of action justifies the conceptualizing of simulation steps, certain arguments point to the indispensable use of simulations, for example in astrophysics. In this context, simulation modelling is guided by an understanding of causality that does not rely on the ideal of experimental interventionism. Consequently, it does not exhibit any scope of definition for criteria where "success" means "success of action." The same applies for problems which cannot be addressed by performing empirical tests for moral, economic, or other reasons. In such tests, *ceteris paribus*, the effects of manipulation are scrutinized relative to its claims of being necessary (or altogether sufficient) conditions that can be balanced.[4] For the vast and indispensable field of "creative" simulations," the rule applies that between simulated situations and the real present of future situations, whose recording would have to be evaluated by pragmatic criteria, a pragmatic theory of truth cannot yet be implemented because the real situation does not (yet) exist. Which definition and which criteria of truth should be applied here? Should an adjustment be made for the requirements of a pragmatic theory of truth?

Even for those in favor of the pro-arguments, there remains the need for some justification, since the reference to "stability of a success of actions" is relevant only under *ceteris paribus* conditions. The intended efforts' lack of success or failure (because the methods were conceived for a different area of expertise) are quite possible when an individual or a situation deviates from presumed standards.

It becomes apparent that the realm of reflection needs to be extended to allow for a transgression from the constraints of a basic pragmatic theory of truth. On the one hand, the theory needs to fulfill its performance in a certain field, and, on the other hand, the documented shortcomings of its implementation have to be accounted for. These shortfalls, due to derivations from standards, are part of the remaining risks and uncertainties, and are furthermore the result of a lack of validation options per se that could refer back to the stability of the expected success of simulation actions. Consequently, the problems on both sides are temporalized by assumptions which cannot be addressed directly by correction models under pragmatic criteria. Conclusively, an examination of the relevance of a pragmatic attitude facing possible errors in simulation research, that is, a pragmatic theory of error, should be elaborated to give support to a pragmatic theory of truth and correct its deficits.

---

[4]Which means that not all toy simulations are accounted for pragmatically.

7 An Amendment: The Pragmatic Theory of Error

The discussion of definitions and criteria of truth is now raised to a higher level. Supposing that the old question of "truth" or "falsehood" focused on objective propositions, that is, assumptions about the state of an area, the question of "right" or "erroneous" is now directed at the recording of sources relative to such error or correctness (e.g., validation strategies recorded as correct or false). The view is raised to a higher level of judgement and validation, shifting from object-oriented observations to real and possible facts. For simulation research, such a theory of error focuses with pragmatic intent on criteria relevant to handling possible errors, when the question is which simulation strategy should be favored in view of possible errors. Constraints which limit the space of error (relative to our varying state of knowledge) would be assumptions about possibly relevant non-knowledge (relative to our interest of being able to act). This is especially true for effects regarding our readiness to even approach new possible risks (risk potentials/meta risks; the same is true for opportunities). The next objective is to find criteria that guarantee on a higher scale the justifi*ability* of actions and decisions when dealing with simulation results. Because an orientation towards stability, or the ability to plan and repeat successful, objective-oriented actions, is no longer a viable option, the problem of how to guarantee the ability to act needs to be addressed. The focus is now *either* on the possibility of orienting the search toward action results, probing their evaluation, assessment, modification, correction, compensation, and future omission (risk and opportunity management) *or* on attempt to test alternatives for all cases in which the possibility of an error cannot be excluded (Hubig 2015, pp. 196–205).

For this task, the classic distinction between real and optional values is the point of reference. Real values are integrated into objective, pragmatic criteria of validity (the discussion of whether values determine performance or vice versa shall not be resumed here). Optional values refer to the possibility or perpetuation, shift, and modification of real value attributes (i.e., the confirmation of real values with which object-layered, pragmatic truth criteria are concerned). In regard to this distinction, we are faced in the most general sense with a problem of optional value (Hubig 2007, pp. 137–146). To be more precise: If the intent is pragmatic, the main objective must be guaranteed to assume real value attributes. Similar to extending the capacity to act with an objective level of orientation rather than a simple pragmatic criterion, the emphasis is now on a guarantee of the ability to act, framed by the possible challenge of error during prognostication and during the assessment of performance. This criterion must not be mistaken for the simple claim that widening of the scope of action is the only point at issue (Foerster 1993).

The higher level reflection called for, then, consists in a weighting of moral, economic, and social burdens of action-guiding, but possibly erroneous simulation results. To uncover the inner structure of the task implicit in such an assessment (cf. Betz and Cacean 2012 with a deviating, but similarly plausible suggestion for structure), the following instances would have to be considered: First, the

distinction needs to be made between the identification of the problem characteristic of "inductive" simulations, which develops a "storyline" of chances and risks
in the framework of probabilities on the one hand and "creative" simulations on the
other, which transgresses pure calculation and also pursues possibilities in the
background of our knowledge, such as, for example, simulation-supported scenario
development.

In cross-reference to this lead difference, there could be possible erroneous
false-positive findings as a claim of non-exclusion of usage or damage that does
not occur. This needs to be differentiated from possible erroneous false-negative
findings as exclusion or mistakes in usage and damage that occurs nonetheless.
Again, in cross-reference to this inner differentiation, there would be on each side
of the equation high costs of error/charges (including opportunity costs) versus low
costs of error/charges (including opportunity costs) to be factored in. This way, a set
of paths for consideration emerges that can function as a working to-do list for the
treatment of possible errors.

It would be beyond the scope of this presentation to introduce the entire
normative dimension (this would require the development of an engineering ethics
of simulation, which is, however, only just beginning; for example, see Betz and
Cacean 2012). Therefore, only the contour or possible outline for a solution can be
elaborated here. There are many good reasons for favoring a false/erroneous
warning over a false/erroneous deceptive certainty. This view is not implied in
the "killer argument" developed by Hans Jonas in the framework of his *Heuristics
of Fear* (Jonas 1984; hereto Hubig 2015, p. 191). In his work, he recommends that
situations affected by error adopt the worst possible prognosis and to avoid planning actions predicted by such prognoses. Following the assessments shown above,
several interim plans unfold. The basic rule for favoring a certain simulation
strategy, as has been proposed here, is a result of the conclusion that investments
in prevention, representing the practical application of this rule, have an altogether
higher optional value than defense, repair, or compensation investments. These
become mandatory if the occurrence of damage is excluded by error and only is
recorded in a regular real-value balance sheet. Furthermore, investments in prevention guarantee the maintenance and future availability of goods whose real value
can be never fully pre-assessed. Beyond that, they ensure that the possibilities for
activity and the use of available means are not excluded (based on error) under
altered preferences. They fulfill a vital role due to their usual multi-functionality
applications, for example, in the technical realm in the wake of climate protection
(increase in efficacy and efficiency), in the social realm (protection and development of sustainable work places), in economics (favoring long-term over short-term
profits and quarter-year balances), in the moral realm (maintaining negative and
positive liberties by minimizing factual constraints, crisis-related-pressures, or the
limitation of elementary human rights, such as the rights to life and health), and
many more. Hence, the spectrum of areas susceptible to error can be examined
relative to the status of the simulations (inductive or creative), to the candidates of
error (false-positive or false-negative), and to the costs associated with possible

errors (high or low). These can enter into the light of critical reflection under a pragmatic theory of error as an extension of the pragmatic theory of truth.

References

Ashby, Ross W. 1974. *Einführung in die Kybernetik*. Frankfurt a. M.: Suhrkamp.
Bacon, Francis. 1963. *Dist. Operis. The Works of Francis Bacon*. Repr., Stuttgart: Fromann-Holzboog.
Betz, Gregor, and Sebastian Cacean. 2012. *Ethical Aspects of Climate Engineering*. Karlsruhe: KIT Scientific Publishing.
Bungartz, Hans-Joachim, Stefan Zimmer, Martin Buchholz, and Dirk Pflüger. 2013. *Modellbildung und Simulation: Eine anwendungsorientierte Einführung*. 2nd ed. Berlin and Heidelberg: Springer, Springer Spektrum.
Caetano da Rosa Caterina, 2013. *Operationsroboter in Aktion. Kontroverse Innovationen in der Medizinethik*. Bielefeld: Transcript.
Caramana, E. J., M. J. Shashkov, and P. P. Whalen. 1998. Formulations of Artificial Viscosity for Multi-Dimensional Shock Wave Computations. *Journal of Computational Physics* 144: 70–97.
Foerster, Heinz von. 1993. *KybernEthik*. Berlin: Merve.
Frigg, Roman, and Julian Reiss. 2009. The philosophy of simulation: hot new issues or same old stew. *Synthese* 169 (3): 593–613.
Goodman, Nelson. 1983. *Fact, Fiction and Forecast*. 2nd ed. Cambridge MA: Harvard University Press.
Gottschalk-Mazouz, Niels. 2012. Toy Modelling: Warum gibt es (immer noch) sehr einfache Modelle in den empirischen Wissenschaften? In *Die Reflexion des Möglichen. Zur Dialektik von Handeln, Erkennen und Werten*, ed. Peter Fischer, Andreas Luckner and Ulrike Ramming, 17–30. FS Christoph Hubig, Münster: LIT.
Gramelsberger, Gabriele. 2007. Computersimulation in den Wissenschaften. Neue Instrumente der Wissensproduktion. In *Wissensproduktion und Wissenstransfer. Wissen im Spannungsfeld von Wissenschaft, Politik und Öffentlichkeit*, ed. Renate Mayntz, Friedhelm Neidhardt, Peter Weingart and Ulrich Wengenroth, 75–94. Bielefeld: Transcript.
Hubig, Christoph. 2006. *Die Kunst des Möglichen*, vol. 1, *Technikphilosophie als Reflexion der Medialität*. Bielefeld: Transcript.
Hubig, Christoph. 2007. *Die Kunst des Möglichen*, vol. 2, *Ethik der Technik als provisorische Moral*. Bielefeld: Transcript.
Hubig, Christoph. 2015. *Die Kunst des Möglichen*, vol. 3, *Macht der Technik*. Bielefeld: Transcript.
Husserl, Edmund. 1962. *Die Krisis der europäischen Wissenschaften und die transzendentale Phänomenologie*. vol. 6 of *Husserliana: Gesammelte Werke*. Den Haag: Martinus Nijhof.
Husserl, Edmund. 1970. *Philosophie der Arithmetik*. vol. 12 of *Husserliana: Gesammelte Werke*. Den Haag: Martinus Nijhof.
Jonas, Hans. 1984. *Das Prinzip Verantwortung. Versuch einer Ethik für die technologische Zivilisation*. Frankfurt a. M.: Suhrkamp.
Kaminski, Andreas, Uwe Küster, Michael Resch, and Björn Schembera. 2016. Simulation als List. In *List und Tod. Jahrbuch Technikphilosophie 2016*, ed. Gerhard Gamm, Petra Gehring, Christoph Hubig, Andreas Kaminski and Alfred Nordmann, 93–121. Zürich und Berlin: Diaphanes.
Kant, Immanuel. [1781/1787] 2009. Critique of pure reason [=CpV]. 15. print. ed. and transl. by Paul Guyer and Allen W. Wood. Cambridge: Cambridge University Press.
Lenhard, Johannes. 2015. Kann Technik die Naturgesetze verändern? Zu den technischen Erfolgsbedingungen fundamentaler Gesetze. In *Ding und System. Jahrbuch Technikphilosophie 2015*, ed. Gerhard Gamm, Petra Gehring, Christoph Hubig, Andreas Kaminski and Alfred Nordmann, 171–186. Zürich und Berlin: Diaphanes.

Lenhard, Johannes, and Hans Hasse. 2017. Fluch und Segen: Die Rolle anpassbarer Parameter in Simulationsmodellen. In *Technisches Nichtwissen. Jahrbuch Technikphilosophie 2017*, ed. Alexander Friedrich, Petra Gehring, Christoph Hubig, Andreas Kaminski and Alfred Nordmann, 69–84. Baden-Baden: Nomos.

Morrison, Margaret. 2015. *Reconstructing reality. Models, mathematics, and simulations*. New York: Oxford University Press.

Oberkampf, William L., and Christopher J. Roy. 2010. *Verification and validation in scientific computing*. Cambridge: Cambridge University Press.

Oberkampf, William L., and T. G. Trucano. 2002. *Verification and Validation in Computational Fluid Dynamics*. In *Progress in Aerospace Sciences* 38 (3): 209–272.

Reisch, Gregor. 1503. *Margarita philosophica*. Freiburg: Schott.

Roache, P. J. 1998. *Verification and Validation in Computational Science and Engineering*. Albuquerque, NM: Hermosa Publishers.

Russell, Bertrand. 1912. On the Notion of Cause. In *Proceedings of the Aristotelian Society* 13: 1–26.

Schiemann, Gregor and Kristian Köchy. 2006. *Natur im Labor. Philosophia naturalis* 43 (1).

Schlaudt, Oliver. 2014. *Was ist empirische Wahrheit? Perspektiven pragmatischer Wahrheitstheorie zwischen Naturalismus und Kritizismus*. Frankfurt a.M.: Klostermann.

von der Weiden, Silvia. 2015. Blutflussmessungen im virtuellen Organ. *VDI-Nachrichten* 35/36, August 28.

Weinberg, Kerstin. 2008. Modelling and numerical simulation of kidney damaging side effects in shock wave lithotripsy. In *8th Wolrd Congress on Computational mechanics WCCM8*, ed. Bernhard A. Schrefler and Umberto Perego. CIMNE.

Winsberg, Eric. 2010. *Science in the age of computer simulation*. Chicago and London: University of Chicago Press.

Winsberg, Eric. 2006. Models of Success versus Success of Models: Reliability without Truth. *Synthese* 152: 1–19.

Wissenschaftsrat. 2014. *Bedeutung und Weiterentwicklung von Simulation in der Wissenschaft. Positionspapier Drs. 4032–14*. Dresden: WR.

Wittgenstein, Ludwig. 1972. *On Certainty*. New York: Harper.

The Demon's Fallacy: Simulation Modeling and a New Style of Reasoning

Johannes Lenhard

Abstract Simulation is based on the vast increase in computational power that is available to researchers. This increase, however, does not by itself characterize simulation. What philosophically matters are the *conceptual* ramifications. Simulation modeling combines extant concepts in a new way. It intertwines different types of experiments and in this way gives rise to a new combinatorial style of reasoning. The argument in favor of this thesis discusses two exemplars of simulation, namely thermodynamics and quantum chemistry. The conclusion reflects upon some of the resulting challenges for the philosophy of science.

1 Introduction

Does computer simulation change the forms of scientific reasoning? While the daily work of many scientists already testifies to the fact that the computer changes scientific practice, the exact nature and scope of these changes remain contested. The philosophy of science has put forward various theses to address these issues.[1] Prominent among them is the controversial discussion around experiments and whether simulation and computer experiments constitute a new kind of experiment. Another, related, line of thinking starts from tractability. According to it, simulation approaches offer innovative ways to broaden or deepen the realm of mathematical tractability. Simulations open up pathways for how to compute, or approximate, mathematical entities, like solutions to a system of equations. Based on simulations, researchers can tackle questions formerly conceived to be out of reach.

It is philosophically tempting to generalize this observation and to characterize computer simulation by its ability to bring within reach what was formerly out of reach. According to this viewpoint, simulation is enlarging the realm of tractability and hence can be taken as an achievement of *computational power*. I would like to

---

[1]Among the standard sources for getting an overview are Winsberg (2014), Parker (2013), Humphreys (2012), and Lenhard (2015, Einleitung).

J. Lenhard (✉)
Department of Philosophy, University of Bielefeld, Universitätsstr. 25, Postfach 100131, 33501 Bielefeld, Germany
e-mail: johannes.lenhard@uni-bielefeld.de

© Springer International Publishing AG 2017
M.M. Resch et al. (eds.), *The Science and Art of Simulation I*,
DOI 10.1007/978-3-319-55762-5_10

call this the gym-picture. Though this picture seems to be straightforward, it is philosophically dangerous, because it obscures interesting *conceptual* changes related to simulation. And in fact, a widely held view on computer simulation sees it as directly descending from classical mathematized science. According to this view, the computer increases the power for calculations and in this way helps to provide a new flowering for the classical form of mathematized sciences. True, computational power is a pillar on which simulation rests, but the *conceptual* ramifications are what philosophically matter. In this chapter, I want to oppose the gym-picture and argue that it throws a misleading light on simulation. Trusting this light means to commit "the Demon's fallacy." Only once one has become aware of the fallacy can one appreciate how simulation affects the form of scientific reasoning.

The chapter proceeds as follows. First, I clarify the established classical (or gym-) viewpoint about mathematical modeling (Sect. 2), which squarely coincides with what has been called rational mechanics. This picture serves as a contrastive background against which I put forward an alternative viewpoint. The main thesis is that the pivotal concept of computer simulation is combination rather than analysis. Simulation modeling intertwines different sorts of experiments and in this way gives rise to a new combinatorial style of reasoning (Sect. 3). The argument in favor of this thesis discusses two exemplars of simulation. After reviewing the basic methodology of simulation modeling (Sect. 4), Sect. 5 briefly introduces thermodynamics and quantum chemistry as two issues where simulation thrives on the combinatorial style. The conclusion reflects upon some of the resulting challenges for the philosophy of science.

2   The Classic Viewpoint: Rational Mechanics

The importance of mathematical modeling for science is widely acknowledged. Mathematics and mathematical tools have shaped modern science since its beginnings. The story of the scientific revolution and the formation of modern science in the sixteenth and seventeenth centuries is familiar to all.[2] The vision to synthesize observation, experiment, and mathematical knowledge deeply influenced philosopher-scientists of such different stripes as Descartes, Galileo, Kepler, and Leibniz. Newton's theory of gravitation, set forth in his *Philosophiae Naturalis Principia Mathematica*, is arguably the paradigm and epitome of modern science. He showed how analyzing mathematically formulated laws allowed to describe motion on earth as well as in the heavens. Newton was able to derive Kepler's somewhat mysterious empirical laws of planetary movement from his own laws that were not only simpler, but also universal, applying to planets and apples alike.

---

[2]Dijksterhuis (1961), Koyré (1968), or Drake and Drabkin (1969) are classical sources about the nature and impact of mathematization.

In short, Newton's approach to mathematical modeling was commonly acknowledged to be superbly successful.

This approach held great promise, namely of finding a rational structure that would allow for a general mastery of physical dynamics by mathematical means. Mechanics quickly became the paradigm of science (though the name "science" was not yet in use) and, moreover, deeply influenced the picture of scientific rationality. Following the Newtonian paradigm and making it applicable to all phenomena is a program that has been called "rational mechanics." In a sense, the program of rational mechanics was to enlarge the Newtonian paradigm so that it would cover the entirety of the sciences. This program gained currency over the course of a century and was championed by Pierre-Simon Laplace (1749–1827), who combined his excellence as mathematician and astronomer with his influence in the scientific and political establishment (cf. Fox 1996 on the Laplacian program).

Laplace's opus magnum is the *Traité de Mécanique Céleste*, which appeared between 1799 and 1823 in five volumes. There, Laplace significantly developed the mathematical analytical apparatus, with the goal of asking and answering refined questions in the framework of rational mechanics. The mathematical details will not be discussed here, but it is important to keep in mind that mathematical tools work only in particular circumstances—Newton, for instance, had to treat planets as point masses.

The whole point of differential and integral calculus is that it is the right kind of instrument for analyzing the interplay of laws that capture the dynamics of a system in the form of differential equations. The goal, then, is to derive a formula—a "solution" for these equations—so that one can specify the particular conditions and the equation spits out the solution. If scientists had something like this in their hands, they could bring natural processes under their control.

This is the promise of rational mechanics, as based on mathematics (calculus). This tool, however, can only be of use under certain strict conditions. Given that a set of (partial) differential equations expresses the dynamics of some system, determining the solution requires knowing the exact initial and boundary conditions. Furthermore, actually obtaining quantitative results obviously also requires numerical evaluation. Both might be critical hurdles. Laplace himself, in a famous passage of his *Essai philosophique sur les probabilités*, expressed the point in the following way:

> We ought then to regard the present state of the universe as the effect of its anterior state and as the cause of the one which is to follow. Given for one instant an intelligence which could comprehend all the forces by which nature is animated and the respective situation of the beings who compose it an intelligence sufficiently vast to submit these data to analysis it would embrace in the same formula the movements of the greatest bodies of the universe and those of the lightest atom; for it, nothing would be uncertain and the future, as the past, would be present to its eyes. The human mind offers, in the perfection which it has been able to give to astronomy, a feeble idea of this intelligence. (Laplace 1902, p. 4)

In other words, Laplace is deeply convinced that the structures and laws that govern the workings of nature can be known. In this respect, rational mechanics is a typical standpoint for the Enlightenment. Laplace, however, also expresses the practical problems posed by the limitations of human intelligence that do not allow for making full use of the mathematical structures. Fostering the uses that science can make of these structures is a major challenge. This view is deeply ingrained in the ways we conceive of why and how the hard sciences are hard.

I quoted Laplace above because he suggests exactly the gap that computers are supposed to fill. They are the right instruments to aid human intelligence so that it can perform the necessary analysis. In other words, the computer is exactly that kind of instrument that makes humans more demon-like by boosting their ability for numerical evaluation. This leads us back to the initial question of this text, namely how computer simulation changes scientific reasoning. The suggested answer boils down to a remake of the classic picture, only with vastly increased, that is, more demon-like, technical abilities.

Does simulation, then, lead to a revival of rational mechanics, now coming increasingly closer to fulfilling the promises made by the original program? To answer this question in the affirmative would be a fallacy—"the demon's fallacy."

3 Combination Rather than Analysis

Why, then, should the affirmative answer be a fallacy? Computer methods surely do thrive on increased computational power. Also, this perspective puts computer simulation into an established and long-standing framework. With only moderate overstatement, it sees the computer as a tool for solving problems conceptualized two centuries ago. The demon's fallacy ignores the conceptual transformation that comes with computer simulation. The innovation, then, appears to be restricted to the new mathematics of numerical solutions. This is an interesting and fruitful topic, of course, but it does not exhaust the conceptual richness of simulation.

My main thesis is that this richness includes the following point: Simulations *combine* theoretical, formal, and empirical components in a new and pragmatic way. I will argue that combining these heterogeneous components is key to simulation's success and that combination in a sense replaces the concept of analysis that was so central to rational mechanics. If this is an adequate way of putting the matter—and I think it is—then the capability of combination is not a mere add-on, but signals that simulation modeling is discontinuous with the rational-mechanical picture of mathematical modeling.

I will argue for this thesis by discussing two pertinent examples in the next section. But first let me add a remark on a situation somewhat analogous to the demon's fallacy. The case I am thinking of is a revolution that truly deserves the name—the industrial revolution. It is often said that this revolution was driven by the steam engine, which increased the available working power in many industries. Of course, this power was important, but was it the main driving force? Karl Marx argued in his analyses (on machinery and modern industry, Chap. 13 of the Capital) that the true driver was not the steam engine, but the tool machine, which led to a fundamental re-organization of how labor was conceived and, consequently, how goods were industrially produced.

The first tool machine was allegedly the Spinning Jenny, a multi-spindle spinning frame. The crucial point is that tool machines replaced what had formerly been a task for human hands and skills. To do this required a new perspective on how the working process was organized and, consequently, how it could potentially be re-organized. Such new organization could then also make use of the mechanical power made available by the steam engine.

I do not intend to directly compare the industrial revolution with the impact of computer simulation. The analogy to my thesis should be clear now: In computer simulation, the process of creating and handling mathematical models is fundamentally re-organized by combining known elements in a new (pragmatic) way. More specifically, the computer permits a new way of combination, in that it challenges the established categories of experiment, theory, and, finally, scientific rationality. Since the simulation-related form of rationality deviates significantly from the established form, simulation modeling amounts to a new "style of reasoning" that is aptly called (so I propose) "combinatorial style." "Styles of reasoning" is a term introduced by Ian Hacking (1992), for whom such a style determines what is right or wrong, or rather what it means to be right or wrong. I do not have space here to discuss why "style of reasoning" is an apt term in the context of simulation. Interested readers can find more material on this topic in Lenhard (2016). For now, let it suffice that the following argument gives examples of how simulation modeling exerts the kind of influence Hacking attributes to styles of reasoning.

4 Schema of Simulation Modeling

It might be useful to review some well-known facts about simulation modeling, before the two examples are discussed. This section[3] highlights a particular feature of simulation model development, namely a feedback loop of model adaptation. The pathway of modeling is depicted in Fig. 1 and leads from some phenomenon (of the world) to a theoretical, often mathematical, model x^{mod}, on to a simulation model implemented and run on a computer. The results of the simulation (x^{sim}) can then be compared to measured data (x^{exp}) that might come from regular (empirical) experiments.

Of course, the nature of experiments is a topic of its own and there are a number of recent studies that show how simulation experiments and empirical experiments are interrelated. This interrelation occurs especially when empirical experiments work with simulation models, which raises the question of to what extent measurements are independent from models.[4] I will not enter into this discussion here, but leave it for another occasion.

---

[3]Section 4 has been adapted from joint work with Hans Hasse (Hasse and Lenhard 2017a).
[4]One prominent example is the LHC at CERN, see Merz (2006), or Morrison (2015).

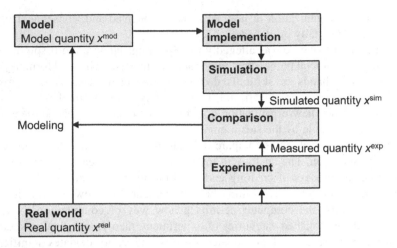

Fig. 1 Schema of simulation modeling, including an arrow pointing to the left and closing the feedback loop of modeling (Courtesy of Hans Hasse)

This paper simply takes the status of x^{exp} for granted and directs attention toward the process of modeling. This process apparently climbs to the level of a theoretical model and then moves top-down through different levels to eventually reach a running program. Philosophers of science have repeatedly scrutinized this movement and have highlighted that there is no straightforward pathway to a running simulation. Simulations cannot be derived from theoretical models—even in those cases where the latter exist. Eric Winsberg (2010), for instance, counts being "motley" among the characteristic properties of simulation. The crucial point in the present context is that the process of simulation modeling in an important way *does not proceed top-down*. Rather, it includes a feedback-loop, as indicated in Fig. 1. In fact, there is even more back-and-forth than indicated in the diagram, but for now, the simple loop suffices.

Although the existence of this loop is not news to anybody who has taken a closer look at simulation modeling, the significance of this loop is widely underappreciated. It is basically a classical feedback control loop, which aims at minimizing the differences between a variable (here: x^{sim}) and a set value (here: x^{exp}). The two quantities that are compared need not be scalar quantities, but may have many entries or be, for example, trajectories over time. There are also many ways of carrying out the comparison.

This feedback loop easily appears as marginal, as a pragmatic handle for fine-tuning and correcting imperfections of the (theoretical and simulation) models. It fulfills, however, a central role. Repeated comparisons between x^{sim} and x^{exp}, i.e. between simulated and measured data, guide the modeling process. During this phase, the model is explored via (simulation) experiments and then modified with the goal of achieving a better fit in the next round of comparisons. We thus have a cooperation of both types of experiments that is the nucleus of model development via adjusting parameters of a model. However, the cooperation becomes even more intertwined when one takes into account that the measured quantities themselves might be partly determined with the help of simulation.

Essentially, simulation modelers have two sorts of actions at their disposal when the comparison does not yield the desired results: (a) They can adapt the model structure, for instance by modifying the equations so that they capture a previously neglected effect; or, (b) they can change the model parameters. This second option is the focus here. Adjustable parameters are arranged in parameterization schemes that can be considered something approximately like auxiliary constructions that are intentionally used for dealing with missing knowledge and the inaccuracies of existing knowledge. The simulation model is *designed* so that it contains parameters that can be adjusted over the course of the further development.

The key feature of adjustable parameters is that they make the model flexible. Adjusting parameters serves to control model behavior without changing the (structure of the) model. I do not claim that the parameter settings are the only pivotal quantities in play, or that they alone would determine model behavior. Rather, this behavior results from how the following components are combined:

- Theory is often crucial for constructing a model in the initial stages. Theory also serves as a platform from which efficient parameterizations can be developed.
- Experimentally measured data are crucial for obtaining criteria for comparisons.
- Adjustable parameters are crucial for achieving a reasonable fit between x^{sim} and x^{exp}.

The overall success is based on how these elements get *combined*, much like the strength of a rope is based on how the single strands are twisted.[5]

The reader might ask whether these observations about adjusting parameters are in fact important in order to appreciate simulation. The question is fitting and I will try to convince the reader of a positive answer by discussing two examples in the next section.

5 The Argument by Way of Two Examples[6]

5.1 Equations of State in Thermodynamics

The first example is thermodynamics, one of the exemplars of a well-grounded theory in physics. The basic and also best known equation of state is that of the ideal gas

---

[5]For an elaboration of the bundle-rope argument, consult Hasse and Lenhard (2017b).

[6]The examples are adapted from Hasse and Lenhard (2017a) and Lenhard (2014), respectively. Both papers offer more detailed argumentation than is possible here.

$$p\,v = R\,T \qquad (1)$$

where p stands for pressure, $v = V/n$ the molar volume (volume per mole of substance), and T is the temperature measured in Kelvin. This equation expresses the relationship between pressure, temperature, and volume. The general form of an equation of state is

$$f(p, v, T) = 0 \qquad (2)$$

All the quantities (p,v,T) are measurable in classical experiments; and R is a universal constant $(8.314 \text{ J mol}^{-1} \text{ K}^{-1})$. It is known that all substances fulfill Eq. (1) if the density $\rho = 1/v$ is low enough (or the molar volume v is large enough)—that makes R universal. The ideal gas equation is a wonderful exemplar of rational mechanics, giving the functional dependency (2) a universal and simple mathematical form.

However, the equation is 'ideal' in that it takes for granted that the particles are so diluted that they do not interact with each other. When thermodynamics is useful in scientific practice—which it definitely is—it has to account for non-ideal conditions, i.e. for interactions of many kinds. This is done by introducing parameters that modify the functional dependency in an adequate and effective way. I want to argue that even in theory-based simulations, like in thermodynamics, adjustable parameters do more than smooth out minor deviations when a theory is applied. Instead, they take on a main role in determining model behavior.

The next-simplest examples of equations of state are the van der Waals equation:

$$p = \frac{RT}{v - b} - \frac{a}{v^2} \qquad (3)$$

and the Virial equation of state in the following form:

$$\frac{pv}{RT} = 1 + B\frac{1}{v} + C\frac{1}{v^2}. \qquad (4)$$

The researchers who introduced these equations, J.D. van der Waals and H. Kammerlingh Onnes received Nobel prizes in 1910 and 1913, respectively. These equations, though both with strong foundations in physics and mathematics, contain adjustable parameters, namely a and b in Eq. (3) and B and C in Eq. (4). These parameters are not universal across substances, but are needed to account for the individuality of different fluids (e.g. water is different from nitrogen). The parameters are not even necessarily simple numbers, but can also be functions of variables. The theory behind Eq. (4), for instance, yields that B and C are functions of temperature, but not of pressure. In the original version of Eq. (3), a and b were numbers. However, in later versions of Eq. (3), *a* was considered to be a function of temperature. Adjusting functions is obviously more flexible than adjusting numbers.

What is the point of introducing these equations of increasing complexity? They illustrate that even the very first steps beyond the ideal Eq. (1) involve parameters. The parameterized equations like (3) or (4) do not work with universal parameters, but with highly specific ones, dependent on the substance at hand (mixtures of pure substances open up a practically unlimited space) as well as on the conditions, such as temperature. Nevertheless, equations like (3) or (4) are great theoretical achievements, as is aptly documented by the Nobel prizes. The parameters there can be interpreted to express pairwise interactions of molecules and, for a long time, fitting these parameters to experimental data was the only way to extract information about molecular interactions. In a way, the particular achievement of Eqs. (3) and (4) is finding a parameter scheme that is informative and tractable.

This task looks very different when seen from a simulation perspective. Automation via the computer can utilize the feedback loop in a new and systematic way. One can introduce many more parameters and adapt them to a great variety of circumstances. Such practices made thermodynamics informative about the behavior of an enormous number of substances. At the same time, its success raises interesting new issues:

1. One can observe that equations of state proliferate: More than 400 equations of state are in use, a veritable "flood of flavors" tailor-fit to particular substances and conditions. It is common that up-to date equations have 30 or more parameters, whose adjustment presents a task that clearly cannot be tackled by non-computer methods. On the top of this, there is the question of how mixtures of substances behave. Mixing rules express the properties of mixtures in terms the properties of the single substances. Normally, such mixing rules are of a heuristic nature. In principle, one could evaluate their adequacy by testing them against measured data. In practice, however, there is a combinatorial explosion of possible mixtures of substances according to different fractions that forestalls any rigorous test scheme.

2. There is a philosophical point about why first-principle predictions are impossible on the basis of equations of state. Or, more precisely, why the term 'first principles' is not adequate in this context. Of course, no mathematical model ever perfectly matches some phenomenon under investigation. Introducing unassigned adjustable parameters is intended to compensate for the slippage. The van der Waals Eq. (3), for example, does not include attractive forces between particles, but contains the parameter "a" that effectively lumps all sorts of attractive forces together, no matter what their exact origin and properties are. And this does not matter, since adjusting the parameter against known data does not require more detailed knowledge. This equation therefore has included some semi-empirical component in its fundaments. From this point onwards, scientists working with this equation cannot claim to use a first-principle approach.

3. It is worthwhile to recall that the van der Waals Equation is much more theoretical than recent many-parameter equations. There are many examples in which parameters do not allow any physical interpretation. One instance out of many is when mixtures of liquids are modeled as if the molecules would be arranged on a lattice, although it is known that liquids are not arranged in this way. Also, in such model interaction energies are fitted, but are never physical. Such parameters, in a sense, combine (physical) interaction energies with inadequacies of the model, and the parameter fit indicates some balance between these partly unknown factors.

4. A further issue is parameters of the implementation. There is a host of potential influences that the particular implementation might have on the simulation's outcome. Two simulation models on the same theoretical basis might differ in the type of discretization, or in the parameters the numerical solvers work with during the process of (automated) adjustment. Even if such parameters significantly increase the performance, they also pose a great threat to simulation, because they depend on the implementation and not on the theoretical model. I will not address that problem here.

Overall, theory alone cannot account for practical success. The theory certainly has a large share, but it is always theory plus adjustment that shoulders the work. Over the course of parameter adjustment—i.e. over the course of the feedback loop in modeling—experiment, mathematical modeling, and simulation have been combined. This combination depends on the particular features of measured data, of parameterization schemes, of the chosen discretization strategy, and so on. All these factors are closely entangled while adjustment and modification are iterated. This combination can hardly be disentangled afterwards and hence it is hard, or rather impossible, to attribute model behavior to one of the factors.

5.2 Quantum Chemistry

The second example deals with quantum chemistry and, in particular, with density functional theory (DFT), which has experienced a remarkable upswing since the mid-1990s. In the nineteenth and early twentieth centuries, chemistry had been firmly established as a discipline with a strong experimental culture, considered to be profoundly different from the rational-theoretical branch of physics. The difference was called into question when the new quantum theory was formulated, and in particular when Schrödinger published his wave equation in 1926. This equation details the electronic structure of atoms and molecules, which in turn determines their chemical properties, like bond energies. Hence, quantum theory seemed to establish a bridge between theoretical physics and chemistry. Shouldn't one be able to *compute* chemical properties from the Schrödinger equation?

More accurately, it was not clear then whether the potential new field would lean more toward chemistry or physics. The early name of "chemical physics" indicates the somewhat combinatorial nature of what later became known as quantum chemistry. In fact, two views of how the combination of physics and chemistry should work opposed each other. The first camp can be called "principled theory" and foregrounds the physics side, while the second camp is often referred to as "semi-empirical" and brought in the experimental traditions from chemistry. Both flourished from the start, that is, shortly after the Schrödinger equation was published. Simply put, semi-empirical approaches, advocated by Linus Pauling among others, led the field in its first decades. With the increasing availability of the computer, so-called *ab initio* methods, which wanted to rely on computation alone and avoid recourse to empirically measured values, became more influential.

The development of quantum chemistry is full of interesting twists and turns. These have been well researched in history of science, cf. Mary Joe Nye (1993) and the monograph *Neither Physics Nor Chemistry* by Kostas Gavroglu and Ana Simões (2012), which cover the history up to the late 1960s. Both end their narratives with the establishment of quantum chemistry as a subfield of chemistry.

I want to look at what has happened more recently. Computational quantum chemistry has experienced a remarkable upswing since about 1990. Among quantum chemists, there is widespread agreement on the special role that density functional theory plays in a couple of *ab initio* methods: "The truly spectacular development in this new quantum chemical era is density functional theory (DFT)" (Barden and Schaefer 2000, p. 1415).

DFT had its origins in the 1960s in condensed matter physics and had continued to be an influential theory in physics since then, though marginalized in chemistry. However, around 1990, an avalanche of applications were developed in chemistry. In the timespan of a few years, scientific papers on DFT went up from around 30 per year to a level of several thousand. This increase is still going on: The web of science data report about 15,000 papers were published in 2015.

What made DFT so tremendously attractive in scientific practice? The following analysis argues that the success of DFT is based on a twist in the conception of computational modeling that now includes adaptive feedback loops between (tentative) models and known empirical data. The findings will be very much in line with those of the first example (thermodynamics).

First, a brief introduction to DFT. Quantum chemistry deals with the *electronic structure* of atoms and molecules. DFT is a theory of this structure that circumvents the problem of solving the computationally overly-complex Schrödinger equation. DFT expresses the energy in a different way, namely in terms of the (joint) electron density—the more likely electrons are to visit a certain location in space, the higher the density. The density, therefore, is an object in space and has only three degrees of freedom.

The theoretical condensed matter physicist Walter Kohn played a major part in advancing this approach to the level of theory. He and his colleague Pierre Hohenberg formulated the two founding theorems (Hohenberg and Kohn 1964) that specify that the ground state energy E is indeed uniquely determined by the corresponding electron density $\rho(r)$, that is, E is a function (only) of $\rho(r)$: $E = E(\rho(r))$.

Thus, the energy can be calculated without reference to the Schrödinger equation, at least in principle.

There is, however, a great practical problem, because the reported 1964 results proved merely that there exists a function f that gives the energy and that is dependent only on the electron density.[7] While the energy entirely depends on the form of this function, the theorem does not indicate what that function looks like or how it can be determined. The space of mathematical functions is extremely large, definitely larger than a haystack, hence to actually determine one particular function might be very difficult.

Kohn was aware of this shortcoming and in the following year he introduced, together with his co-worker Liu Sham, a practical computational scheme (Kohn and Sham 1965). This scheme postulates a reference system of N non-interacting electrons—a deliberately counterfactual assumption—moving in a (hypothetical) effective external potential $v_s(r)$, the so-called Kohn-Sham potential. This is an attempt to deal with the unknown functional relationship by (counterfactually) assuming an idealized situation. It does so to place a numerical handle on the problem of how to approximate the unknown functional and has been the main basis for most of the recent developments in DFT.

The mentioned 1964 and 1965 publications were—and still are—immensely influential papers. One can see this from bibliometrical evidence: They are the single two most highly cited papers ever that appeared in the flagship journal *Physical Review*. Eventually, in 1998, Kohn received the Nobel prize "for his development of density functional theory." The reader might wonder how this story about theoretical physics in the 1960s can possibly throw light upon the 1990s turn in computational quantum chemistry.

The first step toward an answer is the observation that Kohn, a theoretical physicist, received a Nobel prize in chemistry (to his own surprise). The Kohn-Sham potential had been accepted as a workable scheme that provided (approximated) functionals, useful in solid state physics, but not good enough to predict properties of chemical interest. What triggered the success was the exploratory option that opened up for simulation modeling when computers became easily and cheaply available.

How does DFT circumvent the complexity of the Schrödinger equation? After all, the interaction of electrons is the main reason for computational complexity, since any proposed first step in an approximation scheme might be dependent on quantities determined in later steps. Such interaction does in fact take place and hence, electron exchange and correlation effects have to be included in DFT in some way or another. The approximation scheme of Kohn and Sham makes the crucial assumption about the effective potential—an idealizing and deliberately false assumption that greatly simplifies the computational task.

---

[7]The density itself is a function and functions of functions are often called functionals—hence the name "density functional."

What are the ramifications of such modeling assumptions? Given that the (real) exchange and correlation effects can be included in the (hypothetical) potentials to a sufficiently appropriate degree, how are they specified in the context of the model, that is, which (computationally tractable) mathematical form has this potential and, furthermore, which parameter values should be chosen?

The predictive quality of early functionals was only moderate. They employed only a few parameters, often justified by mean value considerations. These functionals were in use, because they were 'computationally cheap' and the low level of adaptability was not a great concern for physicists, particularly for crystallographers whose materials possess highly regular structures. In chemistry, substances are typically much more irregular, requiring a closer approximation, and DFT's predictive quality was, in general, too low to be useful.

This situation changed, however, around 1990, when a number of new functionals became available, all of them with a relatively high number of adaptable parameters. Adjusting these functionals calls for an exploratory mode of modeling that uses extensive feedback loops to adapt parameters and steer model behavior to match known cases. Thus—and this is the key point—we have a two-tiered computational model with a functional that is motivated by theoretical considerations (tier one), but not fully specified by them. The specification, i.e. the adaptation of parameters (tier two), is done via iterative and exploratory studies; in other words, by adjusting parameters.

Like in the first example of equation of state, adapting parameters is more than trial and error. It starts from a highly elaborated parameterization scheme. The widely used functionals of Becke, Parr, Perdew, and others can be seen as ingenious proposals for adequate and tractable parameter schemes. DFT exhibits the very same issues that were noted in the first example. I can repeat the list without changing much:

1. One can observe that functionals proliferate: More than a 100 software packages are on the market, and so-called hybrid approaches allow for the combination of several of them to obtain something like a weighted average.
2. There is a philosophical point about why first-principle predictions are impossible on the basis of DFT. Or, more precisely, why the term *"ab initio"* is not adequate in this context. Adapting the parameters of functionals involves a semi-empirical approach during the process of adjustment, and therefore cannot claim to be a first-principle approach.
3. It is worthwhile to recall that DFT is based on principled theory. Nevertheless, practical success only came with many-parameter functionals, where most parameters do not possess a physical interpretation.
4. A further issue is parameters of the implementation. This is generic for simulation models.

6 Conclusion

Since the last paragraph of 5.1 applies verbatim to 5.2, I offer it again here:

> Overall it is not theory alone that can account for practical success. Surely the theory has a large share, but it is always theory plus adjustment that shoulder the work. Over the course of parameter adjustment – i.e. over the course of the feedback loop in modeling – experiment, mathematical modeling, and simulation have been combined. This combination depends on the particular features of measured data, of parameterization schemes, of the chosen discretization strategy, and so on. All these factors have been closely entangled while adjustment and modification have been iterated. This combination can be hardly be disentangled afterwards and hence it is hard, or rather impossible, to attribute model behavior to one of the factors.

The discussion of both examples should show the very same thing: Combination replaces analysis. Simulation modeling combines theoretical and mathematical modeling with experimentation, notably with both empirical experimentation (data for comparison) and simulation experimentation (feedback loop of adjustment and modification). Whereas simulation thrives on this combination, at the same time, the concept of analysis, so central to rational mechanics, loses significance. The success of simulation modeling hinges on iterated adjustments instead of mathematical derivation, and it proceeds by pragmatic amendments (parameterizations) rather than finding 'the right' mathematical structure. Furthermore, analytical transparency is seriously questioned by the very methodology of simulation, since iterated feedback loops during the modeling process make it hard to attribute particular behavior to particular assumptions.

Yes, the advantage of the computer, i.e. the advantage of simulation modeling over traditional mathematical modeling, is based on the speed with which algorithms are processed. But this does not simply extend the conception of mathematical modeling, but re-structures it in fundamental ways.

References

Barden, Christopher J., and Henry F. Schaefer III. 2000. Quantum chemistry in the 21st century. *Pure and Applied Chemistry* 72 (8): 1405–1423.
Dijksterhuis, Eduard Jan. 1961. *The Mechanization of the World Picture*. London: Oxford University Press.
Drake, Stillman, and I.E. Drabkin. 1969. *Mechanics in Sixteenth-Century Italy. Selections from Tartaglia, Benedetti, Guido Ubaldo, & Galileo*. Madison, Milwaukee and London: The University of Winsconsin Press.
Fox, Robert. 1996. Laplacian Physics. In *Companion To the History of Modern Science*, ed. Robert C. Olby et al., 278–294. London and New York: Routledge.
Gavroglu, Kostas, and Ana Simões. 2012. *Neither physics nor chemistry: a history of quantum chemistry*. Cambridge, MA: MIT Press.
Hacking, Ian. 1992. 'Style' for Historians and Philosophers. *Studies in the History and Philosophy of Science* 23 (1): 1–20.

Hasse, Hans, and Johannes Lenhard. Forthcoming 2017a. On the Role of Adjustable Parameters. In *Mathematics as a Tool*, ed. Johannes Lenhard and Martin Carrier. Boston Studies in History and Philosophy of Science. Dordrecht, Heidelberg, London, New York: Springer.

Hasse, Hans, and Johannes Lenhard. Forthcoming 2017b. Fluch und Segen: Die Rolle anpassbarer Parameter in Simulationsmodellen. In *Technisches Nichtwissen*. Jahrbuch Technikphilosophie 2017, ed. Alexander Friedrich, Petra Gehring, Christoph Hubig, Andreas Kaminski and Alfred Nordmann, 69–84. Baden-Baden: Nomos.

Hohenberg, P., and W. Kohn. 1964. Inhomogeneous electron gas. *Physical Review* 136 (3B): B864–B871.

Humphreys, Paul. 2012. Computational Science. In *Oxford Bibliographies Online*. http://www.oxfordbibliographies.com/view/document/obo-9780195396577/obo-9780195396577-0100.xml. Accessed 26 September 2012.

Kohn, W., and L. J. Sham. 1965. Self-consistent equations including exchange and correlation effects. *Physical Review* 140 (4A): A1133–A1138.

Koyré, Alexandre. 1968. *Metaphysics and Measurement: Essays in the Scientific Revolution*. London: Chapman and Hill.

Laplace, Pierre Simon. 1902. A philosophical essay on probabilities. Trans. Frederick Wilson Truscott and Frederick Lincoln Emory. New York: John Wiley & Sons.

Lenhard, Johannes. 2014. Disciplines, Models, and Computers: The Path To Computational Quantum Chemistry. *Studies in History and Philosophy of Science* Part A, 48: 89–96.

Lenhard, Johannes. 2015. *Mit allem rechnen – zur Philosophie der Computersimulation*. Berlin: de Gruyter.

Lenhard, Johannes. 2016. Computer Simulation. In *Oxford Handbook in the Philosophy of Science*, ed. Paul Humphreys, 717–737. New York, NY: Oxford University Press.

Merz, Martina. 2006. Locating the Dry Lab on the Lab Map. In *Simulation: Pragmatic Construction of Reality*, ed. Johannes Lenhard, Günter Küppers and Terry Shinn, 155–172. Sociology of the Sciences Yearbook, vol. 25. Dordrecht: Springer.

Morrison, Margaret. 2015. *Reconstructing Reality. Models, Mathematics, and Simulations*. New York, NY: Oxford University Press.

Nye, M. J. 1993. *From chemical philosophy to theoretical chemistry*. Berkeley, CA: University of California Press.

Parker, Wendy S. 2013. Computer Simulation. In *The Routledge Companion to Philosophy of Science*, ed. Stathis Psillos and Martin Curd, 135–145. 2nd ed. London and New York: Routledge.

Winsberg, Eric. 2010. *Science in the Age of Computer Simulation*. Chicago, IL: University of Chicago Press.

Winsberg, Eric. 2014. Computer Simulations in Science. In *Stanford Encyclopedia of Philosophy* (Fall 2014 Edition), ed. Edward N. Zalta. http://plato.stanford.edu/archives/fall2014/entries/simulations-science/. Accessed 18 January 2017.

Advancing Knowledge Through Computer Simulations? A Socratic Exercise

Claus Beisbart

Abstract Do computer simulations advance our knowledge and if so, how? This paper approaches these questions by drawing on distinctions and insights from the philosophical study of knowledge. I focus on propositional knowledge obtained by simulations and address two key issues: How do computer simulations give rise to propositional content? And how can we be justified in believing the corresponding propositions? To answer these questions, I describe schematically how propositional content may be constructed from the inputs and outputs of computer simulations. I further argue that this propositional content has an inferential justification. I provide the premises and the conclusion of the inference. But in the end, this inference proves insufficient for knowledge from computer simulation. What is needed too is that there are reasons to believe that the right sort of inference is carried out. This is compatible with a variety of internalism regarding justification and also makes sense of the practice of verification.

1 Introduction

In 2002, Michigan State University launched a campaign with the slogan "Advancing Knowledge, Transforming Lives." (see Pozega Osburn 2002).

Since the campaign with this slogan seems to have run out of steam,[1] we may take the liberty to apply it to computer simulation (CS, for short). To focus on the first part of the slogan, CSs seem to make a significant contribution to the advancement of knowledge. This should be plain even to people who read science news only occasionally. There we often find statements to the effect that CSs have shown this or that. To give just one example out of many, according to a recent report on sciencedaily.com,

---

[1]For instance, we do not find it on the entry of the homepage of the university, checked Oct 2016.

C. Beisbart (✉)
Institute of Philosophy, University of Bern, Länggassstr. 49a, 3000 Bern 9, Switzerland
e-mail: Claus.Beisbart@philo.unibe.ch

© Springer International Publishing AG 2017
M.M. Resch et al. (eds.), *The Science and Art of Simulation I*,
DOI 10.1007/978-3-319-55762-5_11

Computer simulations have shown that offshore wind farms with thousands of wind turbines could have sapped the power of three real-life hurricanes [...]. (Stanford University 2014)

The claim that the CSs have shown this can be aptly characterized as a claim to knowledge: Due to CSs, we now know that ... And it is of course presupposed that we did not know this before.

CSs are thus claimed to provide us with new knowledge. But do they really advance our knowledge? Not all our claims to knowledge need hold true. They may be too hasty, over-optimistic or simply advertisements. And even if the claims to knowledge get it right, we may ask how this knowledge is obtained and thus demand an explanation of knowledge in virtue of CS.

Critically engaging with claims to knowledge is one of the core tasks of philosophy. In the history of Western philosophy, it all started with Socrates, who asked his fellow citizens about what they claimed to know in order to find out whether he was the most knowledgable human being, as Pythia had told one of his friends (Apology of Socrates 21a–23c; see Plato 1977). Famously, Socrates found many claims to knowledge wanting. Other famous philosophers, particularly John Locke, David Hume, and Immanuel Kant followed suit and examined how knowledge can be obtained and what its limits are.

This paper is intended to contribute to this philosophical project with a focus on CS. My main questions are: To what extent can CSs provide new knowledge? And how can they do so? The both questions are intimately related to each other, because the second presupposes that CSs can advance our knowledge, which constrains an answer to the first. Conversely, the first question cannot be addressed without considering the second, because all reasons to say that CSs provide us with knowledge depend on the answer to the second question. To address both questions, I apply philosophical insights about knowledge to CSs. In particular, I draw on definitions of knowledge and on positions called reliabilism, internalism, and externalism.

There is now a rich philosophical literature about CSs,[2] and some authors have addressed CS in relation to knowledge. They have mostly assumed success, that is, taken for granted that CSs produce knowledge and then tried to explain this. In this way, Barberousse et al. (2009, pp. 557–558) ask how CSs can produce desired information (see Stöckler 2000, p. 366 and Beisbart 2012, p. 396 for similar questions). Barberousse et al. (2009) answer this question by comparing CS to experiments (as do Parker 2009 and Morrison 2009, the latter with quite a different result); I compare CS to thought experiment and stress the inferential nature of CS (Beisbart 2012; cf. Stockler 2000). In various papers, Winsberg analyzes the way the results of CSs are justified (Winsberg 1999, 2001, 2003). Despite these works,

---

[2]See in particular Humphreys (2004) and Winsberg (2010) for relevant monographs; Frigg et al. (2009, 2011), and Humphreys and Imbert (2011) for collections and Winsberg (2009, 2015) for overview articles.

the broader issue of how CSs and their results fit the terminology of the philosophical scrutiny of knowledge has not yet been addressed. It is thus time to do so.

Accordingly, this paper is an exercise in relating distinct terminologies to each other—those of the modern sciences to that of the philosophical study of knowledge (called epistemology). My hope is that bringing the terms from both worlds together allows for a fresh look at CS and a better understanding of it.

To begin with, I introduce some basic terminology and recall crucial distinctions from epistemology (Sect. 2). I then address the question of what sort of content knowledge through CS may have (Sect. 3). A necessary condition of knowledge is justification or some suitable substitute for it. I address the question of how results from CS are justified in Sect. 4. Section 5 takes stock.

2 Knowledge

To begin, what do we know about knowledge quite generally?

Philosophers like to distinguish between *knowledge that* and *knowledge how* (e.g., Ryle 1945, p. 4). To give an example of the former, we know that there are infinitely many prime numbers. This type of knowledge is also called propositional; it has a proposition as its content, where a proposition is what is meant by an assertive statement. This explains why the content of propositional knowledge can be expressed in terms of a that-clause. Propositional knowledge is the sort of knowledge that can be written up in books and research papers. By contrast, knowledge how, for instance, the knowledge how to ride a bicycle, is more practical and manifests itself in action.

In this paper, I focus on propositional knowledge. This is very natural because science is aimed at this knowledge, at least among other things, and a lot of scientific results, most notably theories, can be expressed in terms of assertive statements. Furthermore, what science news report is propositional knowledge (at least if the claims to knowledge prove correct). Also, propositional knowledge has been at the center of much work in epistemology. This is why I restrict this paper to knowledge *that*. This is of course not to deny that knowledge *how* is important in science quite generally and for CS more specifically. Carrying out a computer simulation study certainly presupposes a lot of know-how; for instance, the computer simulation scientist has to know how to implement a certain approximation scheme in a computer program, how to set the values for various parameters that need to be fixed in the program, etc. Without such know-how, it would be impossible to obtain any propositional knowledge from computer simulations. Whenever we call CS an art, we refer to such know-how. Nevertheless, in this paper, my focus is on propositional knowledge.

What is propositional knowledge? According to what is often called the traditional or JTB analysis of knowledge (which is given in Plato's "Theaetetus", Plato 2015, 201c–201d), it is justified true belief. That is, an agent knows that something is the case, if and only if she believes this to be the case if she is justified in believing so, and if what is believed in fact holds true. Here, the belief condition links facts in the world to epistemic agents. The rationale behind the truth condition is that we cannot say: "She knows that Bob is married, which is of course plain false." The condition of justification excludes epistemic luck, namely that a person boldly believes something true for no reason whatsoever.

Although this account is ultimately rejected in "Theaetetus," it is a useful start because many other accounts build upon it. We will thus also draw on this account in what follows. When we do so, we may start from the assumption that the epistemic agent who is the subject of knowledge is a human being or, maybe, a group of scientists. We need not say much about truth because, if an epistemic agent wonders whether she knows something or not (that is, if knowledge claims are investigated from the first-person perspective), there is no independent access to truth apart from her reasons that speak in favor of her belief. For the epistemic agent, the question of whether she has knowledge or not thus reduces to the issue of whether her belief is justified. Now, when we (be it laypeople, working scientists who run CSs, or philosophers) reflect on the results of CSs, we take a stance from which we think about the question of whether we know certain things. Thus, truth will effectively play no role in our inquiry. Furthermore, whenever CSs provide *new* knowledge, we do not have any access to the truth independently from the CSs themselves. The only way to establish the truth of the results, then, is to show that the application of the method provides a justification for believing the results. In what follows, we will focus on such instances of CS. We will do so since we are here interested in new knowledge resulting from CS and since our question really is whether we know the results *because* they are results of CSs. We will thus bracket potential reasons for believing the results of a CS that do not depend on the simulation itself.

Nor do we need to say much about belief. For if there are sufficient reasons to believe some content that is taken from a CS, then we can assume that scientists and other people do in fact believe this. There are belief-forming processes that take us from good reasons to beliefs, and why shouldn't they be operative in the case of CSs?[3]

This means that there are only two tasks left for our analysis, if we draw on the JTB analysis: We need to determine what sort of content we can associate with CSs and how we may be justified in taking this content to be true.

At this point, more needs to be said about justification. A first point to note is that, to have knowledge, the epistemic agent needs to be justified in believing what she believes. It does not suffice to have a belief that is justified in the sense that a justification might be provided. Thus, if we speak of justified true belief in what follows, this is a shorthand way of saying that the agent is justified in believing something (cf. Alston 1985, p. 58).

---

[3]There may only be a problem if there are contents that cannot be believed, for instance because they are too complicated. But this does not seem to be the case.

We may say that an epistemic agent is justified in believing something if and only if the belief is based upon sufficient reasons (for this and the following see, e.g., Alston 1988, pp. 265–266). Here, basing has a causal aspect, the idea being that the reasons explain why the agent has the belief. But there is a normative aspect, too, in the sense that the reasons render the belief permissible or even mandatory from the viewpoint of epistemic rationality. The modality of justification—whether it is about permissibility or duty—does not matter for what follows.

It is uncontroversial that a lot of justification is inferential; that is, a belief may be justified by means of an inference from other beliefs, at least if the latter are justified themselves. For what follows, inferential justification is most important. We can bracket the question of whether there are other sorts of justification, as so-called foundationalists claim (see, e.g., Hasan and Fumerton 2016 for an introduction).

Justification comes in degrees and a certain degree of justification is needed for knowledge, the idea being that not all indications suffice for knowledge. But what is the threshold that needs to be exceeded? A plausible answer is that it depends on the context (cf. Lewis 1996). In what follows, we will concentrate on justifications that are sufficient according to the standard that is fixed in the relevant context.

Due to Gettier (1963), the JTB analysis of knowledge has come under pressure. The problem is that there are examples in which the JTB analysis and a plausible assumption about justification imply knowledge, although we intuitively refrain from claiming knowledge because there is too much epistemic luck. In response, epistemology has seen a lot of work about justification and knowledge. One account that is worth mentioning here is reliabilism. According to reliabilism about justification (Goldman 1979b), a person is justified in believing something if the belief was caused in a reliable process, where the latter is of a type of process that has a high objective probability of yielding true belief (e.g., perception). This idea can also be brought to bear on knowledge directly by replacing the justification condition by a condition of reliability (see, e.g., Goldman 1979a; see Goldman and Beddor 2015 for an overview). But in what follows, I assume that, if a reliable process is required for knowledge, it yields justification.

Reliabilism does not require the epistemic agent to know that the process which has caused her belief is reliable. The justification of the belief may thus be external to the subject, i.e., beyond the grasp of the agent (although this will not be so in every example of knowledge). This claim has been much criticized and is at the center of a debate between so-called internalists and externalists. Very roughly, internalists hold that the justification of belief needs to be within the agent, while externalists deny this requirement. There are several ways to spell out the core idea of internalism. One important brand of internalism, also called "accessibilism" (Conee and Feldman 2001, p. 2), holds that the justification of belief needs to be accessible to the epistemic agent. But as e.g. Bergmann (2006, Ch. 1) argues, accessibilism is threatened by a regress problem. Roughly, if the reasons of a belief that p need to be accessible to the epistemic agent, she has to have certain beliefs about her reasons for believing p, and these beliefs need to be based on reasons too, if the agent is to be justified in believing that p, and so on. Some brands of externalism thus deny accessibilism. Another variety of internalism, also called "mentalism" (Conee and Feldman 2001, p. 2), argues that the justification of belief supervenes on the mental states of the agent. This is to say that the justificatory status of a belief can only change if something about the mindset of the agent changes too.[4]

With these distinctions in mind, we can now move on to CSs and ask whether and how they can provide new knowledge. The focus is on the acquisition of new knowledge, which is just knowledge that the epistemic agent under consideration did not have before. In what follows, I will sometimes drop the qualification "new" for convenience.[5]

3 Propositional Content

A lot of scientists claim to have knowledge due to computer simulations. Whether such a claim is true depends of course on what exactly they claim to know. This, in turn, depends on the specific case at hand. Now, we are not interested in a specific CS here. What we can examine in a philosophical investigation is only whether there are general conditions under which CSs do in fact provide new knowledge. Now, if we are interested in general conditions under which CSs advance our knowledge, we need to know a general way in which CSs and their results are turned into propositional content that may eventually become subject of knowledge. The aim of this section is to outline in general terms how one can get from simulations to propositional content.

What propositional content we may obtain from a CS depends of course on what exactly is meant by a CS. It is fairly uncontroversial that CSs try to provide approximations to solutions of dynamical equations from a model of a target system (cf., e.g., Humphreys 2004, pp. 110–111). For instance, so-called N-body simulations of cosmic structure formation are supposed to trace the dynamics of the matter distribution on large scales in the universe. They are built upon what may be called a conceptual model of the matter distribution, i.e., a set of partial differential equations. The equations are in some ways discretized (one crucial idea being that the matter distribution is traced using particles) and implemented in a computer program (see, e.g., Bertschinger 1998 and Dolag et al. 2008 for such CSs). Other types of simulations, e.g., agent-based simulations, also solve equations that trace the dynamics of a system.

What is more controversial is what exactly a CS includes. Minimally, a CS as a type of action includes one run with a simulation program, in which the evolution of

---

[4]More fine-grained distinctions between varieties of internalism are available (Pappas 2014), but do not matter for what follows.

[5]The results of this paper can be extended to the consolidation of existing knowledge by means of CS. In this case, some issues are not as pressing as they are regarding new knowledge.

a system is traced. This view is behind the definition of CS given by Hartmann (1996, Sect. 2.2), according to which a CS is a process imitating another process. But for some purposes, it is useful to say that a CS includes further activities. One may say that the programming and the testing of the program are part of the simulation, too. Furthermore, a simulation program is often run several times; the initial conditions are changed; the program may even be changed to incorporate new insights, the results are interpreted and analyzed and so on.[6] I will follow Parker (2009, p. 488) in calling CSs in a more comprehensive sense *(computer) simulation studies*, leaving open how exactly CS studies are individuated.[7]

Now, the more activities we let a CS include, the more results they can have, and the stronger the results may be. Obviously, the results of running a CS program once will be much poorer than if a program is run many times and if several parameters are systematically varied.

For our purposes, it does not make much sense to commit ourselves to a particular conception of CSs, for instance in the sense of one run of a simulation program. Rather, to capture the results of CSs, I will start from one run of a CS program and then include more and more activities to cover more comprehensive CS studies.

Suppose, then, that a simulation program is run once. The program takes numbers as initial conditions and outputs more numbers. Now, in every simulation, the numbers are considered to be the values that quantitative characteristics (e.g., velocity) take at certain times in certain units with respect to a specific coordinate frame. For instance, in typical N-body simulations,[8] the characteristics are the positions and velocities of N particles (where N is a natural number). We start with the positions $x_i(t_0)$ and velocities $v_i(t_0)$ at some initial time t_0, where subindex i labels the particles from 1 to N. The program outputs the positions $x_i(t_j)$ and velocities $v_i(t_j)$ at later times t_j, where j is a label for times. Since each combination of velocities and positions defines a state of a system, we can say that the program takes the specification of a state $s_0 = s(t_0)$ as input, and outputs a series of specifications of states $s_j = s(t_j)$ that are supposed to follow the initial state. Here, the s_j are specific states characterized in terms of values of characteristics.

Our task now is to construct a propositional result of the CS out of this material. A natural proposal is this:

p If the initial state of the system at t_0 is s_0, then it is in states s_j at later times t_j, respectively.

This proposition specifies a certain time evolution of the system under consideration, conditional on an initial state. The time evolution is conditional on the initial state because, if it were not, then the result of the simulation would implicitly

---

[6]Cf. Frigg and Reiss (2009, p. 596) for a similar distinction.

[7]The term "simulation study" is also used by practitioners; see, e.g., Balci (1989, p. 62).

[8]See Hockney and Eastwood (1988) for an introduction to this type of simulation. The N-body simulations of cosmic structure formation mentioned above are of course of this type.

commit one to the claim that the system started from a specific initial state at t_0. But very often, simulations start out not with what are taken to be the actual initial conditions, but rather with merely possible, merely imagined initial conditions. One can nevertheless learn something from such simulations, namely how the system would evolve if it started out in such-and-such an initial state. So, what we minimally learn from running a simulation program once is expressed in a conditional.

Proposition p may of course be used to infer a proposition according to which the system does in fact run through the states s_j. As a premise for this inference, we need the proposition that the system is, or was, in fact in state s_0 at t_0. But this is an additional inference that goes beyond the immediate result of the simulations.

I have said that the simulation refers to a system because it specifies a series of states through which the system runs, conditional on an initial state. But which system are we talking about? Many CSs are ultimately intended to refer to real-world systems. But this is not universally true; for instance, cosmologists have run CSs with various sorts of assumptions about so-called background cosmology and the nature of dark matter, and the assumptions adopted for the various simulations are incompatible with each other, so it is clear that not all of the simulations can refer to our actual universe. Furthermore, even if CSs aim at insights about real-world systems, they rely on models of the target systems. For this reason, it is safer to say that proposition p refers to a model. Here, a model is regarded as a system that may or may not actually exist and which may be used as a substitute for a real-world target system.[9] So more precisely, the proposition is:

p If the initial state of the model system M at t_0 is s_0, then M is in states s_j at later times t_j, respectively.

But what exactly is the model M? When working scientists talk about a model of their target, they often refer to a set of differential equations that feature the time evolution of their target. For instance, in cosmology, they refer to what are called the Vlasov-Poisson equations (Dolag et al. 2008, p. 230; cf. Peebles 1980, p. 46). These equations model the time evolution of a self-gravitating fluid, i.e., a fluid that is only subject to gravitational interactions between its parts. We may say that these equations define (merely imagined) systems, namely those systems in which they hold exactly true. But strictly speaking, a CS does not exactly follow such a model. The CS cannot solve the partial differential equations. Rather, the partial differential equations are discretized and then solved by the computer. To mark the difference between the model with differential equations and what is really implemented in the computer program, it is common to distinguish between the conceptual and the computerized model (Schlesinger et al. 1979, p. 103). I assume

---

[9]See Weisberg (2007) for modeling and Beisbart (2014) for the relationship between CS and modeling.

that the computerized model is identified from the algorithm that computer scientists intend the program to implement.[10]

In the terms of this distinction, what does the result of a CS refer to? We are on the safe side of it, if we say that the proposition refers to the computerized model, because this is closer to what the computer actually does and outputs.

But we are arguably not yet safe enough, because the algorithm that is implemented in a computer program is not really strictly followed due to errors, e.g., round-off errors (see Press et al. 2007, pp. 8–10). Also, due to a hardware failure, the computer may not execute the program properly.

To take into account such problems, we may define the model *in the computer*, which is a model for which the computer provides an exact solution. We can then say that the states s_j and the result of the simulation refer to the model in the computer. That is, p is first and foremost about the model in the computer.

But the hope is of course that the model in the computer is an excellent indicator of the computerized model. More precisely, the hope is this: Given that the computerized model starts with s'_0 at time t_0, each state s_j that is obtained in the model in the computer under the assumption that $s_0 = s'_0$, is an excellent approximation to the real s'_j in the computerized model (here I use primes to refer to states in the computerized model). Thus, what computer scientists quite often would like to infer and do in fact infer is this:

p′ If the initial state of the computerized model model M' at t_0 is s'_0, then, at later times t_j, M' is in states s'_j, that closely approximate states s_j (for which the values of the characteristics are as the output of the simulation program has it).

Here, the states s'_j are not fully known, but the claim is that the values of the characteristics in these states are very close to those in the s_j that are characterized in terms of the output. It is sometimes specified how close the values of the characteristics such as of velocities are in the models, but we can neglect this in what follows.

p′ may be inferred from p. The inference assumes that the computer program implements the algorithm it is intended to carry out, that the round-off errors are sufficiently small, and that there are no hardware failures that significantly impact on the values of the characteristics that define the states.

But ultimately, the working scientists are very often not as much interested in the computerized model as in the conceptual one. Often, only the latter includes what people take to be laws of nature (see Schlesinger et al. 1979, p. 103). So what scientists would like to infer and often do indeed infer is something like this:

p″ If the initial state of the conceptual model M'' at t_0 is s''_0, then, at later times t_j, M'' is in states s''_j that closely resemble states s_j (for which the values of the characteristics are as the output of the simulation program has it).

---

[10]Some CSs are built upon discrete conceptual models such that the difference between the conceptual and the computerized model is less significant or not existent at all.

p'' may be inferred from p', and the inference assumes that the outputs from the run of the CS program can be used to construct good approximations of the solutions of the equations from the conceptual model. Note here that there may be a significant gap between the conceptual and the computerized model because they may not share the same ontology. In cosmological N-body simulations, the conceptual model system is a continuous fluid that is characterized in terms of fields, i.e., functions that are defined for every possible location in space. The computerized model, by contrast, has the universe consist of discrete particles. Thus, some care is needed to obtain a series of states in the conceptual model from the outputs. This is why p'' refers to states of the conceptual model that resemble (instead of merely approximating) states of the model in the computer.

But ultimately, quite often, the working scientists are not as much interested in the computerized model as in a real-world target system. So what many scientists would like to infer and often do indeed infer is something like this:

p''' If the initial state of the target system T at t_0 is s'''_0, then, at later times t_j, T is in states s'''_j that closely resemble states s_j (for which the values of the character-istics are as the output of the simulation program has it).

Under suitable conditions, p''' may be inferred from p''. The inference assumes that the conceptual model reflects the real target system properly. The inference may again switch between different sorts of ontology. For instance, in cosmological N-body simulations, the conceptual model describes the Universe as a continuous fluid, but there is no presumption that the Universe is filled with such a fluid. The latter is rather supposed to provide a coarse-grained picture of the matter distribution in the Universe.

All in all, out of the in- and outputs of a run of a simulation program, we have constructed a series of propositions: $p, p', p'',$ and p'''. While the first simply translates the in- and outputs into a proposition and can thus straightforwardly be obtained, each of the latter three can be inferred from its predecessor under certain assumptions that turn on the quality of the simulation. We may say that, in each inference, certain type of errors are excluded or at least sufficiently small. The inference from p to p' assumes that the effects of programming bugs, round-off errors and hardware failures can be controlled. The inference from p' to p'' assumes that so-called truncation and discretization errors are small (the errors arise if differential equations are approxi-mated using difference equations). The inference from p'' to p''', finally, assumes that the effects of modeling errors are sufficiently small.

The differences between the propositions p–p''' turn on different sorts of models. I have here distinguished between three types of models. We obtain a different series of propositions when we work with different models. For instance, Winsberg (1999) goes as far as to distinguish five layers of models in the construction of a simulation. For our purposes, it does not matter how exactly we specify the series of models. In any case, the series of models goes hand in hand with a certain classification of possible errors that may affect a simulation.[11]

---

[11]See Roache (1998, pp. 36–43) and Parker (2008, pp. 375–377) for classifications of errors.

Very often, there are not sufficient grounds to run the last inference from p''
to p'''. If the model that is used to represent a target system is very idealized, then
working scientists cannot infer that the target system evolves in a way that can be
specified on the basis of the outputs from the CS. Often, they think that the
simulation is reliable in certain respects, say for one specific characteristic, e.g.,
mean global temperature in climate simulations, but not for other characteristics,
for instance those that describe precipitation. In these cases, p''' has to be weakened
accordingly. Sometimes, what scientists wish to infer is no more than a merely
qualitative statement about the time evolution (e.g., whether it is cyclic).

We may spell this out in terms of a distinction offered by Bogen and Woodward
(1988). The authors discriminate between phenomena, e.g., the phenomenon that a
certain substance has its melting point at such-and-such a temperature (Bogen and
Woodward 1988, pp. 308–312), and data, which are straightforwardly obtained in
observations. Bogen and Woodward claim that what theories explain and predict
are phenomena, not data. The data only provides evidence for phenomena (Bogen
and Woodward 1988, pp. 305–306).

To apply this distinction to CSs, we may say that the outputs of a CS correspond
to data in Bogen and Woodward's terms (this is also claimed by Barberousse et al.
2009). These "data" then provide evidence for phenomena. These may be phenomena within a model, but occasionally also in the real world. Some propositional
results of simulations then describe certain aspects of the phenomena.

If we assume that propositional results are obtained in this way from a simulation, then arriving at these results is less straightforward than has been assumed so
far. This need not worry us because, in the field of data analysis, there are well
established methods to obtain phenomena from data.[12]

Now, to know in which respects a simulation faithfully represents a system and
what phenomena may properly be inferred from the CS, scientists often have to run
their simulation program several times. This is advisable anyway to test whether the
simulations are affected from one or the other type of error mentioned above. For
instance, if the same program is run twice with exactly the same input and different
results are obtained, then at least one run was affected by hardware failures (unless
the program includes pseudo-random elements that do not only depend on the input;
for instance, a randomizer may be initialized using the time at which the program is
started).

At this point, we have to move beyond a single run of a simulation program,
which has been our focus so far. We recognize that this focus abstracts from
important details, since, often, simulation scientists do not want to establish a
proposition from one run of a simulation program simply because they do not
know how well the program works. Rather, their program is run several times, and
they construct propositions out of the entirety of the outputs that they have obtained.

Even if the outputs of multiple runs of a CS program are analyzed together to
arrive at a result, what has been said about a single run of a program and its results

---

[12]Here and in the following few paragraphs, I'm indebted to criticism by Eric Winsberg.

still is significant. For the propositions that we have specified as results provide at least initial indications of what may ideally be learned from a single run of a computer program. We can use these results in a reconstruction that aims to understand how results are obtained using several runs of a program. The idea is simply that the propositions jointly ground further propositions. For one thing, they specify the data that support the phenomenon (mere numbers cannot do this). For another thing, they jointly provide evidence about the quality of the simulation.

If several runs of a computer program are allowed, then further inferences are possible that move beyond a mere description of phenomena conditional on some initial state. For instance, if we obtain the same type of dynamical evolution for a large number of initial conditions of the same class, and no different type of evolution for instances of initial conditions of this class, then we can conclude that, for a certain class of initial condition, a certain type of evolution ensues. This inference is a simple enumerative induction. Or, when we run a simulation program several times and vary a parameter, we may conclude that a certain factor is causally relevant for the occurrence of a type of event. This conclusion is effectively based upon the method of difference (Mill 1843, Book III, Ch. viii).

In what follows, I will, however, bracket such inferences, since they are not closely related to what the computer actually does. I will also continue to focus on a situation in which a CS program is run once and only widen the focus if this proves necessary. One reason for doing so is as follows: What is distinctive about computer simulation is that a computer is used, and its central use is when a simulation program is run. If a CS program is run several times, then the computer does more of the same, but nothing qualitatively new. It is true, though, that several runs of a program and related methods provide material that allows for much more powerful inferences than does a single run of a CS program, and this will be taken into account where required.

4   Justification

Turn now to justification.[13] For definiteness, let us assume that, on the basis of one run of a simulation program and by using some of the techniques mentioned in the last section, a scientist, call her S, obtains the proposition

q If the system is in initial state s_0 at time t_0, its ensuing time evolution has this and
  this feature.

---

[13]Of course, the identification of propositional content for CSs, on the one hand, and issues of justification, on the other, cannot really be separated. For we are not looking for any proposition that one may obtain from outputs of CSs, but rather for propositions that may be justified. Thus, justificatory considerations were important already for the last section. But it is now time to address justification more explicitly.

Here and in the following, the simulations are said to refer to a system, which may be the conceptual model system (cf. p'' above) or the real-world target system (cf. p''' above); we will distinguish between the cases where appropriate. The clause "its ensuing time evolution has this and this feature" is an abbreviation of the then-clause in p'' or p''', respectively.

Now, under which conditions is S justified to believe this proposition? And what is the justification for it?

Here is a natural proposal (which is in the spirit of Beisbart 2012). What a computer does in a CS, at some natural level of description, is to do certain calculations (there are other levels of descriptions, which, however, do not much matter here; see Barberousse et al. 2009). The calculations take us from inputted to outputted numbers. Properly interpreted, the inputted numbers provide a characterization of the initial state of a system; likewise, given the same interpretation, the outputted numbers characterize later states of the system under scrutiny. The working scientist thus can translate the input into a statement about the initial state of the model or the real-world target system, and the output into statements about the following states. This was important for obtaining the result of a simulation in the last section. Now, the numbers that constitute the output are obtained from the input by running through calculations that are supposed to provide approximate solutions to equations from a model. The equations can also be stated in one or more propositions. If q is about a conceptual model, it is natural to say that the propositions state the dynamical equations definitive of the conceptual model. If q is about a distinct target system, we may take the propositions to claim that the evolution of the target approximately follows the conceptual model.[14] Given all this, we can say that the computer derives propositions about the later states from a proposition about the initial state plus propositions that specify how the system runs from one state to others (for more details see Beisbart 2012).

This suggests that what the CS does is, essentially, draw an inference. This inference may naturally be spelled out as an argument with two premises: The first premise states that the initial state of the system is such and such. The second premise provides a general characterization of the time evolution of the system (i.e., either of the conceptual model or of the target system). The characterization has the form typical of a law of succession: It is a universal conditional statement that quantifies over all possible states a system may take at t_i and then specifies the state that the system will take one time step further, i.e., at t_{i+1} depending on the state at t_i.[15] The conclusion is a statement about the states at the later times.

Now, we argued in the last section that this conclusion is not really the result that is inferred from a CS. First, the result of a simulation about a real-world target is sometimes weakened in that only some part of the simulation output is taken into

---

[14]Properly speaking, the propositions may also have to contain information about boundary conditions, parameter values, etc., but we can absorb this in talk of the dynamical equations.

[15]This formulation holds true for discrete time; it needs to be adjusted for continuous time, but this does not make much of a difference for our purposes.

account, simply because the simulation is not supposed to be faithful in every respect. Second, the result is conditional on the premise of the initial conditions. Both points can easily be taken into account in reconstructing the inference: We make the conclusion conditional on the first premise, i.e., the one about the initial conditions, and treat this premise as an assumption that is only made for the sake of the argument. In what follows, it thus does not count as a premise any more.

Furthermore, if necessary, we weaken the second premise as follows: The system behaves as if it followed the equations in some respects, which can be specified. The argument that we have thus constructed seems unproblematic, since the conclusion seems to follow from the premise because the computer essentially takes the premise about the dynamics and derives a conclusion by means of mathematical deductions (see below for qualifications). The argument is in fact valid if the consequent in q, i.e., the statement about the states to follow the initial one, is formulated in such a way that the effects of all errors are properly taken into account.[16]

The proposal, then, is that the proposition q is inferentially justified. The inference is based upon a premise that characterizes the dynamic evolution of the conceptual model or of the target system. The inference itself is run with the help of a computer. Of course, inferential justification is conditional: What is inferred is only justified if the premises are. This means that propositional results from CSs are only justified if the dynamic equations on which the simulations are built upon are. But this is as it should be, for the results are certainly only justified if the model equations are.

Here, it is of course assumed that the CS works properly and runs as intended. If, by contrast, there is a hardware failure, there is a problem because then the outputted numbers are not properly derived from the input, which is to say that the conclusion, which is constructed on the basis of the output, does not follow from the premise. So, succinctly put, the proposal is this: Our scientist S is inferentially justified in believing q if she is justified in believing the dynamic equations used to feature the system under scrutiny and if the simulation works as intended.

---

[16]At this point, the following objection may be raised: The fact that we can reconstruct a computer simulation as an argument is not significant and does not show that knowledge based upon simulations is inferential. In fact, it may be added, any justification, even one through perception, can be reconstructed as an argument, because when we say something to justify our belief, we have to make an argument. This objection is not convincing, however. First, we are not talking about justification in the sense of a speech act, because we may be justified in believing something without saying anything at all (Alston 1985, p. 58). Second, the argument with which the simulation is reconstructed captures the epistemic power of the simulation. In particular, it makes plain what needs to be believed if the simulation is used to advance a certain scientific claim (see Beisbart 2012, p. 400 and pp. 416–419). By contrast, it is doubtful whether perception may be reconstructed as an argument that captures the epistemic power of perception. Third, it may be argued that the run of the simulation program is in fact a process in which, roughly, the argument is gone through (of course, in this process, there are many intermediate inferential steps; see below and Beisbart 2012, Sect. 5).

We can slightly reformulate the proposal by switching to reliabilist terms: S is justified in believing that q because the CS is a reliable process that leads her to this belief. If the reliable process is fed with appropriate input, e.g., input that is itself justified on different grounds, then the result is likely to be true and thus justified.

This proposal has many virtues. It provides a simple explanation of how a CS can advance knowledge. This is so because it is uncontroversial that there is inferential justification, that is, that justification can be transferred from certain premises to a conclusion. Also, the proposal makes sense of the fact that a computer is a computer, i.e., a machine that carries out calculations.[17]

The proposal may nevertheless be objected to, at least for two reasons. Let me discuss these objections and then amend the proposal where needed.

To introduce the first objection, we should note that working scientists often try hard to make a case for the results of their simulation. That is, they argue that the results are genuine. These efforts are now most often called validation (see, e.g., Schlesinger et al. 1979 for a frequently quoted definition). Now, validation is regarded as difficult and messy. Working scientists have complained that it is not well understood. In the words of Kleindorfer et al. (1998, p. 1087),

> There is still considerable doubt and even anxiety among simulation modelers as to what the methodologically correct guidelines or procedures for validating simulation models should be.

According to another researcher (Ghetiu et al. 2010, p. 1),

> [A] cohesive understanding of what scientific validation requires, is not captured by the existing efforts that mainly try to solve pieces of the 'puzzle'.

This diagnosis is confirmed by philosopher Winsberg, who takes the epistemology of simulation to be novel because it is downward, autonomous, and motley (e.g., Winsberg 2001, p. 447).[18] But according to the proposal under consideration, there does not seem any need to validate simulations, and no explanation is given as to why many scientists take pains to validate their simulations.

As a first reply to the objection, we should note that the proposal does leave some need for validation. The reason is that inferential justification does not generate reasons from scratch, as it were. It rather transfers justification from premises to conclusions. So our agent S needs to be justified in believing the premise of the argument if she is to obtain knowledge. According to our proposal, the premise

---

[17]To describe the relationship between CS (in the sense of a single run of a computer simulation program) and knowledge, it is, maybe, more appropriate to say that the CS grounds knowledge instead of saying that it produces or advances our knowledge. The reason is that the output of the CS needs to be interpreted or translated into propositional terms. Furthermore, S only obtains knowledge if the premises of the inference are justified. The CS thus provides the basis for knowledge. Thus, if I say that a run of a computer simulation program advances our knowledge, this is to be taken with a salt of grain. This grain of salt is of course not necessary if the term computer simulation is meant to refer to a simulation study, of which interpretation of the results is an integral part.

[18]But consult Frigg and Reiss (2009) for a dissenting view.

describes the dynamics of the conceptual model or the target system. The proposal can explain the efforts to validate results from simulations to the extent that this premise needs justification.

But this reply does not go far enough. Typical efforts at validation do not only try to show that the conceptual model provides an adequate description of the dynamics of the system under scrutiny. Scientists also try to show that their approximation schemes used in the computer code work well enough, that there are no hardware failures, etc. These attempts are often called verification (see again Schlesinger et al. 1979, p. 103). Here, the term "verification" is a technical one; the idea is certainly not that verification proceeds via proof (cf. Oreskes et al. 1994). Verification makes an important contribution to validation, and the objection now is that our proposal does not make sense of verification.[19]

The second objection has it that the proposal is too externalist. Recall that we need to distinguish between two types of externalism, namely between a denial of accessibilism and a denial of mentalism. The justification that we have sketched is externalist in the first sense, because the inference is very complicated (it rests on millions of calculations) and cannot be expected to be carried out by the agent alone. Perhaps this is not much of a problem because internalism qua accessibilism is controversial. But the proposal is also externalist in the sense of a denial of mentalism: The justification does not only supervene on the agent, but also on the computations done by the computer which are external to the agent. The proposal thus violates internalism qua mentalism, and this is more of a problem because mentalism is less controversial; at least Conee and Feldman (2001) try to make a strong case for it.

But what's the problem with denying mentalism? Consider the following example: Peter is traveling in a foreign country and could not follow the news for a couple of days. At a cafe he meets a stranger who makes a lot of claims about news in Peter's home country. Is Peter justified in believing these news? Suppose, for instance, the stranger is very trustworthy. Or suppose she is not. Does this matter? It does not seem to matter unless Peter has some reasons to assume the trustworthiness of the stranger or her lack thereof. For we are here talking about whether Peter would be justified in believing the news, and this, it seems, turns on what he thinks or has reason to think on the basis of his knowledge, memory, etc. And this is exactly what mentalism claims.[20]

Now, according to the proposal we are considering, Peter is justified in believing q if he is justified in believing the dynamic equations of the model and if the simulation produces the output in the way intended. But suppose that two simulations are run that are built upon the same equations. One simulation suffers from a hardware failure, while the other does not. According to our proposal, there is

---

[19]In the literature, the meaning of "verification" is not unambiguous. In this paper, I mean by verification any attempt to show that a CS traces the conceptual model as intended.

[20]Note that, in defining reliabilist justification, Goldman (1979b, pp. 39–40) likewise suggests that justification turns on the reliability of belief-forming processes *within* the agent.

justification in one case, but not in the other, independently of what Peter thinks. And this cannot be the case according to mentalism.

Both objections can be avoided by a slight amendment of our proposal. The amendment is to require not that the simulation works as intended, but that the epistemic agent has sufficient reasons to believe that it does. The point of this amendment may be put as follows: CSs involve a device external to human beings, namely the programmed computer. If S is to obtain justified belief from this device, she needs justifiably think that the programmed computer works as intended.[21]

This amendment helps avoid our second objection about externalism because the new proposal is not necessarily externalist any more: Whether Peter is justified in believing q turns on whether he has reasons to think that the CS works as intended, and this may depend on his beliefs. The first objection is also avoided: To be able to believe that the CS works as intended, it does not suffice to say that the CS is based upon a model that faithfully represents the system of interest. For there is no guarantee that the dynamics predicted by this model is actually traced by the simulation. So S needs to make sure that round-off errors do not spoil the result, that the approximation schemes do not pile up truncation errors too significant, and so on. In this way, we can make sense of the multifaceted activities of validation and in particular of verification.

The point of our amendment may also be brought out as follows. The justification that we have concocted with the reconstruction of the argument is intransparent in the following sense: No human being can easily check whether the conclusion follows from the premise. We are not talking about a short argument that may be formalized in a simple logic such that the validity can be easily checked. In particular, there may be a mismatch between the premise and the conclusion. The premise in the inference is a description of the dynamics of the system (be it a model or a real-world target). The conclusion is constructed on the basis of the actual input and the actual output of the CS. But the premise only supports the conclusion if the CS appropriately traces the model equations. If it does not, then there is likely a mismatch between the premise and the conclusion. Whether the model is properly traced cannot be read off from the equations. Given some knowledge about the sorts of errors that may in principle affect the results of CSs, a working scientist should be very careful and first make sure that the premise supports the conclusion, that is, that the simulation works as intended.

What is wrong, maybe, with the first proposal is that it assumes success without further ado. But success does not help if it is not justifiably believed to be the case. This is a point that many internalists in the sense of accessibilists will make. So our amendment also accommodates certain intuitions that support accessibilism.

According to our new proposal, a requirement for knowledge by means of CS is that the epistemic agent be justified in believing that the simulation works as intended. Typically, the related justification builds upon several test runs with the

---

[21]This is not very far from the third condition that Clark and Chalmers (1998, p. 17) suggest for belief ascription to people who use computers; more on this below.

computer program. Thus, the requirement is only fulfilled if agent moves beyond a single run of a simulation program.

At this point, it may be objected that we have yielded too much to the temptation of internalism. Computers are devices that are in some sense external to the human mind. But they seem to play an important role in the justification of certain beliefs. So is not some sort of externalism more appropriate than mentalism?

This objection may be discussed in connection with the extended mind hypothesis (Clark and Chalmers 1998).[22] According to this thesis, certain cognitive achievements are carried out by coupled systems. For the purposes of our investigation, the coupled system consists of a scientist and her computer. According to a second crucial claim by Clark and Chalmers, at least some beliefs of persons are partly constituted by the environment, in particular by the states of devices to which the people are coupled.[23]

Now, I have above argued above that, in a CS, the calculation done by the computer may be reconstructed as an argument. Given that the calculation is essentially done by the computer, but that the propositional content of the premises and the conclusion crucially depends on what the working scientists know, why can't we say that we have a cognitive process (running through the argument) that is carried out by a coupled system consisting of the working scientist and the computer (see Beisbart 2012 for this proposal)? But if we say this, then it is natural to argue as follows: The inference is supposed to provide a justification, so the justification is gone through by the coupled system as the simulation program is being run.

From this perspective, it seems inappropriate to require justification to supervene on mental states that are not co-constituted by the states of external devices. So isn't the appropriate reaction to mentalism as follows: Either mentalism claims justification to supervene on the mind and its states in a narrow sense, i.e., without taking into account devices such as computers. Then we should reject mentalism by drawing on the extended mind hypothesis. Or, mentalism only requires supervenience on our mental life, which is supposed to be co-constituted by states of external devices. Then mentalism is not really violated. Either way, there would be no problem for our first proposal. Put differently, Clark and Chalmers claim that the beliefs of a person depend on what she has stored in a lab-top. So why do we not claim that whether a person is justified in believing may depend on states in a computer?

I think we should resist answering this question in the affirmative. The reason is as follows: Even if the extended mind hypothesis is granted (which I have assumed here for the sake of argument), one should note that coupling is subject to certain

---

[22]See Clark (2007) for another defense of the view, and the essays collected in Menary (2010) for more discussion.

[23]This claim is wrong if belief and other mental states cannot be constituted by material systems quite generally. But it may then still be argued that the states of the device determine in a non-causal way what the beliefs of the person are. In the following, I will continue to talk of constitution without endorsing the idea that beliefs have a material constitution.

conditions. Clark and Chalmers do not deal with conditions for coupling regarding justification, but they give conditions that have to be fulfilled for belief. Among other conditions, they require that, for having a belief that something is the case, which is only stored in a computer, a human being has to endorse the stored information when reading it, and the information needs to be stored in the computer because it was once endorsed (Clark and Chalmers 1998, p. 17). Similar conditions are necessary for justification being achieved by a coupled system. A very natural condition is that the person coupled to the device thinks that a certain justification is achieved and also that she is justified in doing so. The second part of this condition pushes us towards the amendment that was proposed. In Beisbart (2012, p. 422), a similar condition was mentioned in the account (if only for each single step in the argumentation). So the amended proposal is compatible with the extended mind hypothesis if the conditions for coupling are taken into account.

To wrap up, my new, amended proposal is as follows: An agent S is inferentially justified in believing a propositional result constructed from a computer simulation if she is justified in believing the dynamic equations used to feature the system under scrutiny and if she is justified to think that the simulation works as intended. The second condition is only fulfilled if the simulation has been verified (in the technical sense mentioned above). So, according to my new proposal, the results of a computer simulation are justified by an argument that summarizes the calculations done by the computer. Verification is needed to ensure that this argument is really gone through.

5 Conclusions

The advancement of knowledge is an age-old dream. This is plain from the frontispiece from F. Bacon's "Novum organum scientiarum" (1620), for instance, on which ships have passed the columns of Hercules and thus the known part of the world. To explore unknown lands or seas, human use technical devices such as ships. Today, they try to advance knowledge with the means of computers, in particular by using computer simulations (this is stressed by Humphreys 2004, among others). That new knowledge is gained by this method and that uncertainties are reduced in this way is often claimed by scientists and in science news.

The aim of this paper was to scrutinize such claims. To this effect, I have confronted the claims with the traditional philosophical definition of knowledge and with ideas from epistemology. To show that CSs give rise to what is knowledge in the traditional account of propositional knowledge, I had mainly to show how the in- and outputs of simulations suggest propositional content and how an agent may be justified in believing the latter. Since the output of CSs comprises numbers that are values of characteristics of a system (e.g., the velocities of its components), they can easily be translated into propositions. The latter are conditional and specify the dynamic evolution of a system conditional on certain initial conditions. Often, such propositions do not really state what the simulations are supposed to show, but they can be weakened and combined with each other to yield what are thought to be the results from simulations. These results are justified in terms of an inference that takes us from modeling assumptions about the dynamics of a system to a description of its conditional dynamic evolution. The inference can be reconstructed in terms of an argument.

This argument alone cannot carry the burden of the justification, however. What is crucial is that there are reasons to think that an appropriate argument has really been carried out. Regarding its form, this justification is inferential too, being based upon what is called verification.

Our conclusion, then, is that the results of computer simulations can provide an agent with new knowledge. They do so whenever the outputs of the simulation are translated into a result as described, if the latter is believed by the agent, and if our condition of justification is fulfilled, that is, if the agent is justified in believing the premise about the dynamic evolution of the system she is interested in and if she has reasons to believe that the CS works as intended, which is to say that the execution of the CS program takes her from the premise about the dynamic evolution to the results by means of a convincing argument. The justification condition also explains how new knowledge due to a CS is formed.

In practice, verification is difficult to attain it because CSs can suffer from all kinds of errors that are often not easily detected. Thus, although simulations can provide the basis for new knowledge and thus help reduce uncertainties, they come with their own, specific uncertainties. If Socrates were to engage with present claims to knowledge that are built upon computer simulations, he would probably address the problems of verification.

Acknowledgments Thanks to the editors for their invitation to contribute and for their patience and to Andreas Kaminski for helpful comments and constructive criticism.

References

Alston, William P. 1985. Concepts of Epistemic Justification. *The Monist* 68 (1): 57–89.
Alston, William P. 1988. An Internalist Externalism. *Synthese* 74 (3): 265–283.
Balci, Osman. 1989. How to Assess the Acceptability and Credibility of Simulation Results. In *Proceedings of the 21st Conference on Winter Simulation*, 62–71. New York: ACM. doi.acm.org/10.1145/76738.76746.
Barberousse, Anouk, Sara Franceschelli, and Cyrille Imbert. 2009. Computer Simulations as Experiments. *Synthese* 169 (3): 557–574.
Beisbart, Claus. 2012. How can Computer Simulations Produce New Knowledge? *European Journal for Philosophy of Science* 2 (3): 395–434.
Beisbart, Claus. 2014. Are we Sims? How Computer Simulations Represent and what this Means for the Simulation Argument. *The Monist* 97 (3): 399–417.
Bergmann, Michael. 2006. *Justification Without Awareness: A Defense of Epistemic Externalism.* Oxford: Oxford University Press.
Bertschinger, Edmund. 1998. Simulations of Structure Formation in the Universe. *Annual Review of Astronomy and Astrophysics* 36: 599–654.

Bogen, James, and James Woodward. 1988. Saving the Phenomena. *Philosophical Review* 97 (3): 303–352.

Clark, Andy. 2007. Curing Cognitive Hiccups: A Defense of the Extended Mind. *Journal of Philosophy* 104 (4): 163–192.

Clark, Andy, and David J. Chalmers. 1998. The Extended Mind. *Analysis* 58 (1): 7–19.

Conee, Earl, and Richard Feldman. 2001. Internalism Defended. *American Philosophical Quarterly* 38 (1): 1–18.

Dolag, Klaus, Stefano Borgani, Sabine Schindler, Antonio Diaferio, and Andrei M. Bykov. 2008. Simulation Techniques for Cosmological Simulations. *Space Science Reviews* 134: 229–268.

Frigg, Roman P., and Julian Reiss. 2009. The Philosophy of Simulation: Hot New Issues or Same Old Stew? *Synthese* 169 (3): 593–613.

Frigg, Roman P., Stephan Hartmann, and Cyrille Imbert. 2009. Models and Simulations. Special issue, *Synthese* 169 (3).

Frigg, Roman P., Stephan Hartmann, and Cyrille Imbert. 2011. Models and Simulations 2. Special issue, *Synthese* 180 (1).

Gettier, Edmund. 1963. Is Justified True Belief Knowledge? *Analysis* 23 (6): 121–123.

Ghetiu, Teodor, Fiona A. C. Polack, and James Bown. 2010. Argument-driven Validation of Computer Simulations – a Necessity rather than an Option. In *VALID 2010: The Second International Conference on Advances in System Testing and Validation Lifecycle*, held in Nice, France, ed. Amirhossein Alimohammad, Andrea Baruzzo, Lydie du Bousquet et al., 1–4. IEEE Press.

Goldman, Alvin Ira. 1979a. Innate Knowledge. In *Innate Ideas*, ed. Stephen Stich, 111–120. Berkeley: University of California Press.

Goldman, Alvin Ira. 1979b. What is Justified Belief? In *Justification and Knowledge*, ed. George Pappas, 1–23. Dordrecht: Reidel. Here quoted from the reprint Alvin Ira Goldman. 2012. *Reliabilism and Contemporary Epistemology: Essays*, 29–49. New York: Oxford University Press.

Goldman, Alvin Ira, and Bob Beddor. 2015. Reliabilist Epistemology. In *Stanford Encyclopedia of Philosophy* (Winter 2016 Edition), ed. Edward N. Zalta. https://plato.stanford.edu/entries/reliabilism/.

Hartmann, Stephan. 1996. The World as a Process: Simulations in the Natural and Social Sciences. In *Modelling and Simulation in the Social Sciences from the Philosophy of Science Point of View*, ed. R. Hegselmann, Klaus G. Troitzsch, and Ulrich Mueller, 77–100. Dordrecht: Kluwer.

Hasan, Ali, and Richard Fumerton. 2010. Foundationalist Theories of Epistemic Justification. In *Stanford Encyclopedia of Philosophy* (Winter 2016 Edition), ed. Edward N. Zalta. https://plato.stanford.edu/archives/win2016/entries/justep-foundational/.

Hockney, Roger W., and James W. Eastwood. 1988. *Computer Simulation Using Particles*. New York: Taylor & Francis.

Humphreys, Paul. 2004. *Extending Ourselves: Computational Science, Empiricism, and Scientific Method*. New York: Oxford University Press.

Humphreys, Paul, and Cyrille Imbert, eds. 2011. *Models, Simulations, and Representations*. New York: Routledge.

Kleindorfer, George B., Liam O'Neill, and Ram Ganeshan. 1998. Validation in Simulation: Various Positions in the Philosophy of Science. *Management Science* 44 (8): 1087–1099.

Lewis, David. 1996. Elusive Knowledge. *Australasian Journal of Philosophy*. 74 (4): 549–567.

Menary, Richard, ed. 2010. *The Extended Mind*. Cambridge: MIT Press.

Mill, John Stuart. 1843. *System of Logic, Ratiocinative and Inductive*. London: J.W. Parker.

Morrison, Margaret. 2009. Models, Measurement and Computer Simulation: The Changing Face of Experimentation. *Philosophical Studies* 143 (1): 33–57.

Oreskes, Naomi, Kristin Shrader-Frechette, and Kenneth Belitz. 1994. Verification, Validation, and Confirmation of Numerical Models in the Earth Sciences. *Science* 263 (5147): 641–646.

Pappas, George. 2014. Internalist vs. Externalist Conceptions of Epistemic Justification. In *Stanford Encyclopedia of Philosophy* (Fall 2014 Edition), ed. Edward N. Zalta. https://plato.stanford.edu/entries/justep-intext/.

Parker, Wendy S. 2008. Computer Simulation through an Error-statistical Lens. *Synthese* 163 (3): 371–384.

Parker, Wendy S. 2009. Does Matter Really Matter? Computer simulations, experiments, and materiality. *Synthese* 169 (3): 483–496.

Peebles, Phillip J. E. 1980. *The Large Scale Structure of the Universe*. Princeton, New Jersey: Princeton University Press.

Plato. 1977. *Euthyphro, Apology Of Socrates, And Crito*, ed. John Burnet. Oxford: Clarendon Press.

Plato. 2015. *Theatetus and Sophist*, ed. Christopher Rowe. Cambridge: Cambridge University Press.

Pozega Osburn, Debra. 2002. The Campaign for MSU: Advancing Knowledge. Transforming Lives. *MSU Today*, September 20. http://msutoday.msu.edu/news/2002/the-campaign-for-msu-advancing-knowledgetransforming-lives/. Accessed Oct 2016.

Press, William H., Saul A. Teukolsky, William T. Vetterling, and Brian P. Flannery. 2007. *Numerical Recipes. The Art of Scientific Computing*, 3rd edn. New York: Cambridge University Press.

Roache, Patrick. 1998. *Verification and Validation in Computational Science and Engineering*. Socorro: Hermosa Publishers.

Ryle, Gilbert. 1945. Knowing how and Knowing that: The presidential address. *Proceedings of the Aristotelian Society* 46 (1): 1–16.

Schlesinger, Stewart, Roy E. Crosbie, Roland E. Gagne, George S. Inis, C. S. Lalwani, Joseph Loch, Richard J. Sylvester, Richard D. Wright, Naim Kheir, and Dale Bartos. 1979. Terminology for Model Credibility. *Simulation* 32: 103–104.

Stanford University. 2014. Offshore Wind Farms Could Tame Hurricanes Before they Reach Land. Science Daily, February 26. https://www.sciencedaily.com/releases/2014/02/140226075019.htm. Accessed Oct 2016.

Stöckler, Manfred. 2000. On Modeling and Simulations as Instruments for the Study of Complex Systems. In *Science at the Century's End: Philosophical Questions on the Progress and Limits of Science*, ed. Martin Carrier, Gerald J. Massey, and Laura Ruetsche, 355–373. Pittsburgh: University of Pittsburgh Press.

Weisberg, Michael. 2007. Who is a Modeler? *British Journal for Philosophy of Science* 58 (2): 207–233.

Winsberg, Eric. 1999. Sanctioning Models. The Epistemology of Simulation. *Science in Context* 12 (2): 275–292.

Winsberg, Eric. 2001. Simulations, Models, and Theories: Complex Physical Systems and their Representations. *Philosophy of Science (Proceedings)* 68 (3): 442–454.

Winsberg, Eric. 2003. Simulated Experiments: Methodology for a Virtual World. *Philosophy of Science* 70 (1): 105–125.

Winsberg, Eric. 2009. Computer Simulation and the Philosophy of Science. *Philosophy Compass* 4 (5): 835–845.

Winsberg, Eric. 2010. *Science in the Age of Computer Simulations*. Chicago: University of Chicago Press.

Winsberg, Eric. 2015. Computer Simulations in Science. In *Stanford Encyclopedia of Philosophy* (Summer 2015 Edition), ed. Edward N. Zalta. https://plato.stanford.edu/entries/simulations-science/.

Varieties of Simulations: From the Analogue to the Digital

Juan M. Durán

Abstract The article analyzes the notions of analogue and digital simulation as found in scientific and philosophical literature. The purpose is to distinguish computer simulations from laboratory experimentation on several grounds, including ontological, epistemological, pragmatic/intentional, and methodological. To this end, it argues that analogue simulations are best understood as part of the laboratory instrumentarium, whereas digital simulations are computational methods for solving a simulation model. The article ends by showing how the analogue-digital distinction is at the heart of contemporary debates on the epistemological and methodological power of computer simulations.

1 Introduction

Nelson Goodman once said that

> few terms are used in popular and scientific discourse more promiscuously than 'model'. A model is something to be admired or emulated, a pattern, a case in point, a type, a prototype, a specimen, a mock-up, a mathematical description. (Goodman 1968, p. 171)

Something similar can be said about the term 'simulation'. A simulation is something that reproduces by imitation of an original, that emulates a mechanism for purposes of manipulation and control, as well as an instrument, a depiction of an abstract representation, a method for finding sets of solutions, a crunching number machine, a gigantic and complex abacus. Paraphrasing Goodman, a simulation is almost anything from a training exercise to an algorithm.

This article presents and discusses two notions of simulation as found in scientific and philosophical literature. Originally, the concept was reserved for special kinds of empirical systems where 'pieces of the world' were manipulated as replacements of the world itself. Thus understood, simulations are part of traditional laboratory practice. The classic example is the wind tunnel, where

J.M. Durán (✉)
High Performance Computing Center Stuttgart (HLRS), University of Stuttgart, Nobelstr. 19, 70569 Stuttgart, Germany
e-mail: duran@hlrs.de

© Springer International Publishing AG 2017
M.M. Resch et al. (eds.), *The Science and Art of Simulation I*,
DOI 10.1007/978-3-319-55762-5_12

engineers simulate the air flow over the wind of a plane, the roof of a car, and under a train. These simulations, however, differ greatly from the modern and more pervasive use of the term, which uses mathematical abstraction and formal syntax for the representation of a target system.[1] For terminological convenience, I shall refer to the former as *analogue simulations*, while the latter are *digital simulations* or *computer simulations*.

On what grounds could we distinguish these two types of simulations? Is there a set of features that facilitate the identification of each notion individually? In what respects is this distinction relevant for our assessment of the epistemological and methodological value of analogue and computer simulations? These and other questions are at the core of this article. I also show in what respects this distinction is at the heart of recent philosophical discussions on the role of computer simulations in scientific practice.

The article is structured as follows. Section 2 revisits philosophical literature interested in distinguishing analogue from digital simulations on an ontological and agent-tailored basis. Thus understood, analogue simulations are related to the empirical world by a strong causal dependency and the absence of an epistemic agent. Computer simulations, by contrast, lack causal dependencies but include the presence of an epistemic agent.[2]

Section 3 raises some objections to this distinction, showing why it fails in different respects and at different levels, including mirroring scientific and engineering uses. Alternatively, I suggest that analogue simulations can be part of the *laboratory instrumentaria*, while computer simulations are *methods for computing a simulation model*. My analysis emphasizes four dimensions, namely, epistemological, ontological, pragmatic/intentional, and methodological.

At this point one could frown upon any featured analogue-digital distinction. To a certain extent, this is an understandable concern. There are deliberate efforts by modelers to make sure that this distinction is of no importance. I believe, however, that the distinction is at the heart of contemporary discussions on the epistemological power of laboratory experimentation and computer simulations. Section 4, then, tackles this point by showing the presence and impact of this distinction in the recent philosophical literature.

---

[1] Andreas Kaminski pointed out that the notion of abstraction is present in laboratory practice as well as in scientific modeling and theorizing. In this respect, it should not be understood that laboratory practice excludes instances of abstraction, but rather that they are more material—in the straightforward sense of manipulating material products—than computer simulations. I will discuss these ideas in more detail in Sect. 3.

[2] Let us note that it is not enough to distinguish analogue simulations from digital simulations by saying that the latter, and not the former, are models implemented on the computer. Although correct in itself, this distinction does not provide any useful insight into the characteristics of analogue simulations nor reasons for distinguising them from computer simulations. Grasping this insight is essential for understanding the epistemological, methodological, and pragmatic value of each kind of simulation.

2 The Analogue-Digital Distinction

Nelson Goodman is known to support the analogue-digital distinction on a semantic and syntactic basis. According to him, it is a mistake to follow a simple, language-based interpretation where analogue systems have something to do with 'analogy,' and digital systems with 'digits.' The real difference lies somewhere else. Concretely, in the way each system is *dense* and *differentiated*.[3] When it comes to numerical representation, for instance, an analogue system represents in a syntactically and semantically dense manner. That is,

> For every character there are infinitely many others such that for some mark, we cannot possibly determine that the mark does not belong to all, and such that for some object we cannot possibly determine that the object does not comply with all. (Goodman 1968, p. 160)

Goodman uses a rather opaque definition for a simple and intuitive fact. Imagine a Bourdon pressure gauge whose display does not contain any pressure units. In fact, think of the display as containing nothing at all, no units, no marks, no figures. If the display is blank, and the needle moves smoothly as the pressure increases, then the instrument is measuring pressure although it is not using any notation to report it (see Goodman 1968, p. 157). This, according to Goodman, is an example of an analogue device. In fact, the gauge is a "pure and elementary example of what is called an analogue computer" (Ibid., 159).

In a digital system, on the other hand, numerical representation would be differentiated in the sense that, given a number-representing mark (for instance, an inscription, a vocal utterance, a pointer position, an electrical pulse), it is theoretically possible to determine exactly which other marks are copies of that original mark, and to determine exactly which numbers that mark and its copies represent (Ibid., 161–164). Consider the Bourdon pressure gauge again. If the dial is graduated by regular numbers, then we are in the presence of a digital system. Quoting Goodman again, "displaying numerals is a simple example of what is called a digital computer" (Ibid., 159–160).

Goodman's notions of dense and differentiated, and of analogue and digital have been conceived to account for a wide range of systems, including pictorial (e.g., photos, drawings, paintings, and icons), mathematical (e.g., graphs, functions, and theorems), and technological (e.g., instruments and computers). Unfortunately, this analogue-digital distinction suffers from significant shortcomings that put Goodman at the center of much criticism.

According to David Lewis, a chief critic of Goodman, neither the notion of 'dense' nor of 'differentiated' accounts for the analogue-digital distinction as made in ordinary technological language. That is, neither scientists nor engineers talk of analogue as dense, nor of digital as differentiated. Instead, Lewis believes that what

---

[3] I am significantly simplifying Goodman's ideas on analogue and digital. A further distinction is that differentiated systems could be non-dense, and therefore analogue and not digital. For examples on these cases, see Lewis (1971).

distinguishes analogue from digital is the use of *unidigits*, that is, of *physical primitive magnitudes*. A physical primitive magnitude is defined as any physical magnitude expressed by a primitive term in the language of physics (Lewis 1971, p. 324). Examples of primitive terms are resistance, voltage, fluid, and the like. Thus, according to Lewis, the measurement of a resistance of 17 Ω represents the number 17. It follows that a system that represents analogous unidigits, such as a voltmeter, is an analogue system. Consider a more complex case: Think of a device which adds two numbers, *x* and *y*, by connecting two receptacles, *X* and *Y*, through a system of pipes capable of draining their content into *Z*, the result of the addition *z*. Consider now that the receptacles are filled with any kind of liquid. Thus constructed, the amount *z* of fluid that has moved from *X* and *Y* into *Z* is the addition of *x* and *y*. Such a device, in Lewis's interpretation, is an analogue adding machine, and the representation of numbers (by units of fluid) is an analogue representation (Lewis 1971, pp. 322–323).

On the other hand, digital is defined as the representation of numbers by *differentiated multidigital magnitudes*, that is, by any physical magnitudes whose values depend arithmetically on the values of several differentiated unidigits (Ibid., 327). For instance, in fixed point digital representation, a multidigital magnitude *M* is digital since it depends on several unidigital voltages. For each system *s* at time *t*, where *m* is the number of voltages, and $n=2$, (see Ibid., 326):

$$M(s,t) = \sum_{i=0}^{m-1} n^i u_i(s,t).$$

Unfortunately, Lewis' analogue-digital distinction also suffers the same shortcomings as Goodman's. Take, for instance, Kay's first *digital* voltmeter. According to Lewis, this digital voltmeter qualifies as an analogue device because it measures a unidigital primitive magnitude (i.e., voltage). Now, the voltmeter is referred to as *digital* precisely because it converts an analogue signal into a digital value. It follows that Lewis' interpretation also fails to account for the analogue-digital distinction as used in ordinary technological language.

A third proponent of the analogue-digital distinction is Zenon Pylyshyn, who has a different idea in mind. He shifts the focus from types of *representations of magnitudes*, prominent in Goodman's and Lewis' interpretations, to types of *processes (i.e., analogue in the case of analogue, and symbolic in the case of digital)*. In doing so, Pylyshyn gains grounds for objecting that Lewis' criterion allows magnitudes to be represented in an analogue manner, without the process itself qualifying as an analogue process. This is an important objection since, under Lewis' interpretation, the modern computer qualifies as an analogue process. The example used by Pylyshyn is the following:

> Consider a digital computer that (perhaps by using a digital-to-analogue converter to convert each newly computed number to a voltage) represents all its intermediate results in the form of voltages and displays them on a voltmeter. Although this computer *represents* values, or numbers, analogically, clearly it operates digitally. (Pylyshyn 1989, p. 202)

According to Pylyshyn, the properties and relations specified in the analogue process must play the right causal role. That is, an analogue process and its target system are both causally related (Ibid., 202). This idea is mirrored by much of the work being done on scientific experimentation. In fact, the so-called 'new experimentalism' holds that, in laboratory experimentation, independent variables are causally manipulated for the investigation of the target system.

As for the notion of *computational process*, Pylyshyn indicates that it comprises two levels of description, namely, a *symbolic level*, which jointly refers to the algorithm, data structures, initial and boundary conditions, and the like; and a description of the physical states of the machine, referred to as the *physical manipulation process*. Pylyshyn, then, carefully distinguishes between a symbolic level, which involves the abstract and representational aspects of the computational process, from the physical manipulation process, which includes the physical states of the computer as instantiated by the algorithm (Ibid., 144).[4]

Closely related to Pylyshyn is Russell Trenholme, who discusses these ideas on analogue and digital processes in the context of simulations. Trenholme distinguishes between *analogue simulations*, characterized by parallel causal-structures isomorphic to the phenomenon simulated,[5] from *symbolic simulations* characterized as a two-stage affair between symbolic processes and a theory-world mapping (Trenholme 1994, p. 118). An analogue simulation, then, is defined as "a single mapping from causal relations among elements of the simulation to causal relations among elements of the simulated phenomenon" (Ibid., 119). According to this definition, analogue simulations provide causal information about represented aspects of the physical processes being simulated. As Trenholme puts it, "[the] internal processes possess a causal structure isomorphic to that of the phenomena simulated, and their role as simulators may be described without bringing in intentional concepts" (Ibid., 118). Let us note that this lack of intentional concepts is an important feature of analogue simulations, for it means that they do not require an epistemic agent conceptualizing the fundamental structures of the phenomena, as symbolic simulations do.[6]

---

[4]Pylyshyn is neither interested in belaboring the notions of analogue and computational process, nor in asserting grounds for a distinction. Rather, he is interested in showing that concrete features of some systems (e.g., biological, technological, etc.) are more appropriately described at the symbolic level, whereas other features are best served by the vocabulary of physics.

[5]The idea of 'parallel causal-structures isomorphic to the phenomenon' is rather difficult to pin down. For a closer look, please refer to Trenholme (1994, p. 118). I take it as a way to describe two systems sharing the same causal relations. I base my interpretation on the author's comment in the appendix: "The simulated system causally affects the simulating system through sensory input thereby initiating a simulation run whose causal structure parallels that of the run being undergone by the simulated system" (Ibid., 128). Also, the introduction of 'isomorphism' as the relation of representation can be quite problematic. On this last point, see, for instance, Suárez (2003).

[6]Unfortunately, Trenholme does not give more details on the notion of 'intentional concepts.' Now, given that this term belongs to the terminological canon of cognitive sciences, and given that Trenholme is following Pylyshyn in these respects, it seems appropriate to suggest that a definition could be found in Pylyshyn's work. In this respect, Pylyshyn talks about several concepts that

The notion of *symbolic simulation*, on the other hand, includes two further constituents, namely, the *symbolic process* and a *theory-world mapping*. The symbolic process is defined as a mapping from the simulated model onto the physical states of the computer. The theory-world mapping is understood as a mapping from the simulated model onto aspects of a real-world phenomenon (referred to as an exogenous computational phenomenon). A *symbolic simulation*, therefore, is defined as a two-stage affair: "first, the mapping of inference structure of the theory onto hardware states which defines symbolic [processes]; second, the mapping of inference structure of the theory onto extra-computational phenomena" (Trenholme 1994, p. 119).[7] An important outcome that I will come back to later is that in a symbolic simulation the simulation model does not necessarily map a real-world phenomenon. Rather, the simulation could explore the theoretical implications of the model.

3   Varieties of Simulations

So far, I have briefly reconstructed canonical literature on the analogue-digital distinction. It is Pylyshyn's and, more importantly, Trenholme's account which facilitates drawing the first dividing lines between analogue and digital simulations. Whereas the former is understood as agent-free and causally isomorphic to a piece of the world, the latter is only an abstract –and, as sometimes also characterized, formal—representation of the target system. I take this distinction to pave the way to the general understanding of analogue and digital simulations, although some adjustments and clarifications must follow.

First, the claim that an analogue simulation is tailored to the world in a causally isomorphic, agent-free sense has serious shortcomings. Take first the claim that analogue simulations are agent-free. One could easily think of an example of an *agent-tailored* analogue simulation. Consider, for instance, a ripple tank for simulating the wave nature of light. Such simulation is possible because water waves and light as a wave obey Hooke's law, d'Alembert's equation, and Maxwell's equation, among other conceptual baggage. Now, clearly these equations have been conceptualized by an agent. It follows that, according to Trenholme's account, the ripple tank cannot be characterized as an analogue simulation. But this appears counterintuitive, as a ripple tank is an analogue simulation of the wave nature of light.

Additionally, *iso*-morphism is the wrong representational relation. One can argue this by showing how causal structural isomorphism underplays the reusability of analogue simulations. Take the ripple tank as an example again. With it,

---

could be related, such as *intentional terms* (Pylyshyn 1989, p. 5), *intentional explanation* (Ibid., 212), *intentional objects* (Ibid., 262), and *intentional descriptions* (Ibid., 20).

[7]Trenholme uses the notions of *symbolic process* and *symbolic computation* interchangeably (Trenholme 1994, p. 118).

researchers simulate the wave nature of light as well as diffraction from a grid. The principle guiding the latter simulation establishes that when a wave interacts with an obstacle, diffraction –or passing through—occurs. The waves then contain information about the arrangement of the obstacle. At certain angles between the oncoming waves and the obstacle, the waves will reflect off the obstacle; at other angles, the waves will pass right through it. Now, according to Trenholme, there must be a causal isomorphism between the ripple tank and the light as a wave, one the one hand, and the ripple tank and diffraction from a grid, on the other. It follows that there should also be a causal isomorphism between light as a wave and diffraction. But this is not the case. The reason why we can use the ripple tank to simulate both empirical systems is that its causal structure includes, so to speak, the causal structure of light as a wave and the causal structure for diffraction. Since the philosophical literature on representation abounds in similar warnings and examples, I will not present any further objections to causal structural isomorphism (see, for instance, Suárez 2003). In order to maintain neutrality on representational accounts, I will talk of -*morphism*.

Despite these issues, I believe that Pylyshyn and Trenholme are correct in pointing out that something like a causally-based feature is characteristic of analogue simulations. To my mind, analogue simulations are a kind of laboratory instrumentaria in the sense that they cannot be conceived as alien to conceptualizations (i.e., agent-tailored) and modeling (i.e., -morphic causal structures), just like the instruments found in the laboratory practice. In addition to Pylyshyn's and Trenholme's ontological analysis, I include a study of the epistemological, pragmatic/intentional, and methodological dimension of analogue simulations. The ripple tank again provides a good example, as it requires models and theories for underpinning the sensors, interpreting the collected data, filtering out noise, and a host of methods that help us understand the behavior of the simulation and its -morphism with the wave nature of light—and diffraction. In fact, contemporary laboratory experimentation—including laboratory instrumentaria—is traversed by modeling and theory, concerns and interests, ideology and persuasion, all in different degrees and at different levels.

The case of digital simulations, on the other hand, is slightly different. I fundamentally agree with Pylyshyn's and Trenholme's characterization in that computer simulations are a two stage-affair. In this respect, computer simulations must be understood as systems that implement a simulation model, calculates it, and renders reliable results. As elaborated by the authors, however, it is left unclear whether the mapping to the extra-computational phenomena requires them to exist in the world, or whether they could be the mere product of the researcher's imagination. A simple example helps to clarify this concern. A digital simulation could be of a real-world orbiting satellite around a real planet (i.e., by setting up the simulation to real-world values), or of a sphere of 100,000 kg of enriched uranium. Whereas the former simulation is empirically possible, the latter violates known natural laws. For this reason, if the simulation model represents an empirical target system, then the computer simulation renders information about real-world phenomena. In all other cases, the computer simulation might still render reliable results, but not of a real-world phenomena. Resolving this issue is, to my mind, a core and still untreated problem in the philosophy of computer simulations. In here, I discuss several potential target systems and what they mean for studies on computer simulation. In addition, and just like in the analogue case, I discuss their ontological side as much as their epistemological, pragmatic, and methodological dimensions.

To sum up, analogue simulations belong to the *laboratory instrumentaria*, while computer simulations are *methods for computing a simulation model*. This is to say that analogue simulations carry out instrumental work, similar to many laboratory instrumentaria, while digital simulations are all about implementing and computing a special kind of model. Thus understood, I build on Pylyshyn's and Trenholme's ontological characterizations, while incorporating several other dimensions. As working conceptualization, then, we can take that an analogue simulation duplicates—in the sense of imitates—a state or process in the material world by reducing it in size and complexity for purposes of manipulation and control. Analogue simulations, then, belong to the laboratory instrumentaria in a way that digital simulations do not. The working conceptualization for computer simulation, on the other hand, is of a method for computing a special kind of model. These two working conceptualizations are discussed at length in the following sections.[8]

3.1 Analogue Simulations as Part of the Laboratory Instrumentaria

Modern laboratory experimentation without the aid of instruments is an empiricist's nightmare. But, what is a laboratory instrument? Can a hammer be considered one? Or must it be a somehow more sophisticated device, such as a bubble chamber? And more to the point, why are analogue simulations constituents of laboratory instrumentaria? There are no unique criteria for answering these questions. The recent history of science shows that there is a rich and complex chronicle on laboratory instruments, anchored in changes in theory, epistemology, cosmologies and, of course, technology. In this section, I intend to answer two questions, namely, what is typically considered as a laboratory instrument, and why is an analogue simulation constituent of the laboratory instrumentaria? To this end, I address four dimensions of analysis: the epistemological, the ontological, the pragmatic/intentional, and the methodological.

---

[8]Let us note that these working conceptualizations mirror many of the definitions already found in the specialized literature (for instance, Winsberg 2015). In here, I am only interested in the analogue-digital distinction as means for grounding philosophical studies on computer simulations and laboratory experimentation.

Regarding the epistemological dimension, I take that laboratory instrumentaria 'embody' scientific knowledge *via* the materials, the theories, and models used for building them. In addition to this dimension, laboratory instrumentaria are capable of 'working knowledge,' that is, practical and non-linguistic knowledge for doing something. As for the ontological dimension, the laboratory instrumentaria belong to a causally-based ontology, something along the lines suggested earlier by Pylyshyn and Trenholme, but that needs to be refined. The pragmatic/intentional dimension shows that laboratory instrumentaria are designed for fulfilling a practical end. Finally, the methodological dimension emphasizes the diversity of sources which inform the design and construction of laboratory instrumentaria. Let us discuss each dimension in some detail.

The claim that genuine laboratory instrumentaria 'embody' scientific knowledge has been interpreted in several ways. One such a way takes that they carry properties and functionalities specifically built-in in order to make them more suitable for the task designed. For instance, the bubble chamber is a vessel filled with superheated liquid hydrogen suitable for detecting electrically charged particles moving through it. Before liquid hydrogen was available, early prototypes included all sorts of liquids, none of which were suitable for the specific purpose of detecting tracks of ionizing particles. The search for a suitable liquid—suitable materials, etc.—embodies knowledge that configures the instruments, the measurements, and the results. Another way to interpret the embodiment of knowledge is that laboratory instrumentaria have been built by following a theory or a scientific model. The ripple tank, as mentioned, embodies Hooke's law, d'Alembert's formula, and Maxwell's equation, which explains the wave nature of light.

Embodying knowledge has some kinship with the notion of 'working knowledge.' The general claim is that scientific activity is not only based on theory, a linguistically centered understanding of knowledge, or on laboratory experimentation, an empirically centered view of the world, but also on the *use* of instruments. This is at the core of what David Baird calls a *materialistic epistemology of instrumentation* (Baird 2004, p. 17). According to Baird, instruments bear knowledge of the phenomena they produce, allowing for contrived control over them. This is the meaning I give to the term 'working knowledge,' that is, a kind of knowledge that is sufficient for *doing* something, despite our theoretical understanding of the instrument (or lack thereof). One example used by Baird is Michael Faraday's electromagnetic motor. Although at the time there was considerable disagreement over the phenomenon produced, as well as over the principle of operation, Faraday and his contemporaries "could reliably create, re-create, and manipulate [a torque rotating in a magnetic field induced by opposite forces], despite their lack of an agreed-upon theoretical language" (Baird 2004, p. 47).

The analysis on working knowledge needs to be complemented with a causally-based ontology. Our previous analysis made use of Pylyshyn's and Trenholme's as part of the ontological assessment of the analog-digital distinction. However, we now need a more refined taxonomy that takes care of the differences in laboratory instrumentaria. Rom Harré provides such taxonomy based on two families, namely, *instruments* and *apparatus*. The first is "for that species of equipment which registers an effect of some state of the material environment, such as a thermometer", whereas the second is "for that species of equipment which is a model of some naturally occurring structure or process" (Harré 2003, p. 20). Thus understood, instruments are rather simple to envisage, since any detector or measurement device qualifies as such. As features, they are in direct causal interaction with nature, and therefore back inference from the state of the instrument to the state of the world is grounded on the reading of the instrument. Apparatus, however, are part of a more complex family of laboratory instrumentaria. They are conceived as material models whose relation to nature is one of 'analogy,' that is, belonging to the same ontological class. As Harré explains, "showers of rain and racks of flasks are both subtypes of the ontological supertype 'curtains of spherical water drops'" (Harré 2003, p. 34). To make matters more complicated, the family of apparatus must be split into two subclasses: *domesticated worlds* and *Bohrian apparatus*. The former are models of actual 'domesticated' pieces of nature. For instance, a Petri Dish can be used for the cultivation of bacteria and small mosses. The latter are material models used for the creation of new phenomena, this is, phenomena that are not found in the wild. An example of a Bohrian apparatus is Humphrey Davy's isolation of sodium in the metallic state by electrolysis.

Following Harré's taxonomy, Faraday's electromagnetic motor falls into the category of *instrument*, whereas the bubble chamber is an *apparatus*. More specifically, the bubble chamber falls into the subcategory of *domesticated world*, since it is a material model for the behavior of particles and it does not creates new phenomena. Analogue simulations, on the other hand, may fall into any of the categories above. For instance, the ripple tank qualifies as an *apparatus*, subcategory *domesticated world*. We could also think of analogue simulations set for measuring observable values, such as a circuit simulation, as *instruments*.

Thus understood, analogue simulations could be identified as constituents of the laboratory instrumentaria based on their epistemic function, as well as on their ontological placement. However, two more levels of analysis are needed for fully identifying analogue simulations and, more to my interests, distinguishing them from computer simulations.

According to Peter Kroes (2003), besides the traditional dichotomy between laboratory instrumentaria as embodying a theory and the material restrictions imposed onto it, there is another equally relevant dimension, namely, the designed *intentionality* of an instrument or apparatus. This term is meant to highlight, along with the nature of a scientific instrument or apparatus, the practical intentions of the scientist when using it. Following Kroes, laboratory instrumentaria are generally analyzed as physical objects, as they obey the laws of nature—and in this respect their behavior can be explained causally in a non-teleological way. Now, they can also be analyzed by their physical embodiment of a design, which does have a teleological character.

Any instrument or apparatus in the laboratory instrumentaria, then, performs a function for which they have been designed and made. This is true for all laboratory instrumentaria, from the early orreries to the latest analogue simulations. As Kroes puts it: "[T]hink away the function of a technological artifact, and what is left is no longer a technological artifact but simply an artifact—that is, a human-made object with certain physical properties but with no functional properties." (Kroes 2003, p. 69). By highlighting this pragmatic dimension, Kroes allows for categorizations based on a purely intentional factor. This means, among other things, the possibility of subcategorizations within the laboratory instrumentaria based on intended functions and purposes.

As for the methodological dimension, there are no common features that tie all the laboratory instrumentaria together. The sources of inspiration, materials available, and techniques for building an instrument or apparatus vary by epoch, education, and location. It is virtually impossible to establish common methodological grounds. To be an analogue simulation, nevertheless, is to be made of a material thing, tangible, and prone to manipulation in a causal sense. Whether it is wood, metal, plastic, or even less tangible things, like air or force, analogue simulations are unequivocally characterized by the presence of a material substrate.

Thus understood, Pylyshyn's and Trenholme's causal structures are only part of the story of analogue simulations. Other perspectives include Baird's embodiment knowledge as the epistemic angle, Harré's refined ontological taxonomy, Kroes' pragmatic/intentional account that brings into the picture the influence of individuals and communities, and a very complex underlying methodology. In this respect, analogue simulations are part of the laboratory instrumentaria in knowledge, nature, purpose, and design. Computer simulations, however, are something else.

3.2 The Microcosm of Computer Simulations

Trenholme's work enables the idea that results on digital simulation are the byproduct of calculating a simulation model. Indeed, calculating such a model corresponds to Trenholme's first stage of the symbolic simulation, which depends on the states of the physical machine as induced by the simulation model (i.e., the *symbolic process*). Let us also recall that Trenholme indicates that the simulation maps onto an extra-computational phenomenon, suggesting in this way that the simulation model represents a real-world target system. As suggested earlier, there is no need to assert such mapping, as it is neither necessary for rendering results, nor for assessing the epistemic power of computer simulations. Boukharta et al. (2014) provide an interesting example on how non-representational computer simulations deliver reliable information on mutagenesis and binding data for molecular biology. Following their example, then, I take computer simulations to be 'artificial worlds of their own' in the sense that they render results of a given target system regardless of the representational content of its model—or mapping relations to extra-computational phenomena.

Thus understood, there are as many ways in which computer simulations are artificial worlds as there are target systems. A rough list includes *empirical target systems*—as I understand Trenholme's extra-computational phenomena—to utterly *descriptively inadequate target system*. An example of an empirical target system is the planetary movement, where one implements a simulation model of classical Newtonian mechanics. Another example stems from the social sciences, where the general behavior of social segregation is represented by the Schelling model. Naturally, the degree of accuracy and reliability of these simulations depend on several variables, such as their representational capacity, degree of robustness, computational accuracy, and the like.

On the opposite end there are *non-empirical target systems*, such as those of mathematical nature. For instance, in topology one could be interested in simulating a Clifford torus, a Hopf fibration, or a Möbius transformation. Of course, the boundary between what is strictly empirical and what is strictly non-empirical is set by the analysis of several factors. In what respect is the Hopf fibration 'less empirical' when it describes the topological structure of a quantum mechanical two-level system? Real pairwise linked keyrings could be used to mimic part of the Hopf fibration. 'More empirical' and 'less empirical', therefore, are concepts tailored not only to the target system, but also to the idealizations and abstractions of the simulation model. Allow me to bring forward another example. The model of segregation, as originally elaborated by Schelling, explicitly omits organized action (e.g., undocumented immigrants leaving due to their status) and economic and social factors (e.g., the poor are segregated from rich neighborhoods) (Schelling 1971, p. 144). To what extent, then, is Schelling's model a representation of an empirical target system, as claimed earlier, as opposed to a mere mathematical description?

A similar issue rises with *descriptively inadequate target system*, such as the Ptolemaic model of planetary movement. In principle, there is nothing that prevents researchers from implementing such models as computer simulations. The problem is that being descriptively inadequate begs the question of what is an 'adequate' model. A Newtonian model seems to be just as descriptively inadequate as the Ptolemaic one, in that neither literally applies to planetary movement. Another example of a descriptively inadequate target system is a simulation that implements Lotka-Volterra models with infinite populations (represented in the computer simulation by very large numbers).

All these examples furnish the idea that computer simulations are 'artificial worlds of their own.' Any representational relation with an extra-computational phenomena is an extra mapping that does not impose constraints neither on the computer simulation nor on the assessment of its reliability. If the simulation represents an empirical target system, then its epistemological assessment is of a certain kind. If it does not, then it is of another. But in neither case does the computer simulation cease to be an artificial world, with its own methodology, epistemology, and semantics. This is why I believe that separating the simulation model from its capacity to represent the 'real-world', as Trenholme does with the two-stage affair, is the correct way to characterize computer simulations.

So much for target systems; what about computer simulations themselves? Their universe is vast and rapidly growing. This can be easily illustrated by the many ways that one could elaborate a sound taxonomy for computer simulations. For instance, if the taxonomy is based on the kind of problem at hand, then the class of computer simulations for astronomy is different from those used for synthetic biology, which in turn are different from organizational studies, although still similar to certain problems in sociology. The nature of each target system is sometimes best described by different models (e.g., sets of equations, descriptions of phenomenological behavior, etc.). Another way to classify computer simulations is based on the calculating method used. Thus, for simulations in fluid mechanics, acoustics, and the like, Boundary Element Methods are most suitable. Monte Carlo methods are suitable for systems with many coupled degrees of freedom, such as calculation of risk and oil exploration problems. Further criteria for classification include stochastic and deterministic systems, static and dynamic simulations, continuous and discrete simulation, and local and distributed simulations.

The most typical approach, however, is to focus on the kind of model implemented on the physical computer. The standard literature divides computer simulations into three classes: *cellular automata*, *agent-based simulations*, and *equation-based simulations* (see Winsberg 2015). Let us note that Monte Carlo simulations, multi-scale simulations, complex systems, and other similar computer simulations become a subclass of 'equation-based simulations'. For instance, Monte Carlo simulations are equation-based simulations whose degrees of freedom make them unsolvable by any means other than random sampling. And multi-scale simulations are also equation-based simulations that implement multiple spatial and temporal scales.

As a result, any attempt to classify computer simulations based on a handful of criteria will fail, as researchers are not only bringing into use new mathematical and computational machinery, but also using computer simulations in cross-domains. I take that the kind of model implemented is only a first-order criterion for classification of computer simulations. Additionally, and within each class of computer simulations, there are also a host of methods for computing the simulation model, and a multiplicity of potential target systems tailored to scientific interests, availability of resources—computational costs, human capacity, time-frame, etc.—and expertise knowledge.

3.3 Computer Simulations Meet the Laboratory Instrumentaria

The previous sections made an effort to show that computer simulations are methods for computing a simulation model embodying knowledge—i.e., by implementing different kinds of models—, and which are conceived with a specific purpose in mind—i.e., representing different target systems. One could also make the case that researchers have a working knowledge of these simulations (as Baird indicates), and that a diversity of sources influence their design and coding. Let it be noticed, however, that neither the epistemological, pragmatic/intentional, nor methodological dimensions appear in analogue and computer simulations in the same way. For instance, while computer simulations embed knowledge via implementing an equation-based model in a suitable programming language, analogue simulations do something similar via their materiality.

The ontological dimension is, perhaps, where the differences between analogue and computer simulations are more visible. Harré's taxonomy explicitly requires both families of laboratory instrumentaria to bear relations to the world, either by causal laws, as in the case of an instrument, or by belonging to the same ontological class, as is the case of the apparatus. Such a criterion excludes, in principle, computer simulations as part of the laboratory instrumentaria. The reason is straightforward: although computer simulations run on physical computers, the physical states of the latter do not correspond to the physical states of the phenomenon being simulated.[9]

Although not exhaustive, I believe that the discussion presented here helps understand the distinction between analogue and computer simulation. In particular, it facilitates the identification of analogue simulations as part of the laboratory instrumentaria, whereas computer simulations are related to computational methods for solving an algorithmic structure (i.e., the simulation model). Before showing in what sense this distinction is at the heart of contemporary discussions on the role of computer simulations in scientific practice, we need to answer the question of whether analogue simulations could be regarded as methods for computing some kind of model. In other words, we are now asking the following question: Could an analogue simulation be a computer simulation? The question, let it be said, is not about so-called *analogue computers*, as is the example of adding two numbers by adding liquids cited earlier. Such simulations, as I have shown, are still analogue, and have nothing in common with the notion of 'digital.' The question above takes seriously the possibility that analogue simulations actually compute a simulation model. I argue that there are a few historical cases where an analogue simulation qualifies, under the present conditions, as a computer simulation. However, these cases represent no danger to the main argument of this article, as they are only interesting for historical purposes. Having said that, allow me to illustrate this issue with an example.

In 1890, the U.S. was ready to conduct the first census with large-scale information processing machines. Herman Hollerith, a remarkable young engineer, designed, produced, and commercialized the first mechanical system for census data processing. The Hollerith machine, as it became known, based its information processing and data storage on punched cards that could be easily read by the

---

[9]For the interested reader, I suggest reading some of the ideas brought up by Wendy Parker a few years ago (2009), as well as my objection to it based on a principle of no multi-realizability in computer software (Durán 2013a).

machine. The first recorded use of the Hollerith machine for scientific purposes was by Leslie J. Comrie, an astronomer and pioneer in the application of Hollerith's punched cards computers for astronomical calculations and the production of computed tables (Comrie 1932). As early as 1928, Comrie computed the summation of harmonic terms for calculating the motion of the Moon from 1935 to 2000.

Now, to the extent that the Hollerith machine implements and solves a model (*via* punched cards) for calculating the motion of the Moon, it qualifies as a simulation. The question is, of what class of simulation are we talking about? Following Pylyshyn and Trenholme, the Hollerith machine does not qualify as analogue since it is not causally -morphic to a target system. Nor does it qualify as digital in the sense we ascribe to modern computers. It follows that, from a purely ontological viewpoint, it is not possible to characterize the use the Hollerith machine as either analogue or digital. These considerations give us an inkling of the limits of characterizing simulations on purely ontological terms. Alternatively, by following my distinction between laboratory instrumentaria and computational methods, the Hollerith machine scores better as a computer simulation. The reason is that it computes and predicts by means of a simulation model in a similar fashion as the modern computer. Admittedly, a punched cards only resemble an algorithm from an epistemic viewpoint, that is, in the sense that there is a set of step-by-step instructions for the machine. Likewise, the machine only bears a similarity to modern computers in its capacity to interpret and execute the given set of instructions coded in the punched cards. For all practical purposes, however, the Hollerith machine, as used by Comrie, implements and solves a model of the motion of the Moon in a similar fashion to most modern computers. I see no objection, therefore, to assert that this particular use of the Hollerith machine qualifies as a computer simulation, however counterintuitive this sounds.

As I mentioned before, the Comrie case is presented only for historical purposes. It is illusory to think of modern computer simulations as implementing punched cards, or to think of the architecture of the computer as anything other than silicon-based circuits on a standardized circuit board (or quantum and biological computers). It is with these discussions in mind that I now turn to my last concern, that is, to evaluate how the analogue-digital distinction influences current philosophical discussions on laboratory experimentation and computer simulations.

4 The Importance of the Analogue-Digital Distinction in the Literature on Computer Simulations

The previous discussion sought to make explicit the distinction between analogue simulations and computer simulations. It is now time to see how such a distinction is at the basis of contemporary discussions on laboratory experimentation and computer simulations.

For a long time, philosophers have shown concern over the epistemological and methodological credentials of laboratory experimentation and computer simulations. Questions like 'to what extent are they reliable?' and 'in what respects does the ontology of simulations affect our assessment of their results?' are at the heart of these concerns. I submit that the analogue-digital distinction, as discussed here, underlies the answers given to these questions. Moreover, I believe that the distinction underpins the diverse philosophical standpoints found in contemporary literature.

In Durán (2013a), I argued that philosophical comparisons between computer simulations and scientific experimentation share a common rationale, namely, that ontological commitments determine the epistemological evaluation of experiments as well as computer simulation. I then identified three viewpoints[10]:

(a) computer simulations and experiments are causally similar; hence, they are epistemically on par. For instance Wendy Parker (2009);

(b) experiments and computer simulations are materially dissimilar: whereas the latter is abstract in nature, the former shares causal relations with the phenomenon under study. Hence, they are epistemically different. For instance Francesco Guala (2002), Ronald Giere (2009), and Mary Morgan (2003, 2005);

(c) computer simulations and experiments are ontologically similar only because they are both model-shaped; hence, they are epistemically on par. For instance Margaret Morrison (2009) and Eric Winsberg (2009).

To see how the analogue-digital distinction underpins these discussions, take first viewpoint (b). Advocates of this viewpoint accept a purely ontological distinction between experiments and computer simulations. In fact, whenever experiments are analogue simulations—in the sense given by Harré's taxonomy—and computers are digital simulations—in the sense given by Trenholme's symbolic simulation—their epistemological assessment diverges. One can then show that this viewpoint presupposes that experiments belong to the laboratory instrumentaria—like analogue simulations—whereas computer simulations are methods for computing a simulation model—like digital simulations.

Moreover, to see how the analogue-digital distinction works to unmask misinterpretations of the nature of experiments and computer simulations, take viewpoint (a). There, Parker conflates causal-related processes with symbolic simulations. In Trenholme's parlance, Parker merges the representation of an extra-computational phenomenon with the symbolic process. In Durán (2013a), I contended with her viewpoint by arguing that she misinterprets the nature of computer simulations in particular, and of computer software in general. In other words, I made use of the analogue-digital distinction to show in what respects her viewpoint is misleading.

---

[10]In that article, I urged for a change in the evaluation of the epistemological and methodological assessment of computer simulations. For my position on the issue, see Durán (2013b).

Let us note that viewpoints (a) and (b) are only interested in marking an ontological and an epistemological distinction. As I have argued earlier, in order to fully account for laboratory experimentation and computer simulations it is necessary to also include the pragmatic/intentional and methodological dimensions.

Viewpoint (c), on the other hand, includes the methodological dimension to account for the epistemology of computer simulations and laboratory experimentation. In fact, Morrison's ontological and epistemological symmetry rests first in acknowledging the analogue-digital distinction, and then in arguing that in some cases it can be overcome by adding a methodological analysis. It comes as no surprise, then, that viewpoint (c) is more successful in accounting for today's notion of laboratory experiments and computer simulations and therefore, for assessing their epistemological power. I believe, however, that an even more successful account needs also to add the pragmatic/intentional dimension as discussed in this article.

Viewpoint (c) also brings up a concern that I have not addressed in this article yet. That is, that modern practice sometimes merges the analogue and digital dimensions together. This is especially true of complex systems, where computer simulations are at the heart of experimentation—and vice versa. A good example of this is the Large Hadron Collider, where the analogue and the digital work nicely together in order to render reliable data. For these cases, any criteria for a distinction might seem inappropriate and otiose. Admittedly, more needs to be said on this point, especially for cases of complex scientific practice where the distinction seems to have ceased being useful.

It is my belief, however, that we still have good reasons for engaging in studies such as the one carried out here. There are at least two motivations. On the one hand, there still are 'pure' laboratory experiments and 'pure' computer simulations that benefit from the analogue-digital distinction for their epistemological assessment. As shown, many of the authors discussed here depend on such a distinction in order to say something meaningful about the epistemic power of computer simulation. On the other hand, we now have a point of departure for building a more complex account of experimentation and computer simulation. Having said that, the next natural step is to integrate the analogue with the digital dimension.

Acknowledgments Thanks go to Andreas Kaminski for comments on a previous version of the article.

References

Baird, Davis. 2004. *Thing Knowledge: A Philosophy of Scientific Instruments*. Berkeley: University of California Press.

Boukharta, Lars, Hugo Gutiérrez-de-Terán, and Johan Åqvist. 2014. Computational Prediction of Alanine Scanning and Ligand Binding Energetics in G-Protein Coupled Receptors. *PLOS Computational Biology* 10 (4): 6146–6156.

Comrie, Leslie John. 1932. The Application of the Hollerith Tabulating Machine to Brown's Tables of the Moon. *Monthly Notices of the Royal Astronomical Society* 92 (7): 694–707.

Durán, Juan M. 2013a. The Use of the 'Materiality Argument' in the Literature on Computer Simulations. In *Computer Simulations and the Changing Face of Scientific Experimentation*, ed. Juan M. Durán and Eckhart Arnold, 76–98. Newcastle: Cambridge Scholars Publishing.

Durán, Juan M. 2013b. *Explaining Simulated Phenomena: A Defense of the Epistemic Power of Computer Simulations*. Dissertation, Universität Stuttgart. http://elib.uni-stuttgart.de/opus/volltexte/2014/9265/.

Giere, Ronald N. 2009. Is Computer Simulation Changing the Face of Experimentation? *Philosophical Studies* 143 (1): 59–62.

Goodman, Nelson. 1968. *Languages of Art. An Approach to a Theory of Symbols*. Indianapolis: The Bobbs-Merrill Company.

Guala, Francesco. 2002. Models, Simulations, and Experiments. In *Model-Based Reasoning: Science, Technology, Values*, ed. Lorenzo Magnani and Nancy J. Nersessian, 59–74. New York: Kluwer.

Harré, Rom. 2003. The Materiality of Instruments in a Metaphysics for Experiments. In *The Philosophy of Scientific Experimentation*, ed. Hans Radder, 19–38. Pittsburgh: University of Pittsburgh Press.

Kroes, Peter. 2003. Physics, Experiments, and the Concept of Nature. In *The Philosophy of Scientific Experimentation*, ed. Hans Radder, 68–86. Pittsburgh: University of Pittsburgh Press.

Lewis, David. 1971. Analog and Digital. *Noûs* 5 (3): 321–327.

Morgan, Mary S. 2003. Experiments without Material Intervention. In *The Philosophy of Scientific Experimentation*, ed. Hans Radder, 216–235. Pittsburgh: University of Pittsburgh Press.

Morgan, Mary S. 2005. Experiments versus Models: New Phenomena, Inference and Surprise. *Journal of Economic Methodology* 12 (2): 317–329.

Morrison, Margaret. 2009. Models, Measurement and Computer Simulation: The Changing Face of Experimentation. *Philosophical Studies* 143 (1): 33–57.

Parker, Wendy S. 2009. Does Matter Really Matter? Computer Simulations, Experiments, and Materiality. *Synthese* 169 (3): 483–496.

Pylyshyn, Zenon W. 1989. *Computation and Cognition: Toward a Foundation for Cognitive Science*. Cambridge, MA: MIT Press.

Schelling, Thomas C. 1971. Dynamic Models of Segregation. *The Journal of Mathematical Sociology* 1 (2): 143–186.

Suárez, Mauricio. 2003. Scientific Representation: Against Similarity and Isomorphism. *International Studies in the Philosophy of Science* 17 (3): 225–244.

Trenholme, Russell. 1994. Analog Simulation. *Philosophy of Science* 61 (1): 115–131.

Winsberg, Eric. 2009. A Tale of Two Methods. *Synthese* 169 (3): 575–592.

Winsberg, Eric. 2015. Computer Simulations in Science. In *Stanford Encyclopedia of Philosophy* (Summer 2015 Edition), ed. Edward N. Zalta. http://plato.stanford.edu/archives/sum2015/entries/simulations-science/. Cited June 2016.

Printed in the United States
By Bookmasters